D0979119

"If you think this is just another Hollywood tell-all book, think again. This story is so much more. It will shock you, but most importantly it will give you hope. It reminds us all that God is alive and is still in the miracle business."
— Rick Burgess and Bill "Bubba" Bussey
    Hosts of the nationally syndicated "Rick and Bubba Show"

"Willie and Maylo's honesty make this book a heartfelt read. Their journey apart and together is both alarming and affirming. It is inspiring to see a couple so devoted to each other and to their faith."
— Lori Loughlin
    Actor and Producer

"*Grace Is Enough* offers an unflinching portrayal of both the grimmest of human nature and the most extraordinary of the human spirit. Willie and Maylo's story is an emotionally brutal one made utterly compelling by uncovering hope and dignity within the midst of fame, greed, lust, excess, and ultimate betrayal. The candid account of these two lives is both touching and disturbing, but in the end, one of the most remarkable and inspiring stories I have ever read."
— Chris Maul
    Executive of Development, Grammnet/Paramount Pictures

"A fascinating true story that could only emerge from Hollywood. *Grace Is Enough* is honest, riveting, and unfolds in a compelling way that only a real-life drama can."
— Tom Russo
    President, Intermedia Television
    Former V. P. of Development, Paramount Pictures

"Willie and Maylo have been the main characters in their own exciting, action-filled, suspenseful, dramatic and sometimes tragic life story. Their devotion to God and to each other inspires us to reach past the pain and the obstacles in our own lives in order to come to the place where we can agree with them . . . grace is enough."
— Kathy Troccoli
    Singer, Speaker, and Author

GRACE IS ENOUGH

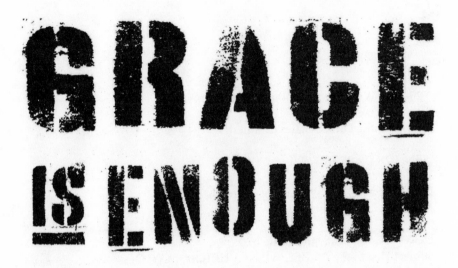

GRACE IS ENOUGH

Willie Aames and Maylo Upton-Aames

with Carolyn Stanford Goss

B&H
PUBLISHING GROUP

Nashville, Tennessee

ISBN: 978-0-8054-4379-0

Published by B & H Publishing Group,
Nashville, Tennessee

Dewey Decimal Classification: 920
Subject Heading: AAMES, WILLIE \ UPTON, MAYLO
                    ACTORS—BIOGRAPHY \ ACTRESSES—BIOGRAPHY

1 2 3 4 5 6 7 8 9 10 11 12 13 14 15   11 10 09 08 07

To Christopher and Harleigh

CONTENTS

CONTENTS

ACKNOWLEDGMENTS

Writing this book was a big undertaking, and I could not have completed my parts without help from some very special people. Before I go any farther I want to say thank you to Cadeau Cavaliers for providing me with Beatrice, the perfect little tricolored puppy that sat on my shoulder and kissed me while I finished the last few chapters of this book.

Then, I want to say thank you to Carolyn Goss. Your talent and humor became evident right up front, and the friendship that grew out of this experience is a treasure.

I also want to say thanks to Len Goss, David Shepherd, and B & H Publishing Group for giving Willie and me the opportunity to tell our story.

Kathy, my beautiful sister, also deserves to be acknowledged. For all the hours spent on the phone talking about Mom and Bernie and the rest of it . . . you helped me remember a lot and you were there to confirm any fuzzy memories that I had. Thank you, Sis!

I want to say thank you to my father for giving me the freedom to write my story the way that I remember it. You never asked to be protected from my feelings or memories. That was really brave, Dad, and was a great gift to me. I also want to thank you for blessing me with a great sense of humor and a good eye for beautiful things. I blame you for that, Dad!

Harleigh, my daughter. What can I say? You are my promise . . . my best friend . . . you have been through so very much and have always allowed me to be myself in front of you. Your depth and humor are unequaled in my eyes!

And finally, I need to say thank you to my husband's parents Jim and Jean. You have been there for me since the very first day that Willie brought me home. I cannot say thank you enough.

Willie . . . I love you . . . we'll talk later.

...Maylo

Nothing is created by the efforts of a single person, especially for the Christian. For us the word single-handedly will never exist. So the first thank you must be given to our Lord Jesus Christ. And hopefully that gratitude is clearly given throughout the entire book.

Recently I found out that on occasion my mother regretted allowing me to be a part of the entertainment industry. Mom, Dad, you have nothing to regret, nothing. I have counted myself incredibly fortunate not so much for my career, but for all of the sacrifices that you and the rest of the family endured so that I would have a shot at television. In the end, no matter how difficult the journey, it has brought us all closer and I love you more with each year. No kid, actor or not, had a finer family.

Many have been hugely influential in my outlook toward Hollywood. Toni Kelman, Chad Everett, Bill Bixby, Michael Landon, and Jackie Cooper are among the most memorable. Dick Van Patten, Helen Hunt, Jodi Foster, John Panozzo, Dennis DeYoung, and Tommy Shaw of "Styx" provided inspiration and affirmation. To those who are no longer with us, may you rest in peace.

During the writing of the book, our lives continued to produce some unbelievable experiences and intertwined with personalities that will no doubt find their way into future works, including

Carolyn Goss, whose quirky warmth and understanding made it most possible to get any of this done. Thanks, too, to Len Goss and all those at B & H.

Steve Stark, Chris Maul, Tommy Russo, your years of honesty, friendship, and creative insight will never be forgotten.

Tony Holden, had it not been for you, I am not sure where we would have ended up. I owe you thanks and debts I can never repay. You are and always will be my close friend.

Thank you to all of our friends who have supported us in so many ways—it would be impossible to name them all—and to the many pastors and ministries that keep us lifted in prayer.

And, the three greatest gifts a man could have. Christopher, I am honored to be your dad and your friend. I am proud of you beyond measure and love every second we spend together. Harleigh Jean, my little sprocket, it is hard to imagine that I could be so in love. I know you have endured much being my daughter. Your laughter, intelligence, and fire are everything I asked God for when we found out you were on your way, and he doubled the dose!

Maylo, how do I express so much? All you are, and have been, is the very reason for my being. It has been true since the first day I met you; there is no person or thing on this earth that I would rather spend time with, no eyes I would rather fall into, no other voice I would have speak to me, no laughter or tears I would rather share. I am completely enveloped and joyfully bound. Aside from God, there is no one more dear than you.

Finally, thank you to everyone who has watched our shows over the years. It is my prayer that we will have many more evenings together!

...Willie

PROLOGUE

Gold shag carpet... Turquoise or avocado-green kitchen appliances. Black-and-white TVs. Transistor radios.

Matt Dillon, Chester, Festus, and Miss Kitty. Mayberry, Opie, Aunt Bea, Andy, and, of course, Barney Fife.

"We're goin' to Surf City. Yeah, here we come." "I wanna hold your han-yan-yand."

Girls with white lipstick. Boys with shocks of long, sun-bleached hair swept across their foreheads. *Beach Blanket Bingo*, Gidget, Annette, Frankie Avalon.

Frank Sinatra in *The Manchurian Candidate*. Charlton Heston in *Ben-Hur*. Norman Bates. Alfred Hitchcock.

These were part of California culture when we were born: I, Willie, on July 15, 1960, and my wife, Maylo, on January 6, 1962.

Do you recognize any of them? They marked the beginning of the '60s in California. No other place on earth was like Hollywood, a land where dreams could be fulfilled—or, more commonly, smashed. Everyone knew that there was no other Disneyland, no other Knott's Berry Farm, no other Sunset Boulevard. Most people had never heard of places like Saigon and Da Nang yet.

Where else could you experience both the dusty Santa Ana winds and an earthquake, maybe even on the same day? Or have

1

to stay inside because the city had issued one of the country's first smog alerts? Welcome to our childhood home, where true locals could describe their state as "where the sewage meets the ocean under the smog." Both the good and bad were essential ingredients for the Golden State.

Ever since the days of Mary Pickford and Errol Flynn, there has been a mystique about making it big in Hollywood. Both of us were eventually caught up in this dream, but for different reasons: my career was born out of a desire to simply be acknowledged by my family, and Maylo's was born as a desire to escape from hers.

I did my first commercial at the age of nine, and by nineteen, I was making a million dollars a year—and doing a killer job of going through most of it. I went from being a teen-idol pinup to cleaning toilets on dive boats for less than minimum wage, while guests on board pointed at the "movie star" and laughed.

But these are not "poor me" stories. It's only after twenty years of being Christians, continually asking and allowing God to enter our lives and remold us, that we can look back and recognize his protective and merciful hand lifting us up in extreme circumstances, whether inflicted by others or ourselves.

~~~~~

While Willie was cashing his checks, I, Maylo, was also living a dream . . . but it was more like a nightmare. At the age of sixteen, I was a Hollywood statistic—a runaway, like so many other girls wandering the boulevards in search of drugs and excitement, looking for escape and hope among the addicted, the lost, the wicked.

On the surface, our stories are as different as the Beverly Hills' palm-tree-lined boulevards were from the stained back alleys where I bought my drugs and witnessed murder and more. But there was an unexpected twist in the plots—God merged our stories together, and they became one.

Years later, we know two things: our stories really belong to and are written by him, and the pain we each went through—and still go through—has prepared us to show others the love and mercy Christ gives us daily.

~~~~~

A one-act play by Thornton Wilder shows Jesus' healing of the man at the pool of Bethesda in John 5:1–4 in modern terms. It's called *The Angel That Troubled the Waters* and describes our hope for the telling of our stories. In the play, a doctor comes periodically to the pool of Bethesda, where from time to time an angel appears and stirs the water, giving it power to heal the first person in the pool. The doctor, hoping to be rid of his melancholy, attempts to step into the water, but the angel blocks him.

"Draw back, physician," the angel warns. "This moment is not for you."

The astonished doctor pleads, "Angelic visitor, I pray thee, listen to my prayer."

Again the angel tells him that healing at the pool is not for him. Then the angel says something surprising: "Without your wounds, where would your power be? It is your very remorse that makes your low voice tremble into the hearts of men and women. The very angels themselves cannot persuade the wretched and blundering children on earth as can one human being broken on the wheels of living. In Love's service, only the wounded soldiers can serve."

We'd like to say that our story has a "perfect Christian" happy ending. Forget it. Christ gave us both a new beginning, but we had to be broken first. As long as we follow Christ, there are chapters of our story still to be written. In the meantime, we have been broken and we are wounded, but we continue to serve, in part through the telling of our stories.

As you read our stories, you may recognize yourself. You may disbelieve all or part of it. You may know the individuals and events we recount and disagree about how things went down. While the events we lived are all as we remember them, we have intentionally changed some names and small details to spare some who could be affected by the public scrutiny that might arise. If you think you know the stories and people involved, let us assure you, you don't.

But why do we share these stories? Because we have endured and have learned what faith is built upon. It is our prayer as a family that reading about the victories as well as the wounds we have received will give you the power to see God's love in a new light and to realize that there is hope. Your story can have new beginnings, over and over, until you meet Christ in his glory.

WILLIE

Daddy's Little Man... At 5:45 a.m., it was still a little dark outside, but the urgency to get to the beach early kept my legs pumping up and down on the half-barren bicycle pedal. The other pedal was just a thin, rusted peg of metal squeaking in protest. No rubber to keep my foot from slipping into the gear chain, tearing off another chunk of flesh from my ankle. Ow! You stupid ———!

My bike swayed wildly out of control right into the teeth of Brookhurst Boulevard, the asphalt dividing line between Huntington Beach, Costa Mesa, and Newport Beach that ended at the Pacific. But with an unintentionally acrobatic recovery, I cheated the surf god one more time. And he got another blood sacrifice to appease his royalness for a while.

It was October of 1977, and summer vacation was fast becoming a memory. *Eight Is Enough* had started filming for the year, but I wasn't on the call sheet to work that day. So, instead of attending private tutoring on the set, I was excused from the usual two-and-a-half-hour, traffic-jammed drive to Warner Brothers Studios and was allowed to attend my regular classes at Edison High School—which I decided to excuse myself from for the day.

Once on the beach, I stood on top of my surfboard to protect my bare feet from the cold sand, mesmerized by *the* classic

California morning. In front of me was a glassy-smooth, windless ocean, broken up by set after set of four- to six-feet-high perfect waves rolling in. The long flawless shoulders, the nice wide tubes, with just a hint of spit (spray that comes from inside the tube) as they broke, peeling cleanly. Lineup after lineup. And I was the only guy on the beach.

Somehow, miraculously, the rest of the world hadn't bothered to watch the news for signs of a swell or, unlike me, they just didn't have the good sense to ditch school that day. It was plain they didn't know the waves were going to be there. After waxing up my board with my favorite brand, Mr. Zogs Sex Wax, I began wading out.

The air temperature was several degrees lower than the water temperature, so it felt like stepping into a lukewarm bath. As I bent down to grab a handful of wet sand to rough up the fresh wax, making it stickier, I noticed that the sun, now just above Saddleback Mountain, was mirrored on the glassy ocean. The dawn sky blew muted colors of red, pink, and orange on the horizon, which I took as a celebration in honor of my escape from academic delirium for the day.

Moments like these reminded me why California was the coolest state in the nation. I knew that the colorful atmospheric display was really just sunlight filtering through tons of dirt, soot, and smog we would no doubt be choking on later that day. Nevertheless, that's California—always a little on the flamboyant side so that the truth becomes dependent on how you define it.

As I looked out to sea, I could see two islands on the horizon. To my south was San Clemente—roughly thirty-six miles from the harbor entrance, used mostly by the Navy and off-limits to most civilians—and to the northwest was Catalina—about twenty-six miles away and full of childhood memories . . .

It was 1963 or '64.

"Willie, you are gonna get it! Wait until Dad gets back . . ."

I was determined not to cry as I looked at my swim trunks with their big wet spot in the middle. I was three, maybe four years old, and the incident is one of my earliest memories. My sister, Kim, eleven months older than I, was with me on the deck of a small powerboat that belonged to a friend of Jim Upton, my father.

Dad was a long-time diver. He wanted to dive that day, and Dad usually did what Dad wanted to do. Mom had to work, so he dragged his two small kids along while he spent the day spearfishing in the rich waters around Catalina Island.

"Sit and don't touch anything! Don't screw around!" Those were his last instructions before throwing himself over the rail and into the water. What the heck? What was that supposed to mean? We were three and four years old. Screwing around was our job! You wait until the worst possible moment when everybody over the age of thirty is stressed stupid, and then you screw around. Makes total sense.

So there we were, stuck by ourselves. And I had to pee!

Being an Upton, I knew this could turn cataclysmic, even if I didn't know the word *cataclysmic* yet. The dictionary's definitions are "a sudden and violent upheaval" or "a terrible and devastating flood." I mean I *really* had to pee. And there was no head (restroom) on board for me to use. I held it as long as I could, asking Kim every few minutes with more desperation each time, "Kim, do you think Dad will be back soon? I have to go to the bathroom!"

But he didn't come and he didn't come. I tried to climb up on the captain's chair, thinking I could pee over the side of the boat, but I was too far from the edge. I had long ago exhausted my own personal version of the dreaded "pee pee Watusi dance."

I gave up and went back to sit on the boat's single bunk. The urine began to run down my legs in spite of my willing it not to happen, and I wet the aqua blue canvas seat. And then I waited for the inevitable, for Dad was not likely to listen to any excuses. His embarrassment in front of his buddy would nix any hope of sympathy; I knew that already.

Looking back at the incident today and being a father myself, my first thought is that we should not have been left alone. We were twenty-six miles from the Newport harbor entrance and from our mother, left to fend for ourselves. I don't recall wearing life preservers, and the boat rocked with the swell of the ocean, making seasickness another of the day's prizes. Had we tried to see over the boat's sides, we could have easily fallen into the water. I guess if the worst thing that happened that day was my wetting myself, I should be thankful. I also believe that today, given the opportunity, Dad would do things differently.

The point is, I wanted to be big that day, and every day. I was the youngest of four children, and I wanted to show what a big man I was. The worst part of wetting myself was not that I would get a whipping; the worst part was that I felt I had let my father down.

I had a lot to live up to if I wanted to be like my father. James Tweedy Upton was totally masculine in the traditional sense. He was a "do it now, don't ask questions" kind of guy. At about five-foot-nine, he was not tall. But the guy was tough. As a firefighter who also worked emergency rescue operations, he was used to acting quickly and decisively, and he expected obedience without question.

Dad could be very intimidating. Not religious in any way, he nonetheless had an innate sense of right and wrong, especially in relation to the treatment of unfairly disenfranchised people at the hands of bureaucracy or government. He had no problem getting in the face of those meting out the injustice. Even as a boy, I admired the way he personified courage. And I was determined to be like him, standing up for the little guy, the so-called common man. This attitude and belief have never left me, even today.

As intense as Dad was, though, don't think for a minute that he didn't have a sense of humor. James Tweedy Upton had reached the age when he and his fellows should personify dignity as men schooled in the finer kinds of classical entertainment. Things like short-sheeting his sons' beds or stealing the distributor cap from his brother's car so he couldn't get to work on time. (It started a practical-joke war that went on for months! Hence, my deep respect for the man.)

My dad's method of teaching me to swim, another of my early memories, was characteristic of both his no-nonsense style and the trademark macho Upton humor. Dad grabbed me by my little hand, and we headed for the water—just him and me, father and son, like a Hallmark commercial. And then the strangest thing happened. I remember an incredible feeling of weightlessness, followed by the sound of a large splash, the taste of salt water, and green foam sloshing over my head. Most of all, I remember an extreme desire to breathe! My grandfather Albert spent a little time with me later, helping me get better at it, but I learned to swim the very day I got thrown into the Pacific. There was no other choice if I wanted to keep up with my father.

The afternoon I wet the boat, I did get the whipping that I knew was coming. There was no other option as a son of James Tweedy Upton. But it was OK—the momentary punishment was a small price to pay for being a disappointment to my dad that day.

Wanting to Matter... The first time I tried to hang myself I was three or four years old. We lived at 721 Center Street. It's funny what we remember. I can't remember whom I talked with on the phone this morning but something as simple as an address before the age of five? Can't get rid of it. It was at our house in Costa Mesa.

I tried it twice, both times by rigging up a rope to our weather-beaten backyard fence. The grain in its dark pickets seemed sand-blasted into a maze of deep channels in the wood. Somehow that fence represented an emptiness to me, ringing our backyard of half grass, a quarter dirt, and another quarter of weeds mixed with grass.

On both occasions, about the time my vision was becoming a blur and my face had begun turning a deep purple, my mother happened to step out into the backyard and find me doing the midair stare. Maybe she went out to take some wash off the line or to turn off the hose that I was supposed to be playing in. What-ever the reason, she discovered me hanging there against the dark brown cedar fence, my head in the noose, or at least a three-year-old's facsimile of one.

"What in the world are you doing, Willie!" Each time she untied the knot and let me down. I don't remember giving any specific answer, but I knew what the answer was: I was curious about what it was like to die and was trying to find out.

Mom didn't seem to see anything more significant in my experimentation than just childish fooling around. At least not that I ever knew of. Nor did she comment or seem concerned about the fact that I also began to climb into the top shelf of the closet in the room I shared with my brother. I would cram myself up into the small space and sleep there, precariously perched five feet or more off the ground on a shelf that was at most twelve or fourteen inches wide.

Neither Mom nor Dad was a *Leave It to Beaver* parent who would sit down and reason with a child about the wisdom or foolishness of certain behaviors. A quick whipping or paddling could solve the problem faster and without testing their already stretched patience.

Or Dad would respond in other ways. One Christmas when I was four or five, I got a double-barreled popgun—the type with two corks at the muzzle—made out of tin and painted to look like it belonged to Davy Crockett. My older brothers teased me about my new toy. To defend my hurt feelings, I raised the gun over my head and threatened them with it. Whoops, that didn't work. In a flash I felt my dad grabbing the gun from me. He quickly and expertly turned it into a pretzel. Then he spanked me.

"If you ever threaten someone with a gun again, you'll really get it!" he yelled, leaving me to wonder, but hopefully not to find out, what the "it" for next time would be.

Similarly, if one of the four of us accidentally left a toy or bicycle in the driveway, it was history. Dad would just run it over, and I don't mean unintentionally. Low gear, up and over. When that happened, I wanted to cry, but being the son of James Tweedy Upton, rescuer of those in distress and an all-around man's man, I knew better than to do so. And I knew that it wouldn't change anything if I did.

It wasn't long after my self-lynchings that I began running away from home, but I can't remember that there was any one event or situation that started my striking out on my own. From time to time after being punished, I'd grab a paper bag and stomp into the bedroom. Then I'd load the bag with an extra T-shirt and a few of my favorite things, including my prized rubber knife, and walk out the front door, informing whoever was in earshot that I was running away.

Off I'd go, dragging my bag of possessions. I'd walk a few blocks—a considerable distance for a child. The early evening would begin fading away, with the California sky changing from a deep indigo into a purplish black. I'd find a large oleander bush or piñon tree in a nearby yard, conceal myself within its branches, and curl up for the night.

Eventually Mom or Dad would send out Ron or Jim, and whichever of my brothers had the duty to find me would kneel down and convince me to come back with him. He'd help me pick up my belongings, and we'd walk home, where I'd go straight to bed. Neither Mom nor Dad seemed surprised or glad to see me. In fact, they gave me the cold shoulder. I suppose it was their version of "using psychology" to discourage my behavior.

Life in the Upton household the next day would go on as usual. There was no delving into the reasons behind my grandstanding for attention. There was no acknowledgment that I was maybe a little too fearless for a boy of three or four.

Was I? As an adult, I see through the lens of memory a small, suntanned, curly-haired little boy who wanted someone to come after him. To say, "We see you. We love you. You're valued." A child of three or four is just on the verge of self-awareness, so I can't say that these cries for attention were conscious ones. I do think that I wanted to act like a man, in whatever way I might achieve that goal. I wanted to be tough and self-sufficient like my father, like an Upton, but at the same time, I wanted someone to acknowledge that I mattered. Mattered to whom? Anyone? Anything? That question took me years to ask in the right way, let alone answer.

On Being an Upton...What was it about the Upton-Tweedy clan that made us all want to be worthy of our name and to carve out our own chapter in the family history? I don't know, but the desire was strong, not just with me but with my brothers and cousins as well.

Our California roots trace back farther than those of just about anyone I've ever met. A fifth-generation Californian, I was born on July 15, 1960, in Newport Beach, California, and named Albert William Upton after my grandfather.

My father, James Upton, and his brother, Tom, had been raised on a ranch about forty miles inland from the California coast. I have sixteen-millimeter footage of him astride Shetland ponies when he was just a toddler. In some ways, Dad and Uncle Tom had a childhood that many boys could only dream of. My grandparents' hired hands were always willing to show young masters Jim and Tom how to bridle and saddle a horse. Jim and Tom hunted and fished and learned to love the outdoors.

The family also owned several boats. One was a ketch they named *The Butcher Boy* because it had been a boat that hauled beef out to commercial vessels. That boat has been completely restored and is now on display at the San Diego Maritime Museum. Later Dad acquired a Catalina catamaran christened *El Gato* (The Cat) and various powerboats. Often one of the boats would be docked on Catalina Island next to Errol Flynn's yacht, *The Zacca*.

Jim and Tom grew up comfortable both in and on the water. They learned free diving as well as scuba diving and were experienced campers under the wide, dry California skies.

Their mother, Aileen Tweedy—called Tippy (later Tip) from her childhood habit of walking on her tiptoes—was the daughter of early California ranchers. James, nicknamed Muzzie, and Aileen (the same name as her daughter) were prosperous orange growers who were part owners with other family members of the only Sunkist packing plant in Southern California.

My grandmother Tippy must have been a brave and bold young girl. When she got angry with a member of her family, she would storm out of the house, jump on her horse, and ride alone and unprotected for two days to visit her Auntie Bunn in Oxnard, which was then just a dusty outpost on the lower central coast. Auntie Bunn lives there to this day in the same house with the same furniture—same everything. Walking into it is like visiting a museum that features a display of late Victorian summer-cottage style.

A woman of great wit and a sharp mind, Tip trained as a biochemist at nearby Whittier College, a prestigious liberal arts school of Quaker origins—though my family was totally secular. She dated fellow student Richard Nixon a few times before she began dating one of her professors, Albert Upton, the dean of the English department and a professor of Russian literature and drama.

Albert, of course, was my grandfather. (He taught Nixon and directed the future president in an undergraduate drama production.) When Albert and Tip married, the family continued as casual friends with the Nixon and Spiro Agnew families. (Later in my story I'll share my experience with Watergate and with Nixon's resignation.)

Albert Upton was a standout even among several larger-than-life relatives who took places of honor in my family tree. Although a professor at a school with religious roots, he was an atheist. Fluent in Russian, he was also highly respected in the field of semantics. In 1941 he authored *Design for Thinking*, a classic textbook for teachers. In 1960, the year I was born, the *New York Times* reported that the Upton Method raised the intelligence of more than two hundred students by ten points in a test group. Educators still borrow from his ideas in their quest to teach their students how to think.

Multi-talented Grandfather Albert Upton was also a dedicated outdoorsman and rancher, skilled in the art of horsewhipping to punish Jim's and Tom's misbehavior. My father carried on his tradition by using new versions of whipping on my brothers and me. Not that Grandpa Albert and my father were unusually cruel—whipping was common among ranching families as a form of punishment in those days.

My grandmother Tip's father, Muzzie, was also known to crack that piece of leather from time to time. Muzzie was a character, no doubt about it. I never knew him, but I sure wish I could have. Whenever my great-grandmother held a large dinner party at the ranch house, he would take the time beforehand to hide a large pitcher of water in a bathroom that adjoined the main dining hall.

Just prior to carving the main course, he would excuse himself to go to the restroom. He would shut the door and pour out into the toilet the large pitcher of water he had hidden, raising it to a height calculated to cause a loud, slow, embarrassing stream that all the guests could hear. He'd save a few drops at the end to make a realistic "dup, dup," flush the toilet, and return to the dining hall.

By this time, the guests had run out of things to talk about and were awaiting the host's return so they could eat. He'd take his place and begin to carve the meat. Meanwhile, the guests would be sure that he hadn't washed his hands because they hadn't heard a faucet running. I don't know if they lost their appetites for the meal as a result, but as a child I thought this stunt was hysterical.

My extended family on my dad's side was prosperous but not aristocratic, though they did live comfortably with a sense of unspoken entitlement to the simple, outdoorsy goodness of life in California. Not so my mother's family. Her childhood was poor and life was pretty harsh. My mother's name was Eva Jean Ingersol, though "Ingersol" was only one of several last names she went by in whatever school she was attending at the time.

Jean's mother, Lois, was half Cherokee and had grown up on an Oklahoma reservation. Her mother was Eva Storm, a full-blooded Cherokee. My mother has told me stories of Grandma Lois, describing a small but tough woman with a keen eye for inventing, and what an invention she came up with. She raised hens and rigged up a nifty device made from two boards for quickly yanking the head off a chicken. She went through seven husbands. Each time she couldn't maintain her marriage or was hard up for money, she would put my mother and her brother, Jim, into foster homes. When her luck would change for the better, she'd come back for them.

Lois did not spare her two children from beatings. Mom says that she and Jim would climb into the tops of trees to escape her wrath, but Lois would casually take a comfortable sitting position beneath the tree, calmly smoking a pipe. She'd remind them that eventually they would have to come down, and she'd be waiting.

As she grew older, my grandmother never did mellow. I remember her only as spiteful to my mother, but her last husband, Ernest Palmero, was kind to me. They were avid square dancers, and I remember the two of them dressed for a night of allemande lefts—she in her many layers of colorful petticoats, he in his cowboy shirt and hat. I think he also had some Native American blood, and he was a World War II hero who had been decorated enough times to fill a box of medals.

My Grandma Lois died of leukemia in 1970. That is all I know of my mother's background except for one detail that I discovered when I was nine years old. Before she met and married my father, my mother had been married to a man who was extremely abusive to her and their two sons. Prior to this news, my sister Kim and I had no idea that our brothers, Jimmy (ten years older than I) and Ronnie (eight years older), were our half-brothers.

After my mother married my father, my brothers were adopted and given the names James Tweedy Upton (after my father) and Ronald Walker (another family name) Upton. As an adult I can see that these names were gifts to them. Names have always held great importance in my family, hence the recurrence of the same ones throughout the generations. I never considered Jim and Ron as any less than full-blood brothers and still don't. They simply are my brothers.

My Upton-Tweedy relatives were crass, witty, jovial, sarcastic, and intelligent. I loved every minute I was with them. I wanted to stack up favorably to them and still do. And that desire, along with the desire to know that I mattered to someone, is a big part of my story.

MAYLO

Glamorous Daddy Bill... "Maylo, climb up onto this ledge and sit with your legs crossed. That's good . . . Oh, you look pretty. Look right at me . . . now, turn your head just a little. Don't smile. Just look right here. Fabulous!"

I was about three years old, and the year was probably 1965. My dad had picked me up from the dirty rented apartment where I lived with my mother. We had gone back to his apartment, and he had dressed me in a pretty little cream-colored dress with a matching white headband that pulled the hair back from my round face. Then we drove in his long black Cadillac convertible to the famous Beverly Hills Hotel, the retreat of celebrities, where every "rag mag" photographer waited in the bushes for a candid shot of Hollywood elite who hid out in the lush, private surroundings. The hotel's bungalows were long known for safely tucking away legendary Tinseltown royalty and keeping them protected from the invasive lenses of the cameras. I spent that day on a ledge and beside the fence of the hotel, posing for my father in a variety of child glamour shots, learning to look straight into the lens . . . to bask in its affirmation.

I loved being with Daddy Bill and his friends. He picked me up on weekends from time to time, lifting me from the oppressive surroundings that were mine during the week and transporting

17

me to a different world where entire afternoons were whiled away driving around Los Angeles with the Cadillac's vinyl top down. He would take me to his lovely little ground-floor apartment somewhere near Hollywood. It was filled with shiny things—bottles and statuettes made of crystal and glass and brightly colored Oriental enamel and art pieces. Everything was colorful and orderly, so different from my weekday existence.

A large woman lived in the apartment above him, and when she moved around upstairs, her footsteps made the ceiling shake as though it might fall down on us. My dad, always amusing, called her Elephant Woman, and we cracked up laughing. Hearing Elephant Woman peeing in the middle of the night would send us into fits of giggles.

Daddy had many gay friends—all of them beautiful, as he was. He had dark, thick hair and tanned, smooth skin. He had a brilliant smile that showcased his straight, white teeth. To me, he was gorgeous. All of his friends were, too, and all of them were exceptionally talented in some way. They were funny and fun to be around, and their lives revolved around a cycle of endless parties and gatherings. Some weekends my father would take me to a local park to fly a kite together, or he'd take me to the house of one of his handsome, flamboyant friends.

I remember one special weekend: Terry, one of my father's best friends, whom I loved dearly and still do to this day, bought me a soft white Easter coat, white gloves, and a little purse. I felt absolutely rich. I felt pretty. They treated me like I was pretty. I was never afraid when I was with them. I knew they adored me.

My father was a backup singer and dancer for Johnny Mathis, a popular singer of the early '60s who specialized in romantic ballads and torch songs. The apartment I shared with my mother had the TV blaring almost constantly, and once when I was very little, she stopped smoking long enough to point to a handsome man dressed in a white tuxedo behind Mathis, doing choreographed dance moves.

"That's him," she said. "That's Bill—that's your dad."

Sitting on my knees, I slid up close to the screen to get a better look. He looked like a stranger to me, and before I could process his image, it was gone, replaced by a commercial.

My father traveled all over the world with Johnny Mathis' entourage. When he returned to California after months away, his arms would be filled with something special for me—perhaps a Japanese doll dressed in a brocade kimono or a tinkling music box with miniature metal milkmaids and woodsmen that revolved to the strains of "Edelweiss."

And off we'd go for the weekend. He had a rich, smooth singing voice, and I spent some evenings with my father at the piano bars around town where he performed. He always introduced me, and I remember him standing me beside the piano once or twice to sing a number of my own.

Occasionally my dad and I sang a duet—"Bridge over Troubled Water" was one of his favorites. I soaked in the bars' atmospheres: the glossy black pianos, the amber smoky rooms, the golden glow from the bar area that reflected off the glasses, and the faces of the men sitting in the audience, smiling those indulgent smiles people get when they watch a child do something "big" and "precocious."

In my father's world I never expected anyone to spit out a string of foul words or blow smoke in my face or seethe with a hot rage that seemed directed at me. I wanted to live with my dad, though, at the time, I did not know that my wish would never be granted.

A Bottom like Hamburger...My mother, Sharon, had

a love-hate attitude toward my father. She loved his charm and humor and the people he surrounded himself with, and he made her laugh. But she hated him, too, not so much because he was gay but because he didn't provide her with the trappings of his glamorous life. It seemed to me that she hated everyone who wouldn't or couldn't give her what she wanted. If there was a chance of squeezing anything—money, possessions, compliments, or attention—out of anyone, her charm and attention would become intoxicating. If her strategies failed, her words would turn ugly, as she spit out her obsession with how victimized we were.

"I haven't heard from your father in months. He won't pay your child support. He doesn't give a fig [she used a much stronger word] about you! He's more interested in traveling the world with his gay friends!"

Many times after my father would drop me off after a weekend with him, I could tell as soon as I opened the door that she had been pacing and smoking. Everything inside me would become tense and on high alert, and I would wish I could just shrink away and disappear into my bedroom. But she would march down the hall toward me with her angry, bloodshot, blue eyes, her tiny black pupils fixed on me like I had committed some despicable offense.

"He is using you! He *has* money, and if he really cared about you, he would take care of you!" The words would increase in speed and volume until she locked into a solid bedrock of anger, and then her voice would abruptly drop as she spewed out low-pitched, seething, growling, hate-drenched words.

"Where do you think he got the money for his car . . . for his clothes . . . his fancy lifestyle? Oh, he has it, he has it; he just doesn't care enough to give any to you! Lowlife liar breezing in here like we should all be so grateful to see him and so impressed by him. He is letting us starve. You go without shoes. He's got eyes. He sees. Don't you listen to his compliments!"

Was my father bad? Was he really using me? I didn't know. How could a small child know? I didn't even know why they were divorced. I only heard whispers about the reasons from my mom's side of the family, and my father didn't talk about it.

~~~~~

Sharon Elizabeth Parker is a native Californian, as were several generations before her. She is one of two daughters born to Grandpa Harry Parker, a fireman, and his beautiful wife, Grandma Peggy. Peggy developed an interest in the teachings of one or more of the self-anointed "prophets" who attracted disciples from around the Los Angeles area.

Sharon and her sister, Judy, were as different as a cucumber and an apple. As far as I know, no one in my mother's family ever went to church, but Judy was obedient, calm, and pleasant. Sharon, on the other hand, was difficult and became promiscuous at an early age. She was a remarkably talented painter and, like her mother, became fascinated with pseudo-spiritual subjects.

Harry and Peggy were close friends with a married couple named Bud and Nikki. They'd get together for a night out at each other's home to play bridge, socialize, and sip a margarita or two. Eventually, Harry and Nikki fell in love. Harry and Peggy got divorced. Peggy eventually married Bud. What I remember is Grandpa Harry and Nikki together, and Grandma Peggy and Bud together.

My dad's family tree was an oil-and-water mix of Irish, Yugoslavian, and Austrian ancestry, with militant Catholicism woven into his mother's side. For reasons perhaps related to her disastrous first marriage, his mother, Rose, was the personification of the phrase "soured on life."

Consider the following story. Two of her five children were fighting in the yard, and she got tired of listening to it. She picked up a baseball bat, marched out to the yard in a rage, threw the bat down in front of them, and demanded, "Here. Somebody kill somebody and get it over with! Please, let's end this. One of you has to die!" The children stood in silent shock until Rose turned and marched back into the house.

Rose's first husband was Francis Barron, a California radio personality. My dad's birth name was recorded as William George Barron, but Bill never knew his biological father because he left Rose soon after my dad was born.

Rose then married Clyde Pero, a Navy officer. Bill spent his high-school years in strict Catholic schools in Hawaii, where his stepfather was stationed at Pearl Harbor.

Clyde Pero's approach to a relationship with stepson Bill was to have no relationship with him. He wasn't overtly cruel, but he wasn't attentive. If young Bill wanted to climb onto Clyde's lap, Clyde would push him away, saying, "No, no, get down. Don't sit on me."

At the age of thirteen, Francis Jr., Bill's adored older brother, died of polio. Bill was thus left on the brink of adolescence with a stepfather who did not seem to care about him, a mother whose main talent was making brilliantly cutting remarks and angry comments, and three younger half-siblings. He was artistic and highly imaginative and daydreamed about two pathways for his life. In one, he was a performer who stood onstage, receiving the loud applause of theatergoers. In another, he was the father to several children and married to a perfectly dressed, nurturing, beautiful wife who kept a lovely house.

Both dreams were just that when Bill's family moved back to the Los Angeles area after he graduated from high school. Already an accomplished artist, he enrolled in some painting courses at the Woodbury Art School. Soon after classes began, he met fellow student Sharon Parker.

To Bill, Sharon was as experienced with men as he was inexperienced with women. She flirted shamelessly with him. Her body language was sometimes brazenly sexual. Bill heard rumors that she had had a boyfriend who was a convict. As ambivalent as his sexual identity may have been or maybe even *because* it was so ambivalent, he was flattered that Sharon would choose him. He didn't stand a chance.

Red-haired Sharon was beautiful. She was a dead ringer for Shirley MacLaine, and when Bill and Sharon were out in public, he always got a kick out of people asking to have "Shirley's" autograph.

Bill was also captivated by her wicked sense of humor, her high intelligence, and her religious curiosity. They sat in a pizza parlor near the campus, and she quizzed him endlessly about theology. Her questions intrigued him and got him thinking about his own early Catholic training.

William Pero and Sharon Parker dated for one-and-a-half years before they got married in late 1960. Bill was twenty; Sharon, nineteen. Sharon joined a Catholic church. They moved into a small apartment near the Los Angeles Sears store where Bill had a job as a sales clerk in men's furnishings. After he'd leave in the morning, Sharon, repetitively twirling a lock of her reddish hair around her finger, would spend hours smoking while she read books about the Catholic saints or books written by psychics such as Edgar Cayce and Jeanne Dixon, who were tremendously popular in the early 1960s. She did little else in terms of housework or laundry.

Within a few months Sharon suffered a miscarriage, and after that she quit even pretending to do much other than smoke and read. Their apartment became more of a shambles with each passing day. Sharon's personal hygiene also became almost nonexistent. She did not bathe, and her makeup remained on her face for days, with her mascara becoming cakey and crunchy on her eyelids.

~~~~~

I, Maylo Elizabeth Pero, was born on January 6, 1962, and was baptized Catholic, though I never recall going to the Catholic church, or any church for that matter. People who knew them both tell me that my mother left me in my crib for most of the day. My mother's method of changing my diaper was to pin a dry diaper over the wet one. When my father came in from work, he would find my diaper was falling off my body due to its soggy, smelly weight. My bottom became so raw and red that it looked like "hamburger," as my father puts it.

My father was alarmed by my mother's lack of interest in me. He accompanied her to the pediatrician for one of my well-baby checkups, and the pediatrician was shocked at the physical evidence of neglect.

"Mrs. Pero," he warned her, "you need to boil the baby's diapers before you put them in the washing machine, and you must change your daughter's diaper regularly. Her bottom has sores that are getting infected, and she's going to end up with scars!" My mother did change my diaper after that—she took it off, rinsed it out a little, and then put the same wet diaper back on my sore bottom.

By the time I was eighteen months old, the marriage was falling apart. At this point, the version of what happened next depends on who tells it.

Whatever the real version, my beautiful daddy was gone. I would be with him only when it was convenient to his travel schedule for him to pick me up. There was an added impediment to my spending time with him: it would sometimes be months before he was able to find out where we were—but that's the next part of my story.

WILLIE

Tony and the Ancient Pottery Caper... Memory comes at us in such funny little whiffs. The smell of citronella candles reminds me of the torches burning around Great-Grandmother Aileen's (Mammaw) back patio on Balboa Island. The organic-dirt smell of beets that I pull from our backyard garden today makes me nostalgic for the seaweed smell that floated on the evening air. I remember the smell of my rottweiler, Gretchen, after she came in dripping wet from a spring downpour, and I think back to Grammy Tip's basset hound, Sidney.

After Great-Grandfather Jim "Muzzie" Tweedy died, Mammaw built a house on Balboa Island, which was just a swamp at the time. Her relatives and friends thought she was crazy, but it became a family gathering place. The house was on the Grand Canal, so she had her own dock. Windows covered almost the entire front of the house, and a bricked-in courtyard with a large patio was in the back.

In the kitchen was a small table with child-sized chairs painted in a Mexican motif of bright greens, reds, yellows, and purples. We smaller children sat at that table for Thanksgiving and Christmas dinners, and we all slept in a small adjacent building (called "the bunkhouse") at the end of the courtyard.

I used to toddle out—I had to be no more than five, since the house passed out of our family in 1965—to observe the adults as they enjoyed one another's company while eating dinner on the patio. The torches were all burning, and lit candles were on the tables. I could smell the fresh fish, probably white sea bass, that my dad would have speared earlier that day. I would inhale the charred fragrance of the grill and of the lemon and cilantro used to enhance the fish's flavor. I would watch and listen silently as the Upton and Tweedy relatives drank wine out of intricately cut cobalt blue goblets that glowed with the reflected candlelight.

Grammy Tip often laughed. She had a knowing, twinkling, winking little laugh that sounded like a chipmunk's chirp. It was infectious, and I loved to hear it because it would make me laugh, too, even when I was not in the mood.

And then Mammaw passed away. Tip, afraid that there might eventually be a squabble over who would get the Balboa house when she herself died, sold it for $65,000. Today it is worth millions, but that is someone else's story.

Grammy Tip's next home was just as striking as the Balboa house her mother had owned but in entirely different ways. Situated in the hills near Whittier, it was like a Bavarian cottage with California flair. It had stone walls, a fireplace in the middle of the great room inside, and a spacious kitchen with a large window that looked out onto the hills. The back of the house sat at the edge of a cliff, and it was ringed by a wide open terrace bordered by a waist-high concrete wall with embedded concrete spindles. Avocado trees created a great canopy above the terrace so that it was always shady, even when the sunset would make the hills behind the house uncomfortably warm.

By the time my father joined the Navy at twenty, Grandfather Albert and Grammy Tip had long since divorced and Grammy Tip had remarried. Carmine Marinzano was a heavyset Sicilian and the grandson of a Sicilian Mafia kingpin. At times it was hard to understand his English, but his voice had a lilting, musical sound. His nickname was Tony, and we called him Grandpa Tony. Tony treated us kindly most of the time and was a wonderful cook.

On a night that I'll remember forever, or at least my backside will, Tony was preparing a feast for the entire Upton clan—Mom, Dad, all four of us kids, and Uncle Tom's family of five. The evening's entertainment was to feature Tony attempting to teach some of us to ballroom dance after having dinner. In the cool evenings, torches cast a romantic, subdued glow on any would-be dancers as they twirled around the concrete floor.

"Hey, Willie, let's go exploring," my cousin and best buddy Jimmy whispered to me. The romance of the setting was lost on us—we were six years old and ready for every chance at adventure, even if we had to manufacture it ourselves. And, oh, could we manufacture. When my cousin Jimmy and I got together, it was pure mayhem.

We climbed up to the rocky area just above the house, where we discovered something amazing buried beneath the thick ivy covering the hill—a line of ancient pottery. This was the stuff of dreams! All those pots begging to be liberated from some awful ancient past. There was nothing to do but to roll those suckers off that cliff. We were heroes, brilliantly and gallantly disposing of all that debris. We took turns pushing them, and they catapulted off the rocky edge, exploding into pieces against the house's stone walls. Our epic adventure ended when we heard the third dinner bell ring. We knew better than to be late.

As we sat down to eat with the rest of the cousins, we saw Tony emerge from the kitchen, butcher knife in hand. He looked menacing. His eyes behind his thick glasses were a bit bloodshot, which meant that Grandpa Tony had probably been drinking. And when he drank, he could turn mean.

"Jimmy!" he called out. The tone of his voice meant we were about to be busted for something. But then, I thought to myself, *He only said "Jimmy."* That's good. I had dodged the bullet.

Then he turned toward me. "Willie!"

Jimmy and I locked eyes. We'd take the fall together.

"What have you kids been doing?"

The room went silent. Across the table, every other cousin, brother, and sister began to smile. They knew what was coming and they had front-row seats.

"What is going on?" interjected Uncle Tom.

For a second, I thought he might be cool about the trouble we'd created. Nope, he was already unbuckling his belt.

Then Mafia Tony ratted on us. "I was planning to put some shrubs in those pots! And now they are all ruined! They are broken all over by the side of the house!"

Reality hit us. Those pots were not artifacts at all! We had just hammered hundreds of dollars of pottery into driveway gravel. We were tongued-tied.

From across the table I could see my brother Jim trying to hide his laughter.

"Whaaaa, whaaa, no more, please no more! Whaaa!" Jim began imitating the sounds we would emit when we took our whipping.

Every brother, sister, or cousin smiled behind their napkins as they waited for our punishment like a flock of turkey buzzards circling roadkill.

The next thing we knew, we were bent over, grabbing our ankles, while Uncle Tom whipped our behinds with thirteen strikes of a very thin leather belt. The air whistled as he swung back at each stroke.

That time I did cry. The backs of my legs felt raw. I was the living illustration of the threat, "I'll spank you so hard you won't be able to sit down." Trust me when I say that my backside and legs stung so bad that when we were sent back to the table with the rest of the kids, who were laughing hysterically, I was afraid to touch my rear to the seat.

But it wasn't the first time, nor would it be the last. My cousin Jimmy and I were closer than brothers. Before I got involved in TV, we had planned to enter the Navy together (I wanted to use that route to become a marine biologist). One or the other of us was always dreaming up some stunt or other. More than once we cooked up ways to get each other out of school for the day, claiming a "family emergency."

One summer at Great-Grandma's on Balboa Island, we hid coins deep within the cracks of the public fishing dock, telling each other that one of us could come back years from that day and find them.

They're still there. I don't know if Jimmy's ever checked to find any, but every time I go back to the beach, I try to find a coin on the dock. As recently as six years ago, I found a couple of them—our own little artifacts of times past. "If one leaves this earth before the other," we had declared, "it is the other's sworn duty to retrieve a coin and place it in the casket with the other. In case it's missing, two new ones are required to keep the connection between us."

I miss those days. I miss that guy. I haven't spent time with him for almost twenty years. We've chatted once on the phone, but that's about it. Jimmy did go on to a career in the Navy, so if there is a next chapter in our saga, it may have to be written in Washington State, where he retired.

Summer Adventures of the Upton Cousins...

I was nine years old when I started smoking cigarettes, a habit that I wouldn't give up for many years. Both my parents were smokers at the time, but I didn't pick up the habit from them.

I started smoking Pall Mall cigarettes on my family's summer trips to Mexico, which we took with Uncle Tom's family every year. Cigarettes were easy to come by in Mexico, and Jimmy and I would buy a pack or sneak one from our parents and then disappear into the rocks near our campsites to light up secretly.

From the time I was two years old, our families would load into our two four-by-fours—Dad's International Scout and my uncle's Jeep—and caravan down the Baja California peninsula. The Baja of those days was a different world from what it is today. The only houses we would see were adobe huts—no one had even thought of building luxury resorts along the water.

Our first real stop was San Quintin, two days' journey at the north end, and then we'd continue south to Cabo San Lucas at the southern tip, camping along the way. When I say we "camped," I mean we really camped. The Uptons could easily be 150 miles from the nearest village or outpost, and they'd sleep on the ground and bathe with lye soap in the ocean. Until 1974 the narrow roads were merely dirt, and we had to go by off-road vehicles, hightailing it across the desert at a dizzying four to six miles per hour—hard to believe that a speedometer could register that low.

We traveled for a month and a half or more every summer— Dad saved up his vacation time, and Tom, who was a biology teacher during those years, had the summers off.

My cousin Jimmy and I spent those long, hot, dusty summer days as explorers and adventurers. Inside caves we discovered things that were the stuff of boys' dreams: turquoise and silver mines, pieces of petrified wood, ammonites, even a piece of dinosaur bone one time. Another time a local Indian showed us where pirates had supposedly hidden boxes of gold coins many years ago. We didn't find any gold ourselves, but what a blast! Two boys in the coastal wilderness looking for real hidden treasure.

Many of the people who lived in those adobe huts became

as loyal and trusting as family. Somehow word would get to the people we'd see every year that we were on our way, and at the final stop our friends Pepe and Tulita would be waiting. We always carried food, clothing, and materials that Dad and Uncle Tom would take to the village elders, and they would pass the goods among the people as needed. We never worked on any buildings or did anything else—we just brought things they could use. And they seemed to prefer it that way.

Some of our adventures were pretty hair-raising. It was not unheard of for one of us to wake up in the morning to find a scorpion, stinger tail up, next to our face. On one trip I woke up one morning with bites of some kind all over my head. They were pus-filled and itched and hurt like mad. We never figured out what cute and cuddly little creature spent an entire night munching on my head and sucking the blood out. Eventually those nasty welts went away by themselves, but I hoped never to visit that particular area again, and we never did.

Nearly driving off of a cliff one summer was a special treat. My uncle's Jeep was a couple miles in front of us when, without warning, Dad brought the car to a dead stop.

"Everybody out the other side!" Dad ordered.

We were hanging off the side of a cliff with an eighty-foot drop below. We had to gingerly open the door and slip out, taking care not to shake the car, which was hanging onto the dirt by two wheels and the differential. Climbing out, we realized just how precarious Dad's position was. He was stuck in the driver's seat with no way out. One wrong shift of weight and my dad would be taking the quick way down the canyon. Dad got on the CB radio to tell Uncle Tom to turn around. Mom, not thinking, slammed the passenger door. Wham!

I'm convinced they heard the string of curse words in Mexico City. Tom arrived with his usual cat-got-the-canary grin, and he must have said something pretty funny to Dad because Dad let fly another string of curses, detailing several things that could end up in several places if Tom didn't get the chain out and pull the stricken vehicle into a more stable position.

Even those adventures were fun. Looking back on those days, though, I realize there were many times my mother hated them. Not all the time, but when things got a little messy, such as when the ice chest containing all of the canned milk, mustard, ketchup, mayonnaise, eggs, and who knows what else, took a jolt from the car bouncing on the road and exploded internally, creating a chest full of "Baja vomit surprise." I laughed, and my sister Kim looked disgusted and turned her head away from it. And Mom? After she stopped crying, I'm pretty sure Dad poured her a stiff drink.

No question that Mom and Tom's wife, Kathy, got the brunt of the cooking for us all—not much of a vacation for them, I think now. At the time, though, I never thought of it as work. I mean, come on. They got to be hundreds of miles from the nearest any-thing, with bugs that chewed their heads, scorpions under their shoes, and dust and dirt that wouldn't come out of their clothes for months. Plus the occasional Mexican Indian riding up on a horse and demanding to spend the night "round the ole campfire" while eyeing the womenfolk. What could be more fun than that?

My sister? Well, Kim was a very girly-girl. I'm not sure she liked it much then, but let's face it, the bragging rights are awesome! And I'm sure she made the most of them, as anyone would.

Eventually the Upton families would make their way back to California, civilization, and school. In 1968, I entered the fourth grade after one of our summer adventures. Suntanned, blond, and fearless from all my outdoor adventures, I was the quintessential California kid. That year none of us knew I would have a teacher who would be instrumental in changing my life.

MAYLO

Apartments, Apartments, All More or Less the Same... We pulled up to the grocery store, and my mother sank down in her seat, trying to keep from being seen. "All right, listen. Just go in and ask for the manager. Take this copy of the bounced check and tell him that your mom has been really sick. Go ahead and cry if you need to. Tell him your mom will be in within one week with cash, OK? I am going to pull around to the side of the building, all right? Tell him you walked here."

I was cleaned up and specially dressed. All the manager could do was look at me and say, "OK, honey. Tell your mother I am holding this check until next week."

In a week we would pull up to the Safeway again. This time my mother would hand me dollars. And in I would go, proud to hand the store manager our money. It felt good and solid to come through. It felt like a small testimony, as if we were saying, "See? We aren't losers. We had the money. My mom was just sick." It felt proper, even though it was a lie. It was a lie for the right reasons, right?

We were on our own, living in a series of apartments in towns like Van Nuys, Sherman Oaks, and Reseda. They were all more or less the same: stained-green shag carpets; sticky kitchen appliances, usually burnt gold with a knob missing; and the classic

33

apartment refrigerator with the little upper freezer that had frozen over like a miniature igloo inside, leaving just enough room for the small unidentifiable Glad-Wrapped package of who-knows-what that we kept taking out, looking at, and throwing back in. The chipped Formica countertop always had to have at least one cigarette burn or one brown circular stain marring it—it wouldn't be home without one of them. Same with the bathroom counters. And the whole apartment, no matter where it was, smelled like cigarette smoke and cooked onions when we first moved into it.

The buildings' exteriors were painted with a thin coat of cheap stucco that was originally pink but had faded to a sickly flesh color. We lived upstairs in a lot of them, and the stairs were made of slabs that looked like gravel stuck together and mounted to a metal rail. You could see right through them between the steps, and I, who was always expecting the worst to happen, just knew I was going to fall through the gap in one of those steps one day.

Mother usually had an easel and oil paints set up in the dining area. If she was working on a painting, the apartment would have a sharp, distinct oil-based paint smell. I liked that smell, and I liked to see her work in progress. Her paints, little smudges of brown, black, blue, and green that she would blend together, would be left out on her palette, which she set down on the kitchen table.

Sometimes people who visited the apartment would offer her money for one of her paintings. One painting in particular was always hanging over our couch, no matter where we lived. It was an emotional, troubled seascape with white foamy tips jumping out of the dark green waters, and I thought it was beautiful.

Our apartments smelled like a mixture of those paints and turpentine, cigarette smoke, and . . . I don't how to explain it . . . a people smell. The same smell you might notice if you put your head on an old couch, maybe a garage couch, and inhaled as hard as you could. They smelled a little old and more than a little dusty.

My mother herself had a strong personal smell that was a combination of Aquanet hair spray and powder makeup and a woman's dirty clothing. She smelled salty and sticky and always had stale cigarette breath. Her red hair was always teased and sprayed. One of her favorite haircuts was a Farrah Fawcett style, cut in layers. She would tease the back and sides so that it had that big "Texas hair" look. She loved long, long nails, and she always wore heavy makeup but rarely washed it off.

I thought my mother was very pretty and very funny. She had an infectious laugh that would somehow seem like a proclamation—"It isn't bad, Maylo; it's going to be OK"—when I felt jumpy or fearful. I loved it when she laughed. That belly laugh made me feel like she wasn't scared—like she had things under control. That was when I still trusted her.

Mom had a lot of boyfriends. In spite of the crusty makeup and her strong body odor, she must have been telegraphing, "I'm available; I'm interested," because the men came around often. I did not like most of them. But Mom would just smile and turn on the charm.

When Mom had a man, we had food. I would come home after school, and the apartment would smell like something yummy was cooking, maybe a roast. When that man's role in Mom's fickle attentions was over, we would be back to ketchup soup and a few slices of bread. There was one time when all Mom had was enough change to buy a cup of coffee. We went to the Denny's restaurant down the street, and Mom ordered a cup. She topped it off with cream, and we took turns sipping it.

From time to time Mom would get jobs as a keypunch operator. We were always tight for money, so when she came home with a paycheck, she would be in a great mood. *Maybe we'll be able to get ahead, to pay some bills, to have the water turned back on,* I'd think. We would go to the grocery store, and I would get any box of sugary cereal I wanted! (To this day cereal has a stable, homey feeling to me.)

Then, while I sat with my bowl in front of the TV, she would more often than not go treat herself to a haircut on Rodeo Drive in Beverly Hills by one of the most famous—and no doubt expensive—celebrity hairstylists of the day, José Eber. And then, as quickly as the money had come in, it was gone. No bills were paid. And the man of the moment was gone too.

Mother's job would be gone soon as well. She'd start calling in sick or would just quit without notice. As she lay around the house, she'd begin to have visions, what she called "imagining."[1] I would go off to school, knowing that more than likely she would lie on the sofa all day long, staring off into a world that I was not part of.

She was extremely sure of herself during those times and often told me of the great future that was ahead of us. She had seen it! She had imagined it! I would come home from school, and she would talk breathlessly of the miniature animals that had been entertaining her and of tongues of fire in the corner of the living room. A young girl wants to believe her mother, and she described her visions to me with such conviction that I had no way to convince her that she was wrong. But I was at a loss, since I saw nothing but shabby carpet, an empty refrigerator, and a stained couch.

Taylor and Lana... "This is my *beautiful daughter*." My dad used to introduce me to his gay friends as if I, too, were one of the Hollywood people he spent his time with—glamorous and glittery people who lived in gorgeous hillside mansions. I felt like a fraud. I was secretly embarrassed about the dingy apartments I really lived in and used to worry that if they knew where I lived, they wouldn't like me as much.

---

1. *Imagining* is an important word in regard to my mother's visions and will appear often in my story. I use it in a specific way because she used it in a specific way—for her visions.

My father had changed his name to Taylor. Though I didn't know it then, I realize now that the name was a tribute to Elizabeth Taylor, one of the Hollywood divas he worshipped from afar. His mother, Grandma Rose, refused to call him by his new name. "Your name is Bill," she would angrily insist.

My father was home from touring. When he could find us, he'd pick me up, and we'd spend weekends with him at lavish parties thrown by his friends or go to the beachfront, beautifully decorated penthouse of the famous movie star Lana Turner.

Lana was truly one of the last glamour girls, a star with a capital S. Her surroundings were the essence of luxury. Everything about Lana was platinum and shimmered. Even in her bathrobe, with her hair swept up in a white turban and with no makeup on, she looked shiny to me.

I'm not sure how Lana Turner and my dad met, but at some point while I was still small, he began serving as her personal manager. My dad seemed happy to be a buddy to her, mostly in the background and a handsome escort to gala events. The pictures around his apartment highlighted him with her at various parties, but the pictures showed only the public face of their relationship—the way things were meant to look for her adoring fans, not what was underneath.

My dad later described an evening event to which he escorted Miss Turner. Lana, dripping in emeralds and diamonds, was attired in a fire-engine red lace gown especially designed for her, while he wore a tuxedo (formerly owned by the popular singer Vic Damone) that he had purchased for twenty-five dollars at The Glamour Shop, a charitable celebrity secondhand store.

By the time my father and Miss Turner began their ten-year relationship, Lana was divorced from her seventh and last husband, the hypnotist Ronald Dante. About ten years prior, Lana and her only daughter, Cheryl Crane, had been involved in a public scandal—the stabbing death of Johnny Stompanato, a minor gangster who had been a lover of Lana's.

According to people who knew him, Stompanato could be intimidating, and Lana had been under his spell but apparently wanted to break off the relationship. Stompanato had choked her almost to the point of strangulation, slapped her, and demanded to accompany her to the glittering events that were on her calendar.

She was nominated for an Oscar for her role in 1957's *Peyton Place* and was excited to attend the Academy Awards in the spring of 1958, but she refused to let Johnny escort her, which sent him into a rage. Later that evening he slapped and punched her, leaving visible cuts and bruises. (You can read more of this story online at Mark Gribben's "Lana Turner and Johnny Stompanato: Hollywood Homicide," http://www.crimelibrary.com/notorious_mur ders/famous/lana_turner/2.html, 02 February 2006.)

A few days later the arguments continued in Lana's bedroom, and Cheryl Crane, Lana's fourteen-year-old daughter from her earlier marriage to the actor Stephen Crane, listened to the escalating fight from her room next door. Cheryl ran down to the kitchen, grabbed a carving knife, ran back upstairs, and begged her mother to open the door. She made such a ruckus that her mother finally let her in. Stompanato was taking some of his clothes out of the closet, but Cheryl later said it had looked to her as if he had a weapon in one hand. As he walked toward her and the door, she stabbed him in the stomach. He quickly bled to death.

At least that's the official version. The unofficial version is that Lana herself may have used that kitchen knife on Johnny and allowed her daughter to take the fall, since Cheryl was a minor. There was an inquest, and Cheryl was put into detention for a while. A grand jury convened, and Lana, who was the only person other than her daughter to witness the stabbing, was given the acting role of a lifetime—having to convince a jury that it was justified. Thanks to her performance and that of one of Hollywood's most famous defense attorneys, Jerry Geisler, Cheryl's act was ruled justifiable homicide.

I knew nothing of the event that Lana Turner forever after referred to as "the happening."[2] By the time I first saw Cheryl Crane, she seemed on good terms with her mother. She was at the penthouse quite often, usually in the company of a woman who I later found out was her long-time lesbian lover.

Miss Turner was somewhat of a recluse by the time my dad started taking me with him. He would fix her a drink of cranberry juice mixed with vodka, at the same time treating himself to one, so that she always had a drink nearby or in her hand. On some days she was sad. Sometimes she would stay in her bedroom, and I wouldn't see her at all. I would play quietly with her mice collection, which she allowed me to do. She had miniature mice of many kinds and colors—crystal, bronze, ceramic, and even one of solid gold, and they were all displayed in a glass curio cabinet.

When she was in a more social mood, though, what a magical time I would have! Her loyal maid of thirty years, Arminda, treated me with kindness. I had learned to read well at a young age, and Lana would give me a copy of a script she was practicing so I could run through the lines with her. Those weekends were glamorous beyond description. I never wanted to leave. I used to dream of becoming her child.

I did not know the whole story of her relationship with my father, but I found out years later. After so many years of being worshipped and courted by so many men, Lana was used to being in control. She would fly into jealous rages, often directed at my father's lover, Bud. If she knew they were together for the weekend, she would call my dad every fifteen minutes, demanding some little service from him.

---

2. I learned about this phrase in Mark Gribben's online article.

Of course, most of what I observed was only what was on the surface, not what went on behind closed doors. As far as I knew, Miss Turner was the very model of graciousness, glamour, and kindness. At least she was to me. The only thing was, I had to go back home at the end of the weekend.

My Daughter Is Not a Tomato!... "Maylo, Maylo, big fat potato! Maylo Tomato! Maylo Tomato!"

The San Fernando Valley is surrounded by hills that turn into mountain ranges like the Santa Anas and the Santa Monicas. It sits still and dusty like a big bowl of brown grit. One of its hundreds of cross streets is Hazeltine Avenue, the busy four-lane street we lived on for a while. I had to walk the sidewalks of that congested street to and from Hazeltine Elementary School.

The air smelled of exhaust fumes, and when cars passed me they made a scary whooshing sound, causing a tense child like me to feel jumpy and nervous. The sidewalk didn't seem wide enough to protect me as I strode with an anxious sense of purpose, clenching my teeth.

Why I was a target was a puzzle to me, but they seemed to think my name was hilariously funny. There they were, right behind me, following me home and into the apartment courtyard—five girls chanting the hated words in a singsong cadence.

I was trying not to acknowledge their taunts, but my mother heard them. With curlers in her hair and days of mascara under her eyes, she ran onto the balcony, screaming, "My daughter is *not* a tomato!"

When the girls saw my mom and heard her angry screams, they burst out laughing and turned around, running back up Hazeltine Avenue. She slammed the door so hard that it shook the apartment, still muttering about those "so-and-so kids" and what she was going to do with them if she caught them.

I went up the stairs into the apartment, wanting to die. Screaming and yelling, Mom took the battle on, and as usual, it became hers. I wanted to shrink down into something so small. I just sat on the couch, looking straight ahead. An occasional hot tear would roll down my cheek, but that's all the emotion I would let her see. I think this incident was the first time that I gave up. There was no one to tell about my mom's rages. I couldn't talk about them or do anything to make my life any better. I was just . . . quiet.

Grandma Peggy was around the apartment a lot in the Hazeltine days because she and Mom were getting along well during that period. I wanted to tell Grandma about my mother's unpredictable moods, but I sensed that my complaints might be not only futile but also betraying. No matter, though. We soon moved, and I didn't see Grandma for months. I never knew the reason we lost touch with Mom's family from time to time. Mom would just pick me up at school, take me back to the apartment, order me to grab my things, and we'd be gone—just like that.

Our next apartment was a lot darker than the one on Hazeltine. It felt like a cave. A hole. It was on the ground floor away from the street, so we didn't hear the din of horns honking and the occasional crashes of fender against fender. But it had only one window that looked out at a shady concrete courtyard, barring all sunshine from reaching our apartment.

Without much to do or friends to play with—"Maylo Tomato Big Fat Potato" was not a girl anyone wanted to hang around with—I watched TV for hours. I sensed that Mom was unhappy. I almost never heard her big belly laugh. She sat on the couch and smoked one cigarette after another, legs and arms crossed in forbidding, distant body language, cursing and complaining about what a spiteful old man (she used much stronger language) her father was, how her mother tried to control her life, and how we weren't going to put up with it.

That was the pattern that defined my childhood. Mom and I—and later my brother and sister—were in and out of Aunt Judy's, Grandma Peggy's, Grandpa Harry's, or my Daddy Bill's lives, depending on whether Mom needed money or babysitting help from them. When she got desperate, she would become suddenly sweet and contrite as she placed a phone call to one of them. Judy, Harry, or Peggy would reappear, and we might spend days at their houses. When my mother got angry again, she'd tell me to grab some things and we'd move.

We'd be out of contact with Mom's family, but she still had plenty of company. In addition to her male "friends" was a group of people she had become involved with. Her visions gave her some notoriety within this group, which was led by a man called Godfrey.[3] When she and Grandma Peggy were speaking to each other, they would go to meetings of Godfrey's followers together. Fellow "Godfreyites" sometimes would come over to our stale-smelling apartment and sit, talk, and smoke around our yellow Formica-topped kitchen table or go into her bedroom and close the door. Sometimes they'd turn off the lamps, light a candle in the middle of the table, and try to contact spirits while passing around a marijuana joint. They had a secretive attitude and mostly talked in whispers, as if afraid someone would hear them. I didn't know what they were talking about, but I felt left out. I didn't like many of them, either—I didn't like the looks some of them gave me, as if they were assessing me for some purpose they had in mind. There was just something about those looks . . .

---

3. Throughout my childhood, this man was a central presence in my mother's life. He had a small but devoted, fanatically devoted, following that does not take kindly to negative comments about him, so for safety's sake I have changed his name. Let me be clear, though: he was an actual, not an imaginary, person and he has since passed away.

WILLIE

Willie Aames Is Born... In the fall of 1966 I began the second grade at Eader Elementary School in Huntington Beach. By the fourth grade I found myself with a new teacher, Miss Jenny Earley. Young and beautiful with hair down to her waist, she was the kind of teacher who was continually involving her students in active learning activities such as games and skits. Every boy in the fourth grade thought she was hot!

Miss Earley had a boyfriend, Reggie, who stopped by the class every now and then. He saw me hamming it up in classroom plays and began asking me if I'd ever thought of trying out for commercials. For the next two or three months, every time he saw me, he brought up the subject. I started thinking that I might like to give it a try.

"Mom and Dad, what would you think if I was on TV?" I asked them one day after school.

"Yeah, great, Willie. Now go outside and clean up after the dog."

I don't think Mom really paid any attention.

I kept asking my mother and father the same question. One day Reggie told me that he wanted to take me to Los Angeles to introduce me to an agent. Reggie had told me that he was a friend of the Mattel brothers and he wanted to introduce me to them. So I told him where my mother worked as a manicurist in a beauty salon in Newport Beach, and he went over to meet her. I wasn't there, but he asked her if he could take me to meet the agent, and she agreed to let me go. Simple as that.

After immediately being thrown out of the Mattel building, we got back in the car, and he drove me to the Sunset Boulevard offices of Toni Kelman, the premier children's film and television agent. Miss Kelman handled most of the kids on *The Brady Bunch*, as well as Johnny Whittaker (who played Jody in the TV show *A Family Affair*), Jodie Foster, and some others.

We were in the office awhile, and after I had talked with Miss Kelman, Reggie discussed my future with her. We finally headed back to Huntington Beach. Reggie had told my mother he'd have me back by 5:00 p.m., but I didn't get home until after 9:00.

"Jean, you're telling me that you let our nine-year-old boy go off by himself with a total stranger!" My dad was incredulous. As I think about it, that's the first time I remember anyone being worried about where I was. My parents argued for quite a while that evening, and after that day I never saw Reggie again. I do not know what happened to him. I don't know if my father threatened him or if Toni Kelman told him to back out of the arrangement. (Toni has passed away, and Toni's daughter, Sandy, whom I spoke with recently, does not know either.) All I know is that Reggie quit coming to the classroom.

A couple of weeks went by. One day, the phone rang and Dad picked it up.

"This is the Toni Kelman Agency. We have an interview for Willie."

"What in the world are you talking about?" Dad sounded annoyed.

"We're Willie's agents," the voice on the phone explained.

"Willie doesn't *have* an agent," Dad said, ready to hang up. "No way. I'm completely against this. He's not going to try out for any commercials."

"Mr. Upton, please at least give it some thought. We think Willie would be perfect for the job we have in mind," said Miss Kelman's assistant.

As soon as the conversation ended, I began a campaign of begging and badgering, and my dad began a counter campaign of telling me why he thought acting was a bad idea. He said the chances were a million to one that I'd even get chosen, I'd never get an education if I did get chosen, and the people in the entertainment business were overpaid egomaniacs.

I began working on my mother too. As with everything else I tried, I was determined to do this. My older brothers were athletes—track captains and high-school heartthrobs, and Kim was probably going to end up a cheerleader. I had . . . nothing. I wasn't even in the game. I finally asked if I could at least do the audition and see what happened. They came around, sort of—actually, they thought they had outsmarted me. They made a deal.

"We'll give you three months," they said. "If you can get a job in those three months, then you can continue. If you don't, you've had your shot, and that will be the end of it."

Two weeks later I got my first job, a commercial for Phillips 66, a nationwide gasoline company. In the commercial I was a little boy selling lemonade on the street. An old prospector came crawling up to me, begging for a glass of lemonade, and I gave him one. In return he gave me a bag of gold. I believe the slogan was "Phillips 66 puts gold in your tank" or some similar classic 1960s slogan.

The commercial was finished, or so I thought. Two days later I got a call at home. The commercial had to be reshot. Why? I had done the entire commercial with my zipper down.

Such was the first in a long line of silly incidents that I apparently had a unique talent for. As a teenager I did two Bob Hope specials. Whenever Bob did a special, he topped it off with a live performance at the Universal Amphitheater. In every one of them, as he introduced my band from the stage, I was just coming out of the bathroom—two Bob Hope specials, two times in the toilet. It got to the point where he said, "Lights on the toilet—Mr. Willie Aames, ladies and gentlemen."

Later on when I started touring with my rock band, I also became famous, or infamous, for splitting my pants open during a show. Not intentionally—I just would get carried away with the theatrics and voila! I would end up revealing almost as much skin as Michelangelo's *David*.

Thus began the career of Willie Aames, child actor. Where did my name come from? People have asked me if it's a family name or if I am related to Ed Ames, a popular recording artist ("Try to Remember" and "My Cup Runneth Over," among others) who also played Mingo on the TV version of *Daniel Boone*. And I tell them the simple truth: there was another Willie Upton listed in the Screen Actors Guild, so I had to have another name. Toni Kelman chose "Aames" for me because with an *A* as both the first and second letters, I would always be sure to get top billing in an alphabetical list of actors. So the mystery of my unusual last name is now revealed.

Welcome to TV Land... "Brandon, take it easy, take it easy. It's going to be OK."

Brandon Cruz was having a meltdown. Bill Bixby's voice was soothing and calm as he sat facing his young co-star who played his son, Eddie.

The studio had given Brandon the Yamaha motorcycle used in the opening footage for *The Courtship of Eddie's Father* each week. It was a prized possession that Brandon kept his eye on all the time. But in one scene with the bike, one of the props crew needed to treat it with dulling spray to tone down the glare on its shiny finish for the camera lenses. Brandon, who was only eight or nine, quieted down a little as Bill walked off the set, saying, "I'll be right back."

In a few minutes Bill drove onto the set behind the wheel of his pride and joy, a light-green classic convertible—an MG, maybe. Whatever it was, the car was obviously an expensive collector's automobile with a leather trundle case on the back, chrome spiked wheels, big tin drum lights in front, and a rich buttery-tan leather interior. He handed the keys to the props manager. "Here, go ahead and spray it if you need to."

Brandon got the message. He looked at his little yellow motorcycle and said, "OK."

One of the crew got on the cycle and drove it off the set to be sprayed.

Bill Bixby was the only other person I've ever met whose family goes back farther into California's early days than mine. He was a sixth-generation Californian; I am a fifth-generation Californian. He died of cancer in 1993 at the age of fifty-nine. I miss him. He was a kind and decent man.

By the time I was in the fifth grade, I had been in several commercials, and it seemed to work for me. *The Courtship of Eddie's Father* series (1969–72) was one of the first major TV shows that I worked on. In March 1971 I got a guest role as a boy named Scott, a friend of Bill's son, Eddie. After that initial appearance I played Harold O'Brien, a friend of Eddie's, for several episodes into the middle of 1972.

By the time I reported for my first job on *Courtship*, I was already a fan of the show and couldn't wait to meet Miyoshi Umeki, a beautiful, soft-voiced Japanese actress who played Mrs. Livingston, the family's housekeeper. Never mind that she was thirty years older than I was—I had a crush on her! I was so smitten that I could hardly look at her when we were on the set at the same time, and I would find an excuse to stand behind her just out of her range of vision when she was having her makeup put on.

The cast and crew of *Courtship* had a familial camaraderie, though they were also somewhat hierarchical, which was traditional in those days. Your place in the hierarchy was based on your position in the show but also on others' respect for your art or craft. At the same time, almost everyone on the set was treated as though they mattered and brought something valuable to the process of putting a show together.

I ate up this affirmation. When I arrived, everyone would be laughing and telling jokes, and they welcomed me to join right in as if I were important to them.

Brandon was a couple years younger than I, and we got on very well. He could be a handful at times—he taught me some risqué limericks and parodies of some familiar songs that he must have learned from one of the grips or wardrobe people. I don't remember Brandon's parents being around the set much. His grandparents were often sitting nearby, but the people on the set became his family—they were the ones watching out for him.

The *Courtship* guest roles led to appearances on other series shows and additional commercials. One commercial offered the opportunity of a lifetime—a chance to appear in the same scene with Henry Fonda. It was for a new version of the Viewmaster. Even my mom and dad, who did not usually seem impressed with anything I did in TV, were in awe that I was working with Mr. Fonda. He seemed like a nice man, but it wasn't until I was in my late teens that I realized how fortunate I had been.

Within a year or two, I had roles on *The Odd Couple*, *Adam-12*, *Gunsmoke*, *Cannon*, *Adam's Rib*, and *Medical Center*—most of them also CBS series shows. On one *Medical Center*, "Nowhere

Child," the series' lead actor, Chad Everett, directed the episode. It was his first chance to direct on the series, and the episode was nominated for a Golden Globe in 1971. I played an eleven-year-old orphan who was up for adoption but who was discovered to have a brain tumor, causing my adoptive parents to have second thoughts about the adoption.

As I lay covered with a white blanket on a gurney, I happened to notice something that made me swell with pride—in the inky blackness just offstage, I recognized Bill Bixby's silhouette and glasses as he stood and watched the scene being shot. I wanted to get his attention so much! I kept trying to sneak a wave to him, and finally he just said quietly, "Hello, Willie."

There was just something about the way he knew my name and singled me out. I don't know why he wouldn't have known who I was—I had been on *Courtship* several times—but his recognition was an acknowledgment from somebody I admired. It was a validation from an adult that meant I was worth something. Later I found out that he had come over from his set because he had heard that I was on the show.

As Bill observed the action, he and Chad got into a mock argument over who had discovered me first. I lay there, a kid with crooked teeth and freckles and a mop of brown hair that had turned blonde from being in the water and sun, and I felt like anything but a nowhere child—I felt like an equal.

I was punchy with happiness. That day it hit me that I was being allowed to do something special that other kids didn't get to do. And when the take was done, I could go sit in a director's chair if I wanted to and hang out with the guys. It didn't even cross my mind that they were many years older than I was. I could stand up with them and be recognized, even if the respect I got was in a make-believe world.

The All-American Boy...I guess I had the look of the all-American boy, whatever that means. At least Toni Kelman thought so. Back at home in Huntington Beach, I was just a typical California kid. I attended public school when I wasn't working and spent as much time as I could scuba diving, fishing off the Huntington Beach pier, or surfing. Then there were the summer camping trips to Mexico, which increased my survival skills and toughened me up. Being outdoors so much bleached my hair, tanned my skin, and increased my freckles, but Toni turned the way I looked into jobs. She was responsible for all the auditions I got for commercials, pilots, guest appearances, and tryouts for weekly series shows.

Because Toni also handled Jodie Foster, we ended up working together in several Reynolds Wrap commercials and *Gunsmoke* episodes from 1971 to 1973. My favorite was a 1971 Christmas episode of *Gunsmoke*, the only Christmas episode done in the entire run of the show. I played Tom, a local boy in some kind of trouble—a type of role that I loved doing. We also screen-tested together for the film version of *Tom Sawyer*, and I think I gave Jodie her first onscreen kiss in that test. I was about thirteen, and she was a couple of years younger.

Jodie already had the part, but I lost it when my foolhardiness landed me in the hospital. My parents had warned me not to take my bike on a rough stretch of road. I got around their restriction by taking a *friend's* bike. I flipped it and broke my jaw in three places. Johnny Whitaker, another actor about my age with red, curly hair and lots of freckles, got the role of Tom. But I didn't care. Everything I was doing was so much fun that I just took it all in stride.

Neither my mother nor my father pushed me to get more roles, to play more parts, to make more money. Mom seemed agreeable enough to what I was doing, and she always managed to get me wherever I needed to be, but she was far from the typical Hollywood mother. She and Dad were almost the other extreme—they never acknowledged that any skill on my part was involved in the roles I got. They'd just tell me I was lucky. Maybe that's why I coveted the validation of my fellow actors so much.

I did forty to fifty commercials and about one hundred guest-starring roles from the age of nine until I was about fourteen. I was in a couple of miniseries (*Rich Man, Poor Man* and *Benjamin Franklin*, among others), a couple of TV pilots, a short-lived TV series called *We'll Get By*, and a couple of TV movies during those years.

Alan Alda created and co-produced *We'll Get By*, which starred Paul Sorvino as a New Jersey lawyer with three children. Sorvino is most famous now for gangster roles such as Paul Cicero in *Goodfellas*. I remember his cute eight- or nine-year-old daughter, Mira, who has become an immensely talented actress, running around the studio. We were in the midst of filming in August 1974. I was all of fourteen years old, playing his son, Kenny. One of the crew burst onto the stage and interrupted our rehearsal. "Get to the TV. You gotta see this."

We all stood and watched. President Nixon began speaking about the trials of Watergate. And then he came out with it: "I have never been a quitter . . . but as president, I must put the interest of America first. America needs a full-time president and a full-time Congress, particularly at this time with problems we face at home and abroad . . . . Therefore, I shall resign the presidency effective at noon tomorrow. Vice President Ford will be sworn in as president at that hour in this office."

I could not keep the tears from streaming down my face. I admired Nixon as president. And the Upton family's ties with the Nixon family dated back thirty years or more to my grandfather Albert's days of teaching him. I stood and cried for a hero in disgrace.

Paul's politics were on the opposite end of the political continuum. He had made no secret of the fact that he hated Nixon and what he stood for. And so he stood and laughed—laughed!— at me, mockingly saying to everyone in the room, "Oh, too bad. I'm sorry, Willie. You actually like Nixon." Paul and I were in no way kindred spirits, though I highly respect him as a fine actor.

One of my favorite memories revolves around a TV movie I was in around the same time. Starring James Olson and Shirley Jones, it was titled *The Family Nobody Wanted*. It was first telecast in February 1975 and was one of those heartwarming stories that nearly everyone likes. It was a true post–World War II story about a minister and his wife who adopted more than a dozen unwanted children of different races. My character was Donny, the natural son of the minister and his wife. Shirley was fun to work with. She had a delightful sense of humor that led to a joke at my expense but which I loved.

On Christmas Eve afternoon in 1973, we were wrapping up some scenes and were tired and wanted to get home. I was full of mischief and decided everyone needed a good laugh. I asked one of the makeup artists to secretly paint "Merry Christmas" on my thirteen-year-old bare posterior with makeup.

Filming began for a scene in which several of the kids were in bed. The room was dark. I was supposed to discover that some of the kids were sick and get out of bed and run to my parents. Well, I jumped out of bed as directed, but I ad-libbed a little. I turned around and mooned the cast, with my co-conspirator shining the light on my greeting.

A couple of weeks later, payback time came, and I didn't expect it. When we resumed filming, I was concentrating on my part when someone walked up behind me and quickly pulled my pants down to my ankles. I stood midstage, dumbfounded. When I turned around, there was Shirley.

She just laughed and said, "Now, that's cute," and pulled my pants up. Everyone laughed, but no one enjoyed the "end" result of this little prank more than I did. I loved playing practical jokes on people, and I took equal delight in having them played on me.

I soon learned that reputations in Hollywood are quickly made. Two weeks later as I walked through Universal Studios, I passed by the great John Wayne, whom I had never met. He stopped me by blocking my path.

"So you're that kid who pulled his pants down for everybody," he drawled. "Nice work."

He yelled at someone over his shoulder. "Hey, Tony, come meet the kid who mooned the suits." Behind Wayne's giant frame appeared another legend, Tony Curtis. Both of them razzed me for a few minutes.

It was a strange claim to fame for a thirteen-year-old boy. What might seem odd is that it also offered me some attention. Was the attention a way to feel validated, like I mattered? At the time, it was a very pleasant substitute.

Fun and Adventure with the Family Robinson...

"My clearest memory about working with Willie Aames was that I was hopelessly in love with him. He, sadly, seemed to have a crush on the best friend I brought to the set who was much more beautiful than me. He was wonderful to work with, though his taste in women left something to be desired."

So wrote Helen Hunt recently when asked about her memories of the time we spent in a TV series together as children. Helen is nearly three years younger than I am. Like Jodie Foster, she has managed to carve out a career for herself in film and TV.

For years after we finished the show, I would occasionally run into Helen, who had mixed success and a few movies before the

TV series *Mad About You* and the film *As Good as It Gets*, for which she won an Academy Award. It's great fun for me to watch the rise of the stellar careers both she and Jodie deserve.

Helen was a pretty girl, but I honestly never saw her as someone to have a crush on. She was . . . well, Helen. My acting buddy. I was fourteen, and at that age, three years is a huge divide. Her comments today are an apt reflection of her sense of humor and lack of pretentiousness. To be truthful, I'm humbled that at her current level of success, she would be so kind as to make mention of those days. Thanks, Helen.

My biggest role to date was to come late in 1974 when I landed the part of Fred Robinson, one of the children—along with Helen, who played Helga, and Eric Olson, who played Ernie—in the TV version of the classic story *Swiss Family Robinson*, which had been made into a Disney movie in 1960. That series was produced by Irwin Allen, nicknamed Master of Disaster for his blockbusters *The Poseidon Adventure* (1972) and *The Towering Inferno* (1974).

I had worked on a series of commercials for Marineland Pacific, a popular Sea World-type tourist attraction in Southern California. I had enthusiastically fulfilled the requirements for those commercials, which included riding dolphins and working with killer whales. I guess Allen had seen those commercials and knew I was game for just about anything, so he requested me, since *Swiss Family Robinson* was an adventure series that took place outdoors. It aired for two years until both our show and *The Wonderful World of Disney* on a rival network were knocked off the air by an obscure news magazine, *60 Minutes*.

Swiss Family Robinson was a Twentieth Century Fox production that was shot in Fox's back lot in Century City and at Fox Ranch, a four-thousand-acre property in the Santa Monica Mountains that was used for outdoor shows and scenes. The famous aerial view supposedly from an Army MEDEVAC helicopter at the beginning of *M*A*S*H* was shot there; outdoor scenes from *Planet of the Apes* were also filmed on the ranch. Just down the road from our set was the set for *F Troop*, and much of the miniseries *Roots* was also being filmed there, soon to be viewed by a whopping 85 percent of American TV watchers in 1977. We'd pull up to the gate to be checked in and hear explosions going off nearby, special effects for any one of the shows.

What a dream come true this was for a boy who loved adventure! On our own set were tigers, apes, chimps, exotic birds, and baby lions, and the animal trainers would let me take some of the animals and birds home for a few nights between studio call days. Want to meet a lot of gorgeous women? Show up someplace with a lion cub in your arms or a beautiful white cockatoo on your shoulder. Talk about chick magnets. *Swiss Family Robinson* was a boy's fantasy come true in more ways than one.

There were pirates, slave traders, and natives in the cast. I sometimes had the option of doing my own stunt if the script called for me to be hanging off a cliff or something similar. Did I do it? No way would I have turned that down! The stunt coordinator would strap me into a harness, and I'd be lowered into the scene.

Meanwhile, Irwin Allen wouldn't speak to me. Every time I'd walk up to him, he'd turn and walk away. I began to get worried, so I asked Martin Milner, who played my father on the show, to see if he could find out what the problem was.

"OK, Willie, mystery solved. You ready for this?" Martin laughed. "Do you remember the first day you met Irwin and how you shook his hand? He said you hurt him!"

When I was a small boy, my grandfather Albert Upton had instructed me in one of those macho Upton lessons that I apparently took to heart. He had taught me that when you shake hands, you do it like a man. For a teenager my size to do that, I had to really clamp down. Turns out, it would sometimes hurt people. Even as

I got older, when I would grab somebody's hand, they'd say, "Wow, Willie." It wasn't intentional. But today it makes me smile to think that Mr. Allen would avoid me because of my handshake.

Sets are funny places, and each evolves into its own unique personality. Everyone in Hollywood knows which sets are fun, which sets have prima donnas for actors, which sets have heavy drug use (Maylo's *Rocky Road* set, which she'll describe in her story, was an example of that), and so on.

As a boy, with a boy's brand of fun, I wanted any show I worked on to become known for its, um, earthy sense of humor. But on a less sophomoric level, I think I also wanted to be acknowledged not only as an actor but as a person. Pranks and jokes, admittedly risqué at times, gave me some sense of personal validation. So, more often than not, I was game. Whether that was good or not so good may have depended on which side of the prank you fell on.

While I was well known for working hard when the job demanded it, I was always ready to do something to loosen up the set. I was once assigned an essay and oral presentation for English class at my public high school (where I went when I was not on the set), and I hated essays. How could I turn a painful assignment into something the whole class would get a kick out of, while leaving the teacher with serious doubts about trying this kind of assignment ever again? I was eating at Don José, a favorite Mexican restaurant, when sheer genius struck with the force of two extra-large Macho Combinacion Burritos. I'd do an essay on, ahem, references to passing gas in literature.

As a result of my "research," I had learned a dubious skill that I was dying to show Martin Milner, the actor perhaps best known for the series *Adam-12*. One day when leaving the sound stage, I felt my moment of glory arrive. Feeling the pressure to perform immediately, I ran to his dressing room, banged on his door, and begged him for a match. Within seconds I had proudly produced a spectacular flame nearly six inches long! Disgusting? Absolutely. Inappropriate? Wholly. The value of seeing the look on Marty's face? Priceless.

Mr. Milner laughed loud and hard. "I've never seen that done before! That's amazing! How did you do that?" I was happy to impart my superior knowledge of such a delicate and precise skill.

Swiss Family Robinson's weekly plots often included parts for some of Hollywood's "old guard," people from the days when actors were somehow larger than life—not like today, when we seem to want them to be just like us. Cameron Mitchell was a regular and a co-star, portraying a marooned sailor already on the island when the Robinsons shipwrecked there. Andrew Duggan guest-starred, and Neville Brand was also a show co-star. All three were old-time 1930s and '40s actors who were usually cast as tough guys.

Neville was a highly decorated military hero who went into acting after the war and had a distinguished career in both movies and TV. He was legendary for his dislike of the tourist trams that would roll through the lots where he was working. At Universal, he would refuse to work while the trams were stopping at the sets, and the story goes that Lou Wasserman, Universal's co-founder and arguably the most powerful man in Hollywood, sent him a letter, stating, "We are here to make money and those trams make money and your job is to make money. So get over yourself."

The next time a tram went by, Neville put on his best smile and nonchalantly walked over to the tram filled with tourists. But, instead of offering a handshake, he quickly unzipped and relieved himself right in front of them. Not surprisingly, the trams quit visiting that particular movie set. Guess he won that battle.

On *Swiss Family Robinson* Neville, Cameron, and Andrew showed us more of what legends are made of. Breaking for lunch in the middle of a scene full of pirates, sword fights, and explosions, the three of them went off together and came back blasted drunk, singing at the top of their lungs. With a flourish worthy of the three musketeers and in perfect unison, they finished their ballad and urinated right in front of the cast and crew. Harry Harris, one of the nicest directors I have had the pleasure to work with, ripped the megaphone from the assistant director's hand, screaming, "All right, all right, call it off. We're done for today." I felt bad for Harry, but I could *not* stop laughing.

As for what Eric, Helen, and I did between takes, we found ways to play some of those tricks that are handed down from movie to movie, set to set. This was a favorite: camera operators and their assistants ("ACs") measure from the actors' eyes to the camera lens to determine the focus. They run out a two-hundred-foot-long measuring tape as far as they need to, take the measurements, and then "ride focus" on the actors.

We'd watch and eventually figure out in which direction they'd habitually wind the tape back up. While Helen would stand guard, I would grab the tape, run it out all two hundred feet, and then wind it back up in the opposite direction. The next time the AC would drag the tape out, he'd try to wind it back, but it wouldn't rewind at all. The more he'd try to rewind the tape, the more it would ball up inside its case until it was one huge mess. Add an assistant director desperate to hurry him up, and the poor victim would finish by tossing the whole mess into the trash just to take the attention off himself. Meanwhile, we angelic children and the rest of the crew would be congratulating one another on our prank. Most of the crew had been on sets for years and joined right in. Gags like this broke up the tension that built up over a twelve- or fourteen-hour workday.

We also played tricks on one another. Helen's personal chair and other possessions mysteriously "climbed up" the tallest tree at Fox Ranch more than once. We each had canvas chairs with our names embroidered on the back of them, and each chair had pockets into which we could put our scripts and papers. They were easy to move and needed to be because we shifted them around continually.

We also used to grab the spritz bottles filled with a mixture of glycerin and water that was sprayed on us to make us look like we were perspiring. Guess it doesn't take much imagination to figure out what I'd do with those. I guess I got a little carried away with the spraying. The guys on the crew would laugh—we were just having fun, right?—but I began to suspect that they were plotting revenge.

One day I just knew something was up. During my last take of the day, they all began to position themselves to block any escape into the dressing rooms.

Still, I had to wait for Harry Harris, the episode's director, to yell, "Cut!" before I could attempt to run to the dressing room as fast as I could.

"Wait! Wait! We've got a hair in the gate!" one of the cameramen yelled, which meant we were going to have to do it again.

Suddenly a couple of the men grabbed me and held me, while one of the others hit me with spray from a fire hose. They just let me have it.

Getting drenched or having my pants yanked down was part of the fun. Wherever Toni sent me, I was happy to go. And when the shooting day was over, Mom and I would trek home, where I was just a typical California surfer boy. I'd go back to my school, and afterward grab my board, tuck it under my arm, and ride my beat-up old bicycle to the beach. I was the all-American boy having all-American adventures—but little did my parents, Toni, or anyone else know that some of the events at the beach, shortly to be revealed, were far from what a wholesome American kid should have been involved in.

Memories of a Hollywood Kid...First, a detour about

those first years as a child in Hollywood. I used to collect scripts from every show I worked on and have the cast sign them, especially for *Swiss Family Robinson*. I displayed them on my bulletin board, and I once said to Marty Milner that I'd like to hang them on a wall someday.

"Yeah," Mr. Milner said. "So you can have a great big shrine to Me." His tone was so derogatory that I took everything down and never put anything up again. I figured that I was supposed to act like I didn't care that I was working with Hollywood legends or that someday I might like to show some of my memorabilia to my children and grandchildren.

The treasures that last are in the mind and in the heart, though. I have a hodgepodge of people, animals, and incidents that remain in my mind from those early days before *Eight Is Enough*.

Tony Randall. I played his son, Leonard, on the sitcom *The Odd Couple*. The man had a mind like a steel trap. I don't think he ever forgot anything ever said to him. Whenever he spoke to me directly, during the scene, he wanted me to kiss him on the cheek. No way! That was not exactly my style in my own family, and it seemed weird to me.

He also loved a challenge. "I don't care how many push-ups you can do; I can do one more," he claimed. And he did. Surprising, isn't it? He didn't seem the type. He was a master of filthy limericks and double entendres, and I recall one directed at Cloris Leachman, which I won't repeat. These days I doubt someone would get away with a pun on her first name . . . and that's enough said of that. Later I worked with him on *Scavenger Hunt*. I didn't think he'd remember me, but when I introduced myself to him he said, "I know exactly who you are!"

Jack Klugman. What a great guy—easy to get along with and perfectly cast as Oscar on the same show.

Slim Pickens. What a character! I got to work with him in a Disney film shot in Oregon called *Runaway on Rogue River*, an adventure movie that was released in 1974. Slim's humor was not exactly *Masterpiece Theatre* level. He wore a hat with a custom-made, gold pin in the shape of a horse's posterior on the front of it. He had given replica pins to both Barry Goldwater and Richard Nixon. So when he gave one to me, it was a huge compliment.

Slim was a perfect target for a prank, so I played one on him. Central to the movie's plot were elephants, and they produce a generous amount of, um, elephant waste. Slim kept saying how he'd like to scoop up a big pile of those droppings and send it to someone as a Christmas gift. Is that a challenge or what? The elephant trainer, Bucky Steele, and I stole one of Slim's drink coolers off the top of his Winnebago and filled it with the elephants' offerings. I expected Slim to say something about his cooler surprise, but he didn't. I didn't see Slim again until 1978, when he was on set for *Beyond the Poseidon Adventure* a few studios down from where I was shooting an episode of *Eight Is Enough.*

When he saw me, he started chasing me, yelling, "You little pill!" in his Old West twang. "If you weren't too big, I'd spank your rear end! I didn't open that chest for four months! You owe me an ice chest!" But he was laughing, and so was I.

Back-lot memories. At one point, I kept seeing people come to the studio in the middle of the summer with down jackets on. I remember wondering what the deal was. It was ninety-five degrees outside. Turns out, one set had been chilled down to about thirty degrees for the filming of *The Exorcist,* so that Linda's breath would show on film.

There was "Dolly Street," where Barbra Streisand came strutting down the avenue in her huge hat. Herbie the Love Bug at Disney Studios. The set of *The Poseidon Adventure*, where everything was upside down. MGM's back lot, which was a wonderland of monolithic castles and Tudor houses and Old West streets. It's gone now, replaced by a subdivision.

Props closets. I remember seeing the Maltese Falcon just sitting there in some closet. In Disney's prop house were the whistles from *Steamboat Willie*—Big Toot, Little Toot—Hollywood animation history, just lying on a shelf.

TV stars, just walking around, eating at the Farmer's Market. Rob Reiner, Sally Struthers, and Carroll O'Connor from *All in the Family*. Richard Dawson of *Family Feud*.

Animal memories. It seemed as if I was always being hired onto a commercial, episode, or movie that featured them.

Chimps. One of the funniest incidents was on a commercial for a short-lived sugar additive called Suga Duga. The other actors in the commercial were chimps, the same ones that appeared in a 1970–71 show called *Lancelot Link*, a clever (to me at the time) spoof of spy shows such as *The Man from U.N.C.L.E.* I was the only human in it. During the filming, the chimps sat in a diner, having breakfast and eating Suga Duga. Unfortunately, the diet gave the chimps the runs. Fifteen hours of chimp poop.

The tiger on *Swiss Family Robinson*. I found out, nearly the hard way, how effective their camouflage is. Their trainers, Steve and Jackie, were sitting by themselves one day at the Fox Ranch. They were two of my favorite people, and I walked over to talk with them. Suddenly they both yelled, "Stop!" I froze. A chained eight-hundred-pound Siberian tiger was lying right in front of me in the dappled sunlight. I had been looking at the trainers and totally missed seeing him.

The elephants in *Runaway on Rogue River*. I remember how their trainer would let them loose to play. They would run at a tree—a full-size, mature pine tree about thirty-six inches across—and hit it with their heads, knocking it down. A big female, Gigi, fell in love with me, or so the trainers said. Wherever I went, she followed two feet behind me. I could not get rid of her. I'd reach up and grab her by the tip of the ear and run her out into the field where the other elephants were. I'd let her go, turn around, and run as fast as I could in the other direction, but she'd be right behind me the whole way.

In one scene I was riding an elephant across a meadow to catch up to where my "dad" was, hoping to save him from a raging river. It had rained, and there were potholes in the ground. When elephants move, they move fast. On a long camera shot, the elephant stumbled into a hole in the meadow and fell, driving its tusks into the ground and launching me several feet into the air. I hit the dirt and got back up, got the elephant up, and kept on going. The director, Larry Landsberg, was one of those old-time directors whose attitude was "real pain is good for the film." So if you rented the film today, you'd see that scene intact.

The animal trainers. They taught me to never, ever, ever turn your back on an animal. Do not treat a wild animal as anything other than wild, even through the second or third generation. These lessons have stayed with me to this day, as I have worked on hunting shows.

Whales and dolphins. When I did the commercials Irwin Allen directed, as well as some later ones, I discovered that whales and dolphins really do have some distinct personality traits. Orky, the female whale in the Marineland commercial, seemingly fell in love with me (maybe I really do have an animal attraction). As I walked around the tank, she'd follow me, with her eye up and pinned on me, slapping the water. I saw dolphins attempting to mate with their trainers. The dolphins would get very attached to the trainers, to the point that if a trainer left them, they were known to commit suicide.

These little bits of memory float through my mind as I write the larger story of my life, and while they seem insignificant by themselves, they are each a piece of what I was and what I have become. There are other memories that are not so pleasant to recall. They may surprise some people. The Willie Upton of the early 1970s had some secrets, oh yeah.

The Jesus Hippies... "Mom, I'm heading down to the beach."

The sun beat down on my tanned skin as I lugged the red-and-yellow-striped surfboard under my arm. The board was a gift from the studio for my birthday. I smelled the salt a couple of blocks away and heard the breakers crashing against the pier.

Yeah. This was living. I was always in my element at the beach and in the water. Though my cousin and best pal Jimmy and I often hung out at the beach together, I also loved being by myself, free to do whatever I wanted to, not having to answer to anybody. I had begun bumming cigarettes off the regular "beach rats" when I was nine or ten years old. At home it was never hard to help myself to a couple of my parents' or older brothers' cigarettes, either, so usually I was pretty well supplied. I'd light up when my bare feet hit the hot sand.

The Jesus Movement was in its heyday in California during the early 1970s, and I used to see what I called "Jesus hippies" wandering around the beach. I thought they were hilarious and pathetic—ragged, scruffy, and down-and-out. Everyone knew that a guy named Chuck Smith was in charge of them,[4] and he or one of his assistants would gather them all around him and begin preaching, trying to attract onlookers.

Why I did what I did when I saw these people listening to the gospel is unexplainable, but I stood on the pier and heckled them, yelling obscenities and throwing trash at them while I dragged on a cigarette. The crowds would swell to several hundred, and the Jesus people would begin passing out tracts. And the more people gathered, the louder I got.

Eventually, whoever was preaching that day would single me out as one of those who refused to hear the gospel. It didn't bother me. I was proud of the recognition.

My family was about as non-churchgoing as a family could be, though Grammy Tip was heavily into séances, channeling, spirit-writing, Tarot cards, Ouija boards, palm reading, and other occult practices. We'd all participate whenever we were at her house in the Whittier foothills. Or Mom would take me to Tarot card readers. Tip believed that the dead could be contacted and that there was another spiritual realm—that could be evil—that people could be drawn into against their will. My cousin Jimmy and I were warned to "stay in the white light." If anyone came to us while we were communicating in our minds with someone who was dead and tried to coax us out of the circle of light, we were to shut down the communication immediately.

As I describe these occult practices, something occurs to me. Though Maylo and I had childhoods that were as different as a Beverly Hills mansion is from a crack house in East L.A., there was an eerie similarity in the way our families were involved in some aspects of the occult—which will become evident as her story unfolds.

---

4. It's ironic that I chose to pick on Chuck Smith in view of my later conversion to Christ—we ended up attending his church. But during my beach-bum days, going to church would have been the last thing on my mind.

My family had no involvement at all with organized religion, and I learned from them not to take any one religion seriously. I was fed the "many paths to God" propaganda.

Still, there was always something inside me that I couldn't put a name to. It had to do with right and wrong, with justice, with wanting to protect people who were being mistreated, with wanting to be a hero like my dad, and maybe with that desire to feel like I was loved and valued. Why I continued to think no one cared about me is a question for someone more knowledgeable than I. But it was true, and the persistence of the feeling is probably why I sought out and was flattered by the attention I got from actors, directors, and crew when I was working. Even being used as an example of an apostate, with the evangelist's finger pointed at me in accusation, fulfilled a need to be noticed by someone.

Was I looking for validation from God himself? If anyone had said that to me as a child or a teenager, I might have responded with "Huh?" And yet small incidents offer clues that maybe I was. When I was eight or nine, probably before I began doing commercials, I was watching TV with my brother Ron, who was about sixteen. We were killing time, flipping through channels, and came across a TV evangelist whose name I can't remember. I got caught up in what he was saying, and when he gave the invitation, I bowed my head, closed my eyes, and started to pray with him. I opened my eyes just the barest bit and saw Ron was staring at me, laughing. I stopped short.

"Hey, Willie, you can do that if you want. Do whatever, man." But his grin made his opinion clear. And I didn't like being laughed at.

I did attend church a handful of times. I attended once with my cousin Jimmy. It was summer, and I was staying with him for a few days. We decided, just the two of us, to go to the local church, which rang bells on Sunday morning every five minutes or so.

The church was close enough to walk to, and Jimmy insisted that we were supposed to kneel in the street every time the bells rang. So we did. Walk, stop, kneel, up, walk, stop, kneel, up. I remember thinking that it was a good thing we were going to church nearby because we'd nearly die of old age before we got there. But we made it. I remember nothing else about the service, but the process of getting there told me enough. These people like to do things the hard way.

I was about eleven when I attended a church service with a friend. About halfway through the service, the pastor excused the kids to go to children's church. All I knew was that, thus far, church had been boring, and I thought it was over. I hightailed it out the sanctuary door, and as soon as I got out, I yelled, "Yeah! All right! Now we can finally get the ——— out of this place!"

I'm positive everyone in the sanctuary heard me. An older boy came up to me and told me that I was going to hell. I was forced to stay for children's church since I was with my friend, but he never invited me to go with him again.

A couple years later, I was actively working in TV and went to church with a friend named Randy. At the end of the service, the pastor invited anyone who wanted to accept Christ to come forward. I readily went, though I had no idea why. Someone took me into an adjacent room, prayed with me, gave me a Bible, and told me that from that point on nothing could touch me or hurt me.

I don't recall going to church again with Randy. But there was something about the idea, or ideal, of being a godly man that intrigued me. I thought of a good man as one who could right the wrongs that seemed to be part of the cruelty of life, and I'd feel frustrated and sad that I was just a kid. When I would see a priest with his clerical collar and serious look, I'd wonder what he was like. I had no idea, no experience, and no frame of reference, though, to know.

Given those feelings, it might seem paradoxical to stand at the pier and ridicule the Jesus people and the street evangelists. But I had my reasons. I was doing more at the beach than anyone knew—that is, anyone but me and two other people, partners in some activities that I'm about to reveal for the first time to anyone, even to my wife, Maylo.

A Friendship with a Heavy Price...When I look at my life, other than my relationship with God or with my wife, my longest relationship has been with the sea. At sunrise or sunset I would sit quietly listening to it, talking to it, and learning from it. Almost all of my earliest memories, and many later ones both good and bad, were in some fashion shaped by the sea. It has been an inseparable part of who I was, am, and most probably always will be. The sea has been a defining element in my life, and when I'm out on it, I feel closer to God than at nearly any other time.

I love surfing. I would feel the wave pick me up; then in one fluid motion I'd stand, pushing hard on the front end of the board and shooting down the face of the wave. Making my bottom turn, I would dig the tail in deep, slashing back up the face, then jam my board hard against the lip of the wave, creating enough energy to slam another 180-degree turn back down the wave. I would allow my left hand to lightly drag in the water to slow myself down, letting the wave catch up until I could feel it begin to break over my head. As I pushed my left foot back toward the skag,[5] almost kneeling sideways, the entire aquatic world would explode into a shimmering golden brown as the wave broke cleanly over my head, putting my entire body in the tube. It was like passing through a giant ice sculpture, bathed in a hundred billion amber crystals.

---

5. The tube of the wave. Other terms for skag are *skeg* or *fin*; a tube is also called a *green room* or *barrel*.

Today it seems hard to believe that my parents would allow me to spend all day at the beach surfing and fishing and not worry about what I was doing, but times were different in the early 1970s. When I wanted to fish, I'd ride my bicycle about five miles to the end of the pier at Huntington Beach and park it at the base. At the other end of the pier, jutting out to where the breakers first began to hurl themselves onto the massively crowded beach, was a series of gangways and ladders—sea-weathered hunks of timber and moss that creaked and swayed with the swells passing thirty feet or so below. I loved the sense of mystery about being underneath the pier with its leftover relics. It was several degrees cooler, the fishing was good, and there were no other people around. The area was underneath the Tackle Box, a live bait concession managed by a guy named Greg, and he controlled access to it. Greg would let me fish there when I wanted to . . . that is, for a price. Greg molested me for more than a year between the end of my *Gunsmoke* appearances in 1971 and the start of *Swiss Family Robinson*—during 1971 and 1972.

I got to know Greg at first by bumming cigarettes from him. He'd occasionally stand on the pier, as I did, and taunt the preachers. He picked a fight with one of the preachers one day, but apparently the preacher had some martial arts training. He used his skills on Greg, and Greg was bruised all over his face and arms for quite a long time. That's how I remember Greg when I first met him—in a fight with someone.

"Hey, we have something in common," he'd say. "We both stood up to the preacher." He soon began to give me fishing privileges, and he also gave me free bait.

Greg was an average-looking guy in his mid-to-late twenties. Thin, about six feet tall, he wore glasses. He was the kind of man who would blend into a crowd. Slowly he inched his way into friendship with me and then, step by step, began to press the friendship further by inviting me to help him sell bait. He had already befriended another kid I'll call David, who was a little older than I was. David also worked for him in the shop.

He invited David and me to go to the drive-in movies, saying he was rewarding us for helping him out so much. I asked my parents if I could go and then spend the night at the shop, telling them that Greg was a nice guy who had hired me to help fishermen choose bait and was taking a gang of us kids to the drive-in movie as a reward for working hard for him.

We did go to the movie, but the only ones who went were David, Greg, and me. The first time Greg actually molested the two of us, I was eleven. He bought some Doritos and beer at the snack bar and gave them to us, and when we were good and drunk from the beer and our defenses were worn down, he molested each of us in turn in the dark car.

After that, it didn't seem to matter where or when. Greg would pressure me to drink so much that I'd throw up all over myself in the car, into the chips and onto the unopened beer. There was a constant swirling in my head, along with the acid taste of vomit, the constant smell of rotting fish and cheap aftershave mixed with the beer and the smell of Doritos. He'd just wait until I was through throwing up and then continue, over and over throughout the night.

When I dare to remember any of this, I can still feel the stubble of beard that scratched until I was nearly raw. After the nighttime episodes I'd eventually pass out and ride with him to pick up his live bait around four o'clock the following morning. To this day the smells of Doritos and beer have a sickening association for me.

As a "reward," Greg taught David and me to steal, so we'd have lots of spending money. I got very good at it. I'd watch and wait, learning to size up the opportunities. When I saw the right situation, I'd run up to a beach blanket where a woman had left her purse, throw my towel over the purse, pick it up under my towel, and take off. The ruse was designed to look like I had been running too hard and tripped. Immediately I'd hide in the bushes near the parking lot, pull the money out of the purse, and ditch the rest—all while she innocently waded in the tide. I never got caught.

In the back of my mind, I knew that what Greg wanted from me was not normal. This was no "friendship" between a man and a boy. In the beginning it was free bait, free fishing privileges, and then, appealing to my ego and desire to be grown up, being told that I was "old enough to make my own decisions" about drinking beer.

And after it started, it seemed there was no turning back. There was something dangerous about him. I was already well aware that he had no problem with using force to get what he wanted—I'd seen him do it. It didn't take long for Greg to begin pointing out all of the stealing and lies. I was guilty just like him, so we had to stay together to keep from getting caught or maybe even going to jail. Honestly, jail didn't frighten me half as much as the beating I knew I would get if Dad ever found out.

Of course I didn't know it then, but I know now that Greg preyed first on my needs and weaknesses and then on my fear and low self-esteem. His predilection for kids like me was premeditated and calculating.

"Hey, Will, I saw you on TV last night. Wow, you were cute. All you TV kids are cute. I moved out to California especially to find a kid like you, one who was on TV. And now I've got you. My special friend."

So he said to me after I had been gone for a couple of weeks to film one of my last *Gunsmoke* episodes. He talked me into riding with him to pick up bait and became so excited about having me back in his rusted old truck that he stopped at a gas station and dragged me into the restroom to molest me.

"Hey, Willie, why don't you come on over? I've got a whole bunch of kids who come in and get naked for me. They like to pretend they're my slaves and I'm the king." I didn't know whether to believe this or not. I never saw it happen, and I never participated. But I began trying to find ways to get away from him.

Free bait. All the fishing behind the pier that I wanted. A secret known by no one but me, Greg, and David. Playing to my desire to be an adult. Playing to my need to be valued by someone. Even the bizarre sense that Greg had singled me out for something "special" could not compensate for the guilt I had about what he wanted me to do and the fear that if I didn't do it, I'd be sorry.

Greg got more aggressive, demanding not just that I let him do what he wanted but that I actively participate. No way! Frightened or not, guilty or not, threats of jail and fear of whippings—I knew I would never be able to do something like that. And the fear of what could happen to me if I didn't participate wasn't enough to convince me anymore. I stopped going down to the pier. I hid or I went the other direction. I cut myself off completely, and I never saw the other boy, David, again.

A couple of summers came and went. *Swiss Family Robinson* had started, and I got too busy to go to the beach as much as I had before. Beach regulars told me that Greg had disappeared. The scuttlebutt was that the owner of the shop had fired him.

At age twelve, I had passed California's state lifeguard certification program, which was so rigorous that whoever participated in it could not help but be in good physical condition. Confident that I could defend myself if I had to, I decided to head back down near the south end of the pier to surf and fish.

"Hey, Willie, come on out back. We've got a friend, and we all hang out." I was about thirteen. A couple of other surfers invited me to where they were camped on the beach. And there, surrounded by a crowd of eight or more boys, was Greg.

I turned around before Greg could see me, or so I thought. I grabbed the arm of the boy who had invited me. "You'd better watch out for that guy," I warned him, my jaw tightening. "That guy is going to want to do things to you. Look out. He's a real creep."

I picked up my board and went back into the water, but when I rode a wave back toward the coast, I saw Greg standing at the water's edge. I had to get out of the water eventually, so I picked up my board and trudged through the wet sand.

His voice was quiet as he confronted me.

"You better keep your mouth shut, Willie, because it would be real easy for someone to just accidentally get hit in the head with a board and drown while they're out there surfing."

It didn't matter that one-on-one I could hold my own by that time, and I would have if I had been forced to. In the water I would have been an easy target for the end of someone else's surfboard if I didn't see the person behind me. Once again I just quit going to the south side of the pier. I never saw Greg again, but I did find myself scanning the water and looking over my shoulder that summer. For years I dreamed of killing him. I also found myself on the lookout for whomever else he may have trapped.

I've lived my entire life never having revealed those experiences. I used to hear jokes about gay men and wonder if what I had gone through had made me gay. What if I had somehow been infected with some sort of fate?

It took years to understand that I would not some day wake up having become my own worst nightmare, like some sick Dracula curse.

Until the writing of this book, I had never told anyone about this. No one. Maylo has suspected something happened and I recently confirmed to her that I had been molested, but even she didn't know the details until now.

As I write, the fear is tangible, constant, and sometimes mountainous. What will my parents say? Did they have a clue back then? Will there be rumors that I am gay? Will it be used against me, my wife, my son, my daughter? How will it be used to hurt us? And there will be hurt. I can't escape it. . . . All these years and the fear is still real.

My case lies at the feet of my Savior. The telling of this story, I have to believe, will be used by the Holy Spirit to help someone else to freedom—freedom from the fear and the guilt of being an outcast, of being laughed at. Without relaying this ugly part of my life, Christ's glory through my story would be drastically diminished.

"Without those wounds where would your strength be?" The angel speaks again, this time directly to me.

MAYLO

Grandpa and Grandma McCaslin... "I have to find a man," Mother announced as the bills piled up and her money for cigarettes ran low. I was five or six.

John McCaslin was an old high-school boyfriend of my mom's. I didn't know it at the time, but my mother had been dating him when she met my dad. He spoke with an Arkansas accent. I loved to hear him talk. My mom married him shortly after she started seeing him again.

Daddy John was a man of few words, but what he did say to me was kind. A son of a dairy farmer, he was a tall, thin man with black hair, blue eyes, and sharp, handsome features. I remember him dressed in a white T-shirt and Levi's, smelling of the Kools he smoked.

I think Daddy John's parents had run into hard times in Arkansas and had moved to California, land of opportunity, as so many other farmers had done back in the late 1930s and early 1940s. They had settled near where my extended family lived, and my Aunt Judy's husband, Don, had been a high-school friend of John's. That's how he originally met my mother, before she went to Woodbury, where she met my dad.

My brother, Lary, was born in 1968 when I was six, and my sister, Kathleen, whom I called Leenie, in 1970. Lary was a red-haired, freckled-faced little pistol who was either laughing or poking a stick at someone all the time. Kathleen was a beautiful little blonde with freckles and blue eyes and a smile that curled up at the corners like an imp's.

When John came into our lives, we got another set of grandparents. Grandpa and Grandma McCaslin were straight out of the country. I had almost no knowledge of what a Christian was other than from the rantings of my mother, who was convinced that Christians were tight-lipped, judgmental Ku Klux Klan members who had no brains or appreciation of art or humanity. I don't remember going to church as a child, but Grandma McCaslin met my child's definition of what a "Christian" was.

Grandma didn't talk about her faith, but she seemed different from Grandma Peggy. People who were down on their luck were always at Grandpa and Grandma's house. Grandma played what I called "church songs" on the piano, one of them with a line in it about an old rugged cross. She also went to church on Sunday mornings. We would sleep over and wake up late Sunday morning, and she would soon return, dressed in a simple, homemade flower-print dress with buttons down the front and smelling of Zest, her favorite bar soap.

Grandma McCaslin had put her expert sewing skills to work by starting a small business in alterations and custom dresses for rich women. Her sewing room was a gigantic cotton heap of a mess. Pieces of batting and fabric were everywhere in piles that looked as if they had been accumulating for years. The scraps were black and red gabardine, blue denim, forest green and bright yellow cotton, plaid, striped, and polka-dotted—and Grandma made colorful, cozy quilts of no particular pattern from them.

"Let's make a pad from 'em," she'd say with a thick Arkansas twang as she spread the quilts in layers on the floor for us to sleep on when we'd spend the night. I loved it there. There was something calm and safe about being with her and Grandpa.

Grandpa McCaslin was tall and square-jawed. Like his son, he hardly ever spoke. His cheeks were always scratchy, and he smelled like vinegar and okra and peppers and wood. He turned the detached garage into a shop where he made cabinets and tables for rich people. His wood shop was like the boy version of Grandma's sewing room. The floor was always covered in sawdust. I loved to sweep it with a long broom, making little fluffy piles. The garage floor underneath was smooth and glossy and cool.

Grandpa would let us make things with his tools. I made birdhouses I wanted to live in with steep roofs and a cozy hole to peek out of. Grandpa also taught us how to feed the squirrels in their backyard. He would get up before the sun every morning— no doubt a lifetime habit from his days of farming—and sit on a bench in front of his workshop. He would gently and patiently feed the squirrels right out of his hands. He told me that if I were very still and quiet, the squirrels would eat out of my hands too. I stood like a statue until my arms felt like they were falling off, but they never came to me. But then, I was tense, not calm as Grandpa was. Maybe the squirrels sensed that.

At night Grandma and Grandpa would make popcorn in a bowl with a glob of cold butter stuck to the side. We'd drag the popcorn through the butter on its way to our mouth. I would sit in Grandpa's lap and eat his popcorn. He was quiet and still and I was not afraid, just like the squirrels he fed. We often watched *The Lawrence Welk Show* with them—"A one-uh and a two-uh and a"—and I often read the comics to Grandpa. I don't think he read very well.

Only one thing scared me about staying with Grandma and Grandpa McCaslin. Down the hall from the sewing room was their bedroom, and in it was a large print of Jesus with long brown hair and blue eyes in a simple wooden frame. I felt like those eyes were staring at me, following me around the room. If Grandma would ask me to get something for her, I would loiter in the hallway, trying to build up the courage to run into the room and get what I needed.

My fear then makes me smile now—but then again, I was ignorant of who Jesus was.

In spite of that picture, I loved almost everything about the McCaslins' house. The backyard had a big plum tree that dropped fruit—purple, squishy, sweet plums you could pick up off the ground and eat. In the yard was also a clothesline where Grandma hung her sheets to dry. She had red geraniums and snapdragons against the back fence. I didn't like the geraniums because they didn't have a fragrance, but I spent hours in the summer on my back in the grass, squeezing the snapdragons until they opened like puppets' mouths.

My mother used the McCaslins whenever she wanted to get rid of us, but we didn't complain. She'd drop us off and leave without even stopping to talk with her in-laws. Back at the apartment, she said spiteful, sarcastic things about them, and there were months at a time when she wouldn't take us there or communicate with the McCaslins in any way. "They're just country trash," she'd sneer at Daddy John. "They're just hillbillies."

One day after Mom dropped us off, I called for Grandpa and he didn't answer. "Grandma, where's Grandpa?" I asked. Grandma told me simply that he had died. She said he had died sitting outside on a bench, feeding the squirrels. Mother had not told us, so we never got to grieve for him.

Imagining Food Doesn't Make It Real...After

Mother married John, we moved into a real house with a detached garage behind it in Reseda in the San Fernando Valley. It had a big tree in the front yard and a swimming pool and grassy lawn in the back. It was a sweet little ranch house with a floor plan that offered what realtors in those days called "a flow."

For a short while, those were the good days. The elementary school was a block away on a small suburban street, so the walk to school didn't make me as tense as it had in the last apartment.

The only dark shadow was the meetings that my mother was still regularly attending. They were held in different places every couple of weeks. I had the sense that the people were hiding from something or someone, because when they met at our house, they talked in whispers, as they had when we were in the apartments. The meetings were sometimes held in a hall somewhere, and they drew a large crowd of people, including Grandma Peggy—she and Mom were on good terms for a while. Even though I had very little knowledge of what "church" was, I knew even then that these assemblies were not church. They were something else.

My mom and Grandma Peggy and sometimes some other people would come home from the meetings and sit at the kitchen table, talking about Godfrey, who they said was Jesus come back.[6] The confusing thing to me was that they said they were Jesus too. I didn't understand what they meant.

---

6. I should clarify their teaching: they thought Godfrey was Jesus, and yet, so were they. Godfrey thought he was especially appointed by God at birth to impart what he called "the promise" and that the promise had been fulfilled in him. (See why people would think of him as a modern Jesus?) He taught the use of imaginative power as a means to see one's dreams come true. According to his teaching, even this special power (my mother's "imagining") will pass. At death you'll enter through a door and be restored to life in a world just like our own. In the meantime you'll have the same problems you had before and will not lose your identity. This process will keep happening until Christ is formed in us—however, you are only born once through a woman and once from above. There is no hell or damnation, for we are God, and God could not condemn himself. It's a confusing set of beliefs, even if a person is not suffering from delusions, as my mother undoubtedly was.

My mother was obsessed with Godfrey's teachings. After John picked up his black metal lunchbox in the morning and left for work, Mom lay on the couch for hours. She listened to tape recordings of Godfrey over and over as she went into that trance that she called imagining.

Mom was having visions again too. She would pop up suddenly, with her teased hair standing straight up and flat in the back, and say, "Oh! Oh, wow! I saw a man, but he had no face, and I knew it was Godfrey!"

In her visions she and Godfrey had sex—weird, out-of-this world sex, or so she told me. My mother talked openly and in great detail about sex to me. She was often nude or wore little baby-doll, see-through nighties around the house. She had raised me with the belief that sex was what got you the man, and the man is what you need to pay the bills. Somehow I understood, though, that sex with Godfrey was not about paying the bills, while sex with John was.

Mom told me that she saw balls of fire around the room. She described being transported to some other world, where she would see battles in the sky and golden chariots with spikes on them coming out of the clouds.

"Maylo, imagining creates reality," she told me. She said I could lie on the couch as she did and dream up what I needed and it would come. But her beliefs were not just positive thinking; she would tell me that everything created came from her mind, and that her mind was the same as Godfrey's mind—the same as God's mind. As a ten-year-old girl, I sensed that this new fixation was more than just "being religious," but I didn't know what it was. Her words scared me. She would tell me that she had powers, that she was getting stronger, and that she could hurt people with her powers—that she could use her dreams to hurt them. She had séances, and she and a friend regularly used the Ouija board for guidance about what to do next.

Eventually the house became more and more of a mess. Nothing got done. She was into nothing but Godfrey. John would come home from work, and his wife would pop up off the couch for the first time all day. She had obviously not taken a bath, combed her hair, or even washed her face.

"Oh, John. I just had the most incredible vision! There were rats running all over my feet and big balls of fire floating in each corner of the living room!"

John would stand in the middle of the room, seemingly struck dumb. How can a person carry on a conversation with someone who is talking of imaginary rodents and fireballs in the room?

So he would just ask, "What's for dinner?" He'd put a country music album on and lie on the couch to rest and listen to music.

Mother would amble into the kitchen to find something to eat. The inside of our refrigerator always had some old something-or-other that had turned into green fuzzy mold on the top shelf that squished in your finger if you tried to pick it up. There was always a puddle of sticky, orangey goo that had dripped from something, and in the vegetable bin were limp, drippy, rotting vegetables. Not many possibilities in there for dinner. I always wondered why, if she could create things from her imagination, we never had anything to eat.

Guess We Won't Make It to China... "Come on,

Leenie." I had just gotten home from school, where I was in the fifth grade. I lifted Kathleen out of the crib. Her ragged rubber pants hung so low that they almost dragged the floor. I changed her and then cut a hole in a small piece of an old bed sheet and pulled it over her two-year-old head and tied a red hair ribbon around her chubby middle. Mom was lying on the couch, imagining, oblivious to my sneaking a tube of her reddest lipstick, blue and green eye shadow, and a brown eyebrow pencil out of her bathroom. I put Leenie in the high chair while I made up her face to look like a clown, giving her an ear-to-ear exaggerated smile and great big balls of red on her cheeks.

"Lary, come here a minute. I'm going to make you look like a clown." Four-year-old Lary stopped arranging miniature plastic soldiers in rows on the kitchen floor. He climbed up in a kitchen chair, and I used the eyebrow pencil to put giant, brown freckles all over his face, and then I gave him a wide, red, silly grin. I handed him a pair of my cutoffs to put on, and the crotch sagged down almost to his knees, giving him a satisfyingly ridiculous look.

"You guys look so funny!"

Lary climbed up onto the bathroom counter to see himself in the mirror, and I held Leenie up so she could wave to herself. They both giggled. I took them outside and told them to climb into Mother's old, red Radio Flyer wagon, and I pulled them up and down the street.

After I got home from school, I always concocted some way to entertain Lary and Leenie and get them outside. Sometimes I pulled them over to our neighbors' house. Mom hardly noticed— she was too busy with her visions.

When I had time alone, I often climbed the maple tree in our front yard and hid in the branches and leaves so that I could spy on other people. I sat up there in my hidden perch and wondered what other kids' families were like. I suspected that other families were not like ours. How many kids had mothers who lay on the couch all day in a trance?

I walked to school, where I knew that two boys, Christopher and Mark, would continue their mission from yesterday and the day before, which was to make my school day miserable. *Why do they pick on me?* I used to ask myself. *Why?*

They would break my pencils and throw big, pink gym balls at me so hard that the hot rubber would burn my skin when the ball hit me. If I was playing hopscotch, they pushed me while I was on one leg and laughed when I fell over, skinning my knee on the asphalt. I hated them. Anxiety nearly ate me alive during recess or lunch because I knew that Chris and Mark would find me. I began to hide in the bathroom, counting off the minutes while I waited for the bell to ring so I could go to class. I was no good at all in sports and didn't have an aggressive bone in my body to fight back, and they exploited my timidity and small stature. I had been promoted to the next grade and was the youngest girl in my class—a distinction that provided ample material for teasing from Chris and Mark. "Baby! Maylo Potato is a bawl baby!"

In spite of the harassment, I got good grades, even though sometimes I couldn't concentrate because I was worried about Lary and Leenie. I sat in class, hoping that Mom had taken Lary and Leenie out of their cribs and changed their diapers, yet experience told me that they probably would not have been attended to all day. When I got home, I picked them up, changed them, and fed them something—anything I could find in our science project of a refrigerator. Then I tried to entertain them.

Besides giving them wagon rides, I played in the dirt with them. In the backyard was a garden area right up against a wooden fence. My brother had a collection of Hot Wheels cars, and I helped him and Leenie build valleys, hills, streets, and whole lands where tiny people lived happy lives in alternate universes from our mixed-up world.

One day I was vigorously trying to make a tunnel. I tossed out piles of dusty red dirt, determined to get to China. It could be done—I had heard the stories. Someone knew someone who had dug to China! If I could dig to China, we could get out of here and start over. I pulled handful after handful of dirt out of the hole and finally stuck my hand in as far as it would go.

"Youch!" Something clamped down on my finger and pinched hard. I yelped and lifted up my hand. A grub—a fat, putty-colored, prehistoric-looking, wormy creature with a black head—was hanging from my finger and wiggling around like it was angry with me. It was disgusting! And it stung! I shook it off and ran into the house to get a Band-Aid. Guess the three of us would have to get to China another way.

How I Officially Became a Loser...Eventually everyone in Reseda had a story they could tell about the McCaslin family. The neighbors suspected that our family was not like other families, and my mother was bent on confirming that suspicion by the way she behaved for all to see.

One of my mom's latest imaginings was that I was destined to be a famous dancer, so she enrolled me in ballet classes. A familiar pattern emerged—the other girls at ballet classes *hated* me. They were all well-scrubbed, pretty little girls in black leotards and pink tights, and they had pretty mommies who all waited in the lobby during class or watched their daughters through the window. Not my mother—she'd pull up to the front of the building and barely stop long enough for me to open the door.

We had a dusty old Rambler, with the name on the back of the car between two pointy taillights that looked like fins. Under the dust, the car was light yellow. The interior was torn up with stuffing oozing out of the peeling upholstery. And it rumbled loudly, embarrassingly.

I cringe when I remember the day Lary fell out of that car. We were going to my dance lesson. I was riding in the front seat, and Lary and Leenie were in the backseat. The little crowd of wannabe ballerinas was waiting outside. I saw the group of girls before we got to the curb and begged my mom to keep going and not stop.

Lary was crawling around inside the Rambler and had made his way over the seat and into my lap. Mother was yelling at me to get out. Lary sat up on his knees on my lap with his hands up against the passenger window.

Mother tried to encourage me in the only way she knew how. "Maylo, you have every right to be here, and those girls are no better than you are. This is your destiny! I know it because I've imagined it! Nobody is going to hurt you! Now pull your head up and get out there!"

I flung open the car door as we pulled to the curb in front of the girls. My brother fell off the seat and landed on his head in the gutter. He immediately started screaming, and my mother lunged across the front seat like a mad woman. As usual, once she got started, she was on a roll.

"Maylo! ———— it! You threw your brother out of the car! Pick him up! Now!" A nonstop artillery of cursing followed.

The girls started laughing. My face turned hot and red, and I could not see straight. I was also in a panic about my brother. I wanted to pick him up and just go home. But she grabbed him from me, slammed the car door, and sped off, and I had to walk up to the crowd and wait for the door to be unlocked.

"Nice goin'," remarked one of the pretty little girls. I didn't go to those classes for long. Although my mother kept having visions about me, we eventually ran out of money again, and, alas, I had to conclude that I was not meant to be a ballerina.

Apparently I was not meant to be a cheerleader either. This became painfully apparent not long after the ballerina funds ran low. I was a fan of both *The Carol Burnett Show* and *The Flip Wilson Show*. I decided to try to write some comedy skits like those on the shows and put on a revue. I dressed my little brother in his clown suit and attached balloons to his tricycle, so he could ride around really fast to circus music, while Annie, a friend of mine for the littlest of whiles, and I got ready for whatever the next show-stopping number was going to be.

Annie was one of those pretty girls who end up as cheerleaders and homecoming queens of everything. I was just sure that she was from a rich family too. She had long, thick brown hair and was super-popular at school. In stark contrast, I was thin and wiry and sported a hacked-off haircut that Mom and Grandma Peggy had given me. Annie and I planned to do a cheer together. I hoped that the cheer would be my ticket to popularity like hers.

We had sold tickets on our block, and a few people actually came to our garage to watch, including a neighbor boy I had a crush on. I thought he looked just like Kurt Russell. He had always been friendly to me and had even given me a St. Christopher medal one day, telling me it would protect me from harm (I think he knew the neighborhood stories about my family).

When I saw him, I began to act just as cute as I knew how to be, or so I thought. I wiggled and shook and kicked as high as I could. The only problem was, I was wiggling, shaking, and kicking right next to Annie, who was also wiggling, shaking, and kicking. Truthfully, she looked great, and I'm sure I looked, well, desperate.

My part turned out to be a disaster. After that day, no one really spoke to me anymore. I realized soon that "Kurt" and the girl who I now called "Annie Bananee" were becoming good friends. All the activity on the block seemed to be centered near her house, and the neighbor kids always seemed to be together, laughing and having a good time without me.

I was frustrated, angry, and consumed with jealousy. I was out and didn't know how to get in. So I made up a horrible lie about Annie Bananee—I told everyone in the neighborhood that she was bald. Her thick, luscious hair was a wig, I insisted.

One day I was in my front yard, pretty pleased with myself . . . until I saw Annie Bananee coming my way, followed by the whole gang (including Kurt). What could I do? Run into the house? That would look dumb. So I stood up and waited. Annie marched right up to me with everyone standing behind her. Eye to eye with me, she screamed in my face, "You told everyone I wear a wig! That is a lie, and you know it! My hair is not a wig!"

I had too much pride to admit that I had lied. I didn't know what to do. I did the smartest, most street-savvy thing anyone could do. I looked her straight in the eye in front of everyone and yelled, "It is too a wig, and you know it!"

She snorted in disbelief. "What? Omigosh! Pull my hair! It is not a wig! You are dead! You are so dead!"

She pointed at me and yelled threats as she and the others backed away. They all were laughing. I had made a complete fool of myself. It wasn't so bad, though. It wasn't like I was popular to begin with or that I had lost anything.

Each day on the walk home from school after that, Annie and her friends followed behind me, resuming the old "Maylo Tomato" taunts. They threw things at me and mocked me or jumped in front of me and pushed me.

I didn't hold it against any of them. I never did. I thought I deserved the abuse. I agreed with everyone else—I was officially a loser by that point.

Mother's First Betrayal...Oh well. I still had my dog, Raisin, and I had weekends to look forward to when Daddy Bill was home from touring, though, as the years went on, I saw less and less of him.

There was always the backyard pool, although I didn't yet know how to swim. My mother's father, Grandpa Harry—a fireman who was all too familiar with drownings of children in swimming pools—argued with my mother over my not knowing how to swim. One day he came over, got in the pool, and called, "Maylo, come here."

"I can't, Grandpa. I can't swim."

"This is the day when that changes," he said calmly.

I got into the shallow end of the pool. He stood with me and had me bend over and put my head into the water. He had me open my eyes underwater and look around. Then he told me that my body would naturally float if I would just relax. He wanted me to lie on my back while he held me and showed me how to float. He was solid. Safe. He spoke right to me without being distracted.

I did as instructed, and while I lay on my back, I tried to calm my panicky feelings. The water threatened to go over my face and into my nose, but my grandfather kept looking right in my eyes and saying, "I have got you. I have got you." I did learn to swim that day, and from that point on, no one could keep me out of the pool.

Raisin would sit nearby and watch me jump recklessly from the diving board into the cool, chlorinated depths. He was a short, fat, black, shiny dachshund with a pointy snout. The way he tried to chase after me on his little legs made me laugh.

One of the things that Raisin did—something I secretly thought brilliant and hilarious—was urinate on Grandma Peggy's feet. Every time she and her husband, Bud, would come to visit, Raisin would run over, lift his leg, and let it fly. Why Raisin singled out my grandma, I don't know. He never did it to anyone else.

After they left, my mother would break into one of her huge, contagious laughs, and we three kids would laugh with her. Mom had created an "us against Peggy" atmosphere in the house, and I thought Raisin was smart to take our side. Mom had us convinced that Peggy was out to take us kids away or to control her. I thought we made a strong team: Mom, Raisin, and us kids.

As I walked in the house after school one day, I saw Grandma Peggy sitting on a chair in the living room. Something felt wrong. My mother was sitting on the couch, and Bud was standing. When I looked at him, he turned away but not before I could see an ashamed expression on his tanned, kindly face.

Everyone froze. Somehow I knew immediately that Raisin was gone. I dropped my books and ran to my room.

"Raisin? Raisin!" I cried, then didn't say a word. I went back into my bedroom, slammed the door shut, and sobbed. I was enraged at my mom. Mother, who sat on the couch with her head down. Mother, who sat with her hands in her lap.

Allowing Raisin to be taken away was a huge betrayal. I had thought Mother loved Raisin. She knew I loved Raisin. Mom was supposed to be the boss. Mom didn't protect my dog. I had a glimpse that day of who Mom really was. Eventually I discovered that she would not protect any of us—from situations that were far more threatening than the loss of a dog.

Caught in a Trap... "I'm caught in a trap. I can't walk out. Because I love you too much, baby."

Elvis's song played over and over again. "Suspicious Minds" was the first thing John played every day when he came home from work. And the chorus rolled around in my head for years after I had grown, connecting my present life to my past, trapping me in memories of that old house . . . memories of Daddy John and his drinking . . . of my mother and her rages.

John had quit working for a landscaping company months ago. He and Mom had bought a lawn mower so he could go into business for himself. She pushed him to work harder and harder, and eventually he was working seven days a week.

When he was home, his drinking was constant. I never heard John yell, and he was never fall-down drunk or obnoxious. He just seemed looser, as if a burden had been lifted off his mind, and he'd smile quietly, not speaking to anyone, as he lay on the couch beside the stereo, picking up the needle arm when the song was over and setting the needle again at the beginning of the track.

Mom would scream at him and humiliate him. John would simply walk out the front door and go to his mother's house to spend the night. I felt lost when he left. Somehow, his quiet smile grounded the living room.

In spite of her frustrations with John, Mom seemed to be in high spirits. She went to her meetings nearly every evening and often talked to me about Godfrey's teachings. She spoke with great authority and quoted passages that sounded like Bible verses, explaining to me about the "apostles" and about her own special position in the hierarchy. She had been singled out for a higher level even than the apostles, she explained, and she told me over and over of her sexual encounters with Godfrey. I didn't know if those encounters were real or imaginary.

One morning before school, we were all sitting at our little breakfast table. John's black, metal lunch pail with the silver snap on the front sat on the counter, ready for him to pick up before he left for work. Mom, cooking an actual breakfast for a change, was frying bacon, and the smell filled the morning with a rare "good day" feeling.

Everything was fine until Mom started laughing. Bent-over, holding-her-stomach, tears-in-her-eyes laughing. Out of the blue.

John and I looked at each other and at Mom. Did we miss something?

"Sharon, what's so funny?" John asked.

"There is a creature like a dinosaur standing over the frying pan, John! He's been looking right at me! He's been dancing over the bacon! It is hysterical!" She held onto the stove, trying to get her breath.

A strange change would come over my mother if we caught her in the middle of a vision. She exuded a sense of superiority. She acted as if she were singled out for this special gift of sight, and we would never belong or be involved in it. Her exclusive little club was so special, so advanced, that we would never make it. She was big and we were small.

I looked back at John; he wasn't laughing. He just looked really, really tired. He didn't say a word. He just sighed, got up, and left for work without even saying good-bye. I finished my bacon and convinced myself that we were fine. At least, Mom was laughing.

But the family was cracking apart, just as our house nearly did one morning in February 1971. I was awakened by an odd rumbling. The house was shaking, and I could hear glass trembling and threatening to crack. The shaking and rolling got more intense, and soon it sounded like a freight train was rolling through our living room. My bed's headboard was placed against the middle of the wall, and on the next wall directly across from my bed was my dresser. Atop my dresser was a bookcase crammed full of books. I sat up in my bed and watched the dresser and bookcase wobble and lean.

Then I heard John calling my name. "Maylo! Maylo! Get off the bed!"

"I can't!" The floor was moving so violently that I was afraid if I stood I would fall down. The next thing I knew, John was standing in the doorway in his underwear, holding onto the frame with both hands as he was thrown from side to side. He finally threw himself toward my bed and grabbed me and pulled me onto the floor. We crawled to the door as fast as we could. As I looked back, the entire bookcase moved to the edge of the dresser and then crashed directly onto my bed—right where I had been sitting.

The neighborhood was quiet after the quake but busy at the same time. News trickled in of heavy damage nearby. People assessed the destruction, and everyone seemed hyper and shaky.

My mother had a spiritual explanation for what the news stations began calling the San Fernando earthquake. She talked as if she had known the earthquake was coming. "And now the truth would be known to everyone," she declared. "You can't stop the truth!"

She smoked what seemed like a million cigarettes that day and talked nonstop about the heavens and how people would be blown away when they saw the truth—whatever the "truth" was (we certainly didn't know).

After the quake John was almost never at home. When he was in the house, he'd just lie on the couch with a bottle of beer, listening to his country music albums, not saying a word to anybody.

One morning he left for work as usual but didn't come home that evening.

Lary kept asking, "Maylo, when *is* Daddy coming home from work?"

I finally had to explain to him that his father wasn't coming home.

That night I held both Lary and Leenie in my lap on the couch, and we all crunched up together and cried.

Weeks passed. Then one evening after I had climbed into bed, I heard a voice from outside the window.

"Psst, Maylo. Psst, Maylo." I opened my eyes, but I didn't move a muscle. I lay still with my heart pounding hard.

"Psst . . . Maaaayyyloooow? It'sth John." He sounded drunk. "It'sth Daddy John. . . . Go get yer motherrrr an' tell 'er to come to this window."

"No," I whispered.

"Ah've gotta gun," he said casually.

I lay silent, frozen to the mattress. A long time went by and then I heard the voice again.

"Maaaayyyylooow . . . Call yer mother!"

Without sitting up, I yelled, "Mom?" And again. "Mom!"

I could still hear him breathing. When she came to the door, she did not come in. I don't know why, but as she stood at the doorway in her satin nightgown, incongruously I thought, *My mom looks pretty.*

"Mom, Daddy John is here, and he wants you to go to the window."

"What? No! No!"

Even in the dark, I could see that Mom was shaking. She came no closer than the doorway.

"Shaaaaron, come to this window," John said.

"Mom, please!" I started to cry. "Please do what he says and come to the window!"

Mom was panting. "No, no, no, no. Maylo, you need to come here to the door." Her eyes were bearing down on me. I could still hear him breathing.

"No, Mom. I can't . . . I can't. Please go to the window! I can't get out of the bed, Mom! Please . . ."

"No!" she croaked in that guttural voice she used when getting agitated. She shoved herself out of the doorway and ran down the hall.

I heard the cracking of sticks and branches outside the window. Then all was still. I lay in my bed, looking up at the ceiling, too afraid to move.

After a time I called softly, "John? John?" No answer. I got out of bed and ran to the bedroom door and shut it. I tried to get my heart to stop pounding and leapt from the doorway to the mattress without touching the floor, so no monsters could reach their yellow, pointy fingernails out and scratch at my feet from under my bed. I pulled the covers tight around me. For the rest of the night, I lay still, listening to the silence. I never saw John again.

WILLIE

Tommy Bradford Comes to Life... "I'm sorry to show up dressed up like this. I have a concert tonight, and I have to go directly there."

I arrived at the audition for the new ABC "dramady" (a term coined to describe the show, which was to be part comedy and part drama, with a laugh track) *Eight Is Enough* dressed in a tuxedo. I was fourteen and a member of Edison High School's madrigal ensemble, a select vocal music group. The drive to the studio took two hours from Huntington Beach, and to make it back to the concert on time, I had to audition already outfitted for the spring concert performance.

As it turned out, the producers liked the way I was dressed. It reinforced that I was a normal teenager, exactly what they had in mind for the character Tommy Bradford, the second youngest of eight children of the widower Tom Bradford, a newspaper journalist. We began filming in 1976 when I was still fifteen, and the show ran four years, starting as a midseason (what they called a "third season" replacement at the time), from spring 1977 through 1980. Throughout the show's run, being in *Eight Is Enough* brought major changes in my personal and professional lives—some exciting, some painful.

I had not been cast for the series pilot, but I already had a recurring role in the drama *Family,* another TV series that ran from 1976 to 1980, and at the time I began my regular role in *Eight Is Enough,* I was more well known for the character of T. J. Latimer, one of Kristy McNichol's onscreen boyfriends. I had, in fact, given Kristy her first onscreen kiss.

My all-American, normal teenager persona landed me my most major role to that point. When I was on the *Eight Is Enough* set, I was tutored and completed grade-level work in accordance with California law. When I was not on call or the show was on hiatus, I would go back to my regular high school, where I tried to blend in as a real normal teenager, with mixed success.

It was becoming increasingly difficult to be just Willie Upton, and some students and teachers seemed to resent my celebrity status. I learned to walk with my head down. In fact, I spent my entire public high-school career looking at my feet. Why? I think it started as a mannerism but quickly became a manifestation of my low self-esteem. I walked that way well into my twenties until someone I respected pointed out that most people walk with their heads held up to meet the world.

While on set or on location I felt validated, but away from the studio that old feeling of not mattering to anyone would come back. I didn't know how to deal with it, so sometimes I'd act cocky and sometimes I'd act like I wanted to be invisible.

Sometimes when I'd enter a classroom after having been gone for quite some time, the teacher would look at my paperwork and inform me that I'd have to make up the assignments missed. I would protest loudly that I already had—that the teacher just didn't understand the arrangement, that the studio tutor had already given me the listed grade for the portion I had completed. I had some heated arguments with some of my teachers, though others just accepted my completed work and welcomed me into the class.

Some even had a sense of humor about my wanting to push the envelope with school assignments (such as my previously mentioned essay on passing gas). I would get my assignments back with comments scribbled across them in red ink: "Well written. Totally inappropriate."

Then there were other teachers who thought I was a bit too full of myself for my own good. One altercation soon after *Eight Is Enough* began airing brought out some hostility that I'm not proud to say has surfaced at other times in my life.

I walked into a social studies class, sporting photosensitive lenses, which were somewhat of a necessity by that time due to my years spent under the bright light of the carbon arcs on the sets. They didn't lighten up as quickly as they do these days, and they looked like sunglasses. The teacher, Mr. Johnson (not his real name), was beginning to show a filmstrip. He peered at me over his own glasses, which were perched low on his nose.

"Well, well, Hollywood! Not too bright for you in here, is it, Hollywood? Better take your glasses off now, Hollywood! Think you can do that, Hollywood?"

I took the laughter and ridicule only for a short time. "You know what, Mr. Johnson? I paid more in taxes last year than you made! I'm outta here!"

I grabbed my file off his desk and walked right down to the principal's office, where I demanded to be put into another section. When the principal asked me what had happened, I told him the truth. He said that I had been disrespectful, and he was right. But I felt as if I had been unjustly belittled for no good reason.

Whenever an injustice was directed toward me or someone else, I was never afraid to take on the offending party. We had a tradition on the set of *Eight Is Enough* every year called the Tush Bowl. Each year we'd all be filmed playing in a family football game at a local park, and it always became part of the show's plot, portraying some family conflict that got resolved.

At the first Tush Bowl, standing on the sidelines with his mother was the boy who had played Tommy in the pilot. He looked miserable, and I could hear his mother berating him. "Watch Willie. See how he acts. That's why you didn't get the job! You should have acted like him!"

Everyone in the scene picked up on the same theme. I could hear them criticizing the boy's acting abilities and personality.

I couldn't stand it. "Leave the kid alone! He's a good kid!"

That comment, loud enough for the boy's mother to hear, only made her pick on him more, pointing out the way I had defended him: "See? That's why he got the job and you didn't! You need to do what he does!"

As the show's episodes made me more recognizable to the American public, my fan mail increased. I had been receiving mail for quite a while and had tried to respond to it personally as much as I could, using an old Royal typewriter. I wasn't very good at typing—the paper inevitably came out crooked with the letters slanted. I started receiving letters from places like Trinidad and Tobago from boys and girls begging me for a package of shoelaces. Shoelaces! They were that poor. The injustice of that poverty so far away was one I was powerless to take on.

Meanwhile, my income and fame were increasing, and I was becoming a "Hollywood kid," whether I wanted to be one or not. I was good at portraying a normal teenager onscreen, but being normal was becoming an act in itself. My attitude toward working was changing due to sheer self-protection and -preservation, a small but growing disinterest, and my old friend, low self-esteem.

Also, my off-screen life had some far-from-normal aspects. And I had become aware of how fickle a friend TV was. You might be a series star one moment and not even able to get on the lot the next. I had been on seven series, and after each one I had moved on, saying good-bye to people with whom I had spent most of my waking hours. It was a fact of life in television, but it didn't help a person feel valued.

I also discovered a major fact of television: TV shows were not much more than filler for commercials. Related to this cynicism, or maybe just realism, was the belief that we were there to do a job, and we were not there to waste the directors', other cast members', or the studio's time. The crew began to call me One-Take Willie, a nickname I didn't mind because it expressed my beliefs.

Theater actors such as Betty Buckley, who played my step-mother, and Laurie Walters, who played my sister Joannie, used to talk about all of us "getting together as a team" to sit down and discuss the motivation for their characters. Motivation? Back history? I could not have cared less. My attitude was this: "Those are the words of the script. Your motivation is that you're ticked off; now go in and act ticked off, and get it done."

I wanted to get in there and finish the job, do it right, and get everybody else out on time. I hated it when other members of the cast showed up late—Betty was known for her late arrivals, which put us all behind schedule. The rest of us got a good laugh from her tardiness once at Columbia Ranch, where we were shooting around a pool. Betty came out of makeup several hours late, hair and wardrobe finally ready to go, and the rest of the girls began needling Betty and making sarcastic comments. They kept on, and she got so frustrated that she just jumped into the pool—clothes, makeup, and all. And when she jumped out, her clothes fell off. She was standing there nearly naked and embarrassed, which made her predicament that much funnier to the rest of us. Betty and I later became good friends—today, I have huge respect for her and her work.

Though I later grew more detached, those first couple of years playing the role of Tommy were pleasant ones. We male cast members got along very well. Dick Van Patten, who played my father Tom Bradford, and Grant Goodeve, who played my older brother David, both had a great sense of humor. We had private jokes between us and would do guy things, such as making embarrassing noises behind the girls' backs. We also enjoyed the antics of Adam Rich, who was only eight years old when the show's episodes began.

Dating is common within a TV cast, since those are the people in your circle of acquaintance. I dated Connie Needham, who played my sister Elizabeth in the show. I developed a crazy, out-of-control crush on her and would stay up very late, buy some roses, and leave them on her doorstep so she'd find them early in the morning. It took me a year to get over her after she began dating a guy in another state.

Later I developed a crush on Dianne Kay, who played my sister Nancy. Dianne was fresh, fun, and pretty, and became like a real big sister to me.

I became friends with Grant, who was about eight years older than I. After I learned to drive and bought a car, I spent many evening hours at his house. He had a nice singing voice and was a good songwriter. We'd play guitars, sing, and drink beer on his front porch and come to the set hammered the next day.[7]

One thing was certain: Grant didn't teach me to drink. I was already an experienced drinker by the time I got roles in *Family* and in *Eight Is Enough*. Jack Daniels had become a good friend of mine. I can remember drinking it straight up as early as age twelve, and Sandy Mirisch, my agent Toni Kelman's daughter, recently reminded me about me drinking the whiskey and spilling it all over a hotel in Palm Springs when I was about that age.

I don't remember exactly how I was able to get hold of the

---

7. Grant later became a Christian, which I discovered during the filming of one of our reunion shows. He and I later worked together under very different circumstances, and Maylo and I visited him in Washington when our daughter was a small child.

whiskey so easily, but my temptations were probably not much different from those of the average person. As I made more money and attracted more people who wanted to hang around with a TV star, my access to those temptations just became easier.

The Truth about My Two Families... The life of Willie Upton behind my Willie Aames/Tommy Bradford persona was very different from what people saw. I never thought that our TV family portrayal was true to reality. I didn't believe a single scene we did. It was all fantasy in my eyes. That's not meant as an indictment of the show itself—it was the high point in my young acting career—it's just that it didn't gel with what I knew about families.

I loved the extended family gatherings that Dad, Mom, my older brothers, my sister, and I would participate in on the holidays. Grammy Tip was always able to make us younger Uptons smile. I recall one family gathering at which she lectured us about the virtues of wearing a condom.

"Willie, Jim, Ronny, Jimmy, come here and listen to me. You boys need to start carrying condoms when you go out on dates. Don't you go out with any girl, no matter how nice she seems to be, without them. Don't you go and get any girl pregnant, you hear?" The laugh lines around her eyes creased as she spoke.

In spite of those times that I remember with fondness, my immediate family was no fantasy. We never played board games or football together like the Bradfords.

The Bradfords solved problems by talking things out, with both parent and child learning something by the show's end. In the Upton house, a similar situation would go like this: if one of us had an argument with Dad, he would "talk things out" by saying, "You're living under my roof, and if you don't like it, we'll go in the backyard if you're man enough. I'll teach you who's boss, and if you don't like it, you can get out."

On the show, problems between family members got solved. In my family, conflicts were ongoing. My TV mother's and father's characters openly and deeply loved each other. For years my real mother and father had not seemed like they were in love at all. I would often hear them arguing when I was supposed to be in bed.

People often told me that the Bradfords were just like their family. I could hardly believe it, sad to say. Soon the TV cast began to drift apart as well. I often got asked, "Is it like a family between you all on the set?" I always answered the question honestly— "No, not really"—surprising people who probably had the answer they wanted to hear already scripted in their minds. By the fourth and last season, most of us began to, at least mentally, move on to other things. We had all become very business-savvy, and most of us were asking for more money—or in my case, developing interests in other areas of performing.

I remember an instance that illustrates the cast's changing attitudes. We were on location in San Francisco, sitting in a station wagon out of the fog, waiting to shoot a scene, when Betty announced, "You know, we all ought to get together and ask for a raise! What do you think, Willie?"

That kind of question directed toward me was typical of Betty. Her treatment of me ran the gamut, from standoffishness one day to extreme friendliness the next, and I never knew what to expect.

I didn't even think before answering. "I think we'll all get fired."

Everyone in the station wagon laughed. We didn't take that course of action, at least not together.

I did get a raise, but it was totally confidential. I was warned not to say one word about it to anyone. The next thing I heard,

Adam Rich's family was demanding a raise for him, based on their knowledge that I had received one. The show's finance manager came to me and asked whom I had told. I answered truthfully, "No one."

I eventually figured out that my agent (not Miss Kelman by that time), who also handled Adam, was at the bottom of the demand. I fired him on the spot.

And so my daily on-set routine continued. Mom would drive me to the studio every morning. (Dick Van Patten recently reminded me that he was always impressed by how, though I lived the farthest of any of the cast members from the studio, I was always there on time and ready to get to work.) I owe her thanks for getting me there promptly because that was no small feat, considering Los Angeles' traffic.

And so one year turned into two, and two into three . . . .

White Powder and Paradise...As we filmed episode
after episode, my interests began to migrate more toward performing as a rock musician than as an actor. Ironically, *Eight Is Enough* was largely responsible for this change in focus because they featured my band, Paradise, as a part of some of the episodes, similar to the way *Ozzie and Harriet* had featured Ricky Nelson years earlier, jump-starting his career as a rock star.

I had played the guitar and sung lead vocals for Paradise, a band composed of high-school friends from my off-screen life before *Eight Is Enough* was even a part of my experience. We had played county fairs, theme parks, and other local gigs. When the show became a hit, we were offered larger venues and began performing and touring on weekends and between seasons. We got some national gigs—an Easter Seals Telethon, a United Cerebral Palsy Telethon, and others. Due to my celebrity, we quickly became part of the 1970s teen-idols craze, joining a huge touring show called Hollywood Teen that flew all over the United States.

My life during this time was pretty frenetic. During 1978 I had begun filming the movie *Scavenger Hunt* in San Diego. I was unusually confident during this period though I can't say why. Probably because I was busy. It was one of those rare streams of time when I actually felt like I could turn out to be somebody. *Eight* was a hit, my band and I were getting along and touring constantly, and I was "so-starring" in this huge comedy with tons of names to it.

Yeah, I said "so-starring," which means my name wasn't as big as my ego—instead of a single credit at the head of the movie (reserved for those truly starring), we came up with the "introducing" title that celebs use to single themselves out when they're young and well known but can't carry a movie by themselves. When people ask what they did during a hiatus, they make a big deal out of doing a "feature film" and the result is . . . so?

But being that busy did have a positive effect on my self-image if nothing else. I had become so busy that I hired a private plane to stand by while I shot *Eight* or a movie. As soon as the director yelled, "Cut!" and "Print it!," I would run to my dressing room, yell good-byes to the set crew, grab my $5,000 Don Feld-designed stage outfit, hop into a waiting limo, and race to the airport.

At that time you could do practically anything at airports, so my limo sporting AAMES license plates would pull up to the private plane's stairs. I'd hop out, climb into the plane, and immediately the plane would start rolling for takeoff. Depending on the gig, in an hour or so I would be buzzing the five thousand or more screaming thirteen-year-old girls surrounding the stage that was meant for me to perform on. The pilot would wag the wings and begin to land at the nearest executive airport, where of course another limo waited on the runway. My plane would roll to a stop next to the car. I'd hop out and jump into the limo, and it would speed all the way to the gig, stopping at the stairs of the stage as my band began warming up. Having changed into my stage clothes along the way, I could step out of the limo and walk directly on stage, grab the mike, and start straight into the opening song—just like clockwork. Neat trick, huh? It cost me a fortune.

The show also featured Scott Baio, Jimmy McNichol, Todd Bridges, and others who played and sang mainly bubblegum pop songs. I wanted to perform the harder, more serious rock or our own material. (I also wanted to perform without the then-common practice of lip-synching.) At one performance, I remember Mario Baio, Scott's father, sitting in the audience and looking shocked when Paradise played a Styx song, "Loralei," with a wall of sound—loud, full, and all-encompassing. Not what the thousands of screaming girls filling the concert hall had expected, I don't think, but I didn't care.

The more we performed, the more involved I wanted to be with hard-rock music. But I was still going on photography shoots for teen magazines like *Tiger Beat*, which catered to girls who shrieked in adolescent frenzy when we'd walk onstage to sing one of the lightweight songs chosen for us by the tour's producers.

As the band began to make a name for itself, we were asked to open for Tanya Tucker, Hall and Oates, Rod Stewart, and others. I'd talk with members of those bands, expressing my frustration over the conflict between the teen-idol music demands and what I really wanted to play, and they'd tell me, "Stick to your guns. Don't change anything. Do the kind of music you want."

That's what I was determined to do, but practicalities entered the picture and forced me to part ways with my band members. We went in to do our first serious record and the producer, Cory Wells, who was also in the band Three Dog Night, told me my high-school buddies weren't good enough. He said I needed to replace most of the members if I wanted to go anywhere musically.

This was, in effect, a death notice for the band. Although we did play a few more gigs together, I think we all knew what was coming. When I told the guys we had to split up, they were livid. They loudly blamed me and my "spoiled Hollywood brat" attitude.

I was becoming spoiled, all right, but maybe not in the way they might have meant. I had been smoking pot for quite a while, and so did members of the band—but in my growing acquaintance with members of other bands, toward the end of *Eight Is Enough*, I was introduced to cocaine by one of Frankie Valli's band members. We were rehearsing at the same location, and I walked over to hear Frankie's high tenor voice backed up by the Four Seasons.

"Hey, Willie, wanna try something?" I don't remember who specifically asked me or who gave it to me.

Let me be honest: I liked it immediately. I liked the sense of euphoria it gave me, and I told myself that I deserved a break from the frenetic pace of my life.

I had bought a house of my own when I was seventeen. Located in the same neighborhood as my parents' home, it was great for parties, with a pool and Jacuzzi in the front yard. I had been so anxious to get out of my parents' house that I was packed for two months beforehand, and at 12:01 a.m. on the morning of my eighteenth birthday, I was gone.

It didn't take me long to figure out where I could find some. "Who's holding?" I'd ask crew or cast members. The grips and other crew always had easy access to cocaine. If it wasn't within reach, I'd send someone out for it, and they'd soon return. That night we'd have plenty to go around, especially since some of my guests would show up at my house with their own supply.

During those days, drugs were everywhere in Hollywood. We used to joke that if it weren't for cocaine, we wouldn't have had disco. We used to call the show *The Dukes of Hazzard, The Drugs of Hazzard.* Not that that show had more drugs than other shows.

That nickname just comes to mind and illustrates the la-de-da attitude we all had. Everyone seemed to be using and dealing—assistant directors, crew, and series cast members.

By the time I was eighteen, there was so much going on in my life besides my role as Tommy that it now seems a blur. It's hard to remember details because there were so many—I had live TV appearances on *Merv Griffin, Bob Hope* specials, *Dinah Shore,* and others; I was regularly featured in photo spreads in *Tiger Beat, Teen Beat,* and other teen mags; I was attending awards shows; and I was trying to cut records and tour with the band. I rode in limos, flew on airplanes, and signed autographs.

Meanwhile, my drug and alcohol use gravitated to daily combinations of four Jack Daniels and an "eight-ball of blow."[8] The more people I met who were into it, the more I got into it.

One incident during this time illustrates a new low, or maybe I should say a new high, in my behavior: I was riding in the annual Hollywood Christmas parade, which I had been participating in for several years. I got the bright idea to call my dealer and have a supply delivered while I was on national television, right in the middle of the festivities. The parade came to a small stop to get around a street corner, so I jumped off the float, went to a pay phone, called him, and within twenty minutes he was on the float with us. We soon had all the coke we needed for the night, supplied right under the noses of the cops who rode horseback between the floats and parade watchers.

I often bought blow for other people. No one wants to party alone. And believe me when I say that almost everyone I knew in television was doing cocaine in the late 1970s and early '80s, including people who would seem to be the most unlikely of users. It was plentiful and it was easy to get. One thing it was not—it was not cheap.

---

8. A slang term for three grams of cocaine, a typical measurement.

Buying cocaine was hardly a problem by that point, though. I was making about a million dollars a year. I was on the top of the world, on a quite literal high. I had money. I had fame. I had the adoration of thousands of fans. I got to travel. I sang in a rock band. I dated some of the most beautiful women in the world.

It seemed like all was well. But it wasn't, though I didn't know it yet.

Viewing the Reruns of My Life...Let me stop again
momentarily to recall some memories of those days. The sheer number of events, interviews, talk shows, and concerts that surrounded the four and a half seasons of *Eight Is Enough* makes individual memories harder to pinpoint. Sometimes a memory will be triggered by seeing someone on TV. I'll say, "Oh yeah, I know that guy" or "I did a movie with that person."

When I catch the Los Angeles Christmas parade on TV, I think of one I was in the year I was fifteen. I knew the teen pop star Leif Garrett and his younger sister, Dawn, who was in the TV version of *Born Free*. Their beautiful mother was dating Burt Reynolds at the time. After the parade she invited me over to the house for Dawn's thirteenth birthday, and while I was there, she kept insisting that I take Dawn on a date to dinner that evening. The demand was odd, but I caved and took her. I walked Dawn to the door afterward, and Dawn's mother met me, asking me a strange question: "Well, aren't you going to sleep with Dawn tonight?"

"Uh, excuse me?" That was about all I could manage from my slack-jawed mouth.

"Aren't you going to sleep with her? She's never slept with anyone before."

"Um, no thanks," I answered, turning around and running for my car.

I also remember that earlier during the birthday party I had told them that I had landed the part in *Eight Is Enough*.

Leif had gotten very upset. "Hey, that was supposed to be my part!"

Oops, I didn't see that coming. I later traveled with him on the Hollywood Teen tours, but we lost touch years ago. We never talked about that evening.

Daily memories of life on the set of *Eight Is Enough* border on the surreal. "Don L." was a makeup artist, a huge African American. He could turn on the charm to women who made a fuss over him, but if they didn't give him any attention, he'd get his revenge—he'd paint blood-red tears around their eyes. They wouldn't know what their face looked like until they turned around and saw themselves in the mirror. Needless to say, Don L. was a little unstable.

I had become friends with Phillip, a thin little wardrobe man. He and I would sit and smoke at a table off by ourselves while we talked about jazz and the blues. Don L. came over one day and demanded—not asked—that Phillip put out his cigarette.

Phillip was not fazed. "Go away," he said, barely looking up.

"You're ruining the air! Put it out!" shouted Don L.

Phillip answered calmly, "Why don't you just go somewhere the smoke isn't?"

In a second Don L. grabbed a stainless steel makeup chair and slammed the headrest into a nearby table. It broke the table in half. He then grabbed me and threw me off my chair and onto the floor. But he was just getting started—while I was struggling to get out of his way, he picked up another chair and started beating Phillip over the head with it.

Six people had to pull Don L. off Phillip, who ended up in the hospital. Don L. was fired, no surprise. What was surprising was that some of the women tried to save his job. Two years later I saw

Don L. on the news—he was in a standoff with ATF, the FBI, and the police, who were attempting to arrest him for making bombs.

I also remember that I became one of an unwilling fraternity of actors when a stalker began calling me. In the last year of *Eight Is Enough*, I started getting calls and messages from a gay man in New York who said he wanted to come to California and be my boyfriend. He described in sickening detail the perversions he had in mind. Not too worried at first, I just hung up the phone, but before long he began telling me things that he should not have known—comments about where I had been that day, what I had been doing, and who I had been hanging around with.

"I'm a friend of Dick Van Patten's son Vince, and he gave me your number," he said.

Um, ri-i-i-ght. I knew very well he was lying, and Dick certainly knew that his son would never have become friends with such a sicko. Dick was and is a true gentleman, but when the man called me on the set, Dick took the receiver from me and ripped him up one side and down the other. Never before had I seen him that angry, and I never did after that. He demanded that the stalker leave me alone.

I appreciated Dick's standing up for me. Still, I was uneasy. We didn't know for sure where the faceless stalker was, and the studio refused to get involved (the old negative PR excuse), so I hired off-duty policemen to sweep the house. I also kept a loaded firearm close by. Eventually the man showed up at the studio, and a security guard called the police while another security guard hustled me out the studio's back exit. The studio escorted the stalker off the lot, and as far as I know, he's still out there.

And finally, perhaps my favorite memory, though not on *Eight Is Enough*: On *Swiss Family Robinson* we once had a director who seemed to delight in ticking everyone off and in treating everyone with disrespect. The final scene he was to direct involved a close-up of a beautiful blue and gold macaw, the type of bird you picture sitting on a pirate's shoulder. The goal was simple: place the bird on a wooden keg and get him to move his beak as though he were speaking. The macaw was trained to talk and the shot should have been easy. But the bird would not cooperate.

The director went into a fit of rage and screamed, "Just move your ——— beak, you ——— pigeon!"

With the cameras rolling, the bird looked calmly at the director and said, "——— you!" The entire set exploded into cheers.

It seemed that I was always being paired with members of the animal kingdom. Ah, those chimps—people do not realize how dangerous they can be. On location in Israel for the movie *Paradise*, which I did in 1982, I was supposed to order a chimp named Doc to do certain things. I had to be aggressive with him on film, yelling at him to follow my lead. Unfortunately, there is no in-between with any animal—you're either friend or foe. I'd try to treat him kindly when we weren't filming, but when I was in character I'd have to treat him roughly. He began to get confused and jumped around on all fours, visibly agitated.

I was safe as long as I was in the water, which I often was. Since chimps hate water, he'd run up to the water's edge then back off. For weeks Doc exhibited the same pattern.

Then came a story segment that involved me "saving" my co-star, Phoebe Cates, from a tent. I was supposed to yell at Doc, "Tear the tent down!"

On the first take, everything went well, but Doc was jumping up and down excitedly and his hair was standing on end. I wanted to leave well enough alone, but the director insisted that we redo the take "just in case." This time Doc came straight at me as soon as I got out of the water. Knowing I was about to be attacked, I bent and tried to lock my arms underneath his, but he was quick and strong. He picked me up, threw me down, and quickly bit into my knee. The trainers went after him with lead pipes, and soon the crisis was over. As two cameramen carried me off to a hospital, I could see Doc sitting in the sand, just playing.

One of the things I remember most about that day was the confusion of the doctors. I was taken to an Israeli military outpost, and as I lay in pain on the table, the doctors were screaming to each other in Hebrew. Even though I don't speak the language, I could tell they were flipping out, trying to figure out how a chimpanzee had gotten all the way up from Africa to the Israeli desert. They wanted to put us both into quarantine. Eventually, we got matters sorted out.

A side memory from a bit later: I saw Doc at the trainers' compound a couple of years after *Paradise*. He got so agitated that if he had been able to get to me, he would have torn me apart.

Memories such as these are, of course, not as significant as others. Still, they fill in some gaps about what it was like to be a teenage TV actor in those days. They also reveal some aspects of my own character, both the blooms and the warts. They're Willie, and they'll always be a part of me.

MAYLO

Mom Trades John for Bernie... The blue station wagon had been slowly circling the Reseda house for several days, while Mom worked her keypunching job on the three-to-twelve shift and I took care of Leenie and Lary. I got a good look at the driver while I was getting the mail.

The man had on a white undershirt. He had one tattooed arm resting on the open window. His other hand hung limply over the top of the steering wheel, holding a lit cigarette. His head was big, and his pockmarked skin was olive brown. He turned his face directly toward me and grinned from behind his large aviator sunglasses. I stopped what I was doing and stared as he rolled by. A few minutes later he came by again.

That night I left a note for my mom about the creepy man who was driving by the house. I didn't feel safe. What should I do?

The next morning she seemed giddy and excited. "What kind of car? What color?"

When I described the blue wagon to her, she smiled as if she knew a delicious secret.

"Did he say anything to you?"

113

"Mom, who is the man?" I pleaded with her to tell me, but she smiled that knowing smile and began another round of questions.

"You said he smiled. Was it a big smile, or was it just like a little no-teeth smile?" She giggled.

"Mom! Who is it?"

"You need to go to school," she answered.

About a day later I saw the blue station wagon again. It rolled to a stop, and the man looked at me. His smile was big, with lots of teeth.

"Hey, Fresh, where's your mother?" I didn't answer, but I didn't move either. "Did she tell you who I am?"

No, I thought. *Did she tell you that she's an apostle with special supernatural powers?*

"Come 'ere. Don't worry. I'm a good friend of your mom's. What's your name? I'm Bernie. I work with your mother. You're a pretty girl."

"No." Awkward silence.

"Tell her I was here. Would you do that for me?"

Bernie moved in with us in about two seconds flat. My mother told me he had gotten out of prison recently. He was muscular, tall, tough, and tattooed. Some sort of car accident had messed up his face. Trails of scars ran across it from the surgeries that sewed his face back together. His teeth came out—all of them. I had never seen dentures before. He would pop them out to be funny. *What a keeper,* I thought sarcastically.

Still, Bernie brought a lot of laughter to the house. When he laughed, he laughed so hard that his face would turn purple, and he would begin to wheeze. Like my mom's laugh, his was contagious, and there was something else about him, maybe his size, that made me feel safe. He was a good cook, and he made dill pickles, borscht, and other interesting foods. He spoke with a staccato, tough-sounding Brooklyn accent, and he talked about opening a deli someday.

Mom was flirty and happy, and the days seemed sunny. She didn't listen to as many Godfrey tapes when Bernie was around. Our lives calmed down a bit, and we established more of a family routine.

One day soon after Bernie had moved in—I was about eleven—my father dropped me off after a weekend visit. As usual, I had not wanted to go back home. I went into the house obviously upset but trying to hold my disappointment inside.

"Whazza matter, Fresh?"

I just stood there.

"Come 'ere. What's wrong?"

Bernie lifted me onto his lap, his big arms wrapping around my little shoulders as he pulled my head to his chest and held me. He felt strong and safe, and I started to let loose and sob. As I calmed down, I realized I had smeared snot and tears all over his suede sweater.

"I messed up your sweater." My eyes welled up again. "I'm sorry. I'm sorry," I blubbered.

"Hey, kid." He lifted my chin to look at me. "I'll never wash that sweater again," he smiled, and he put his face almost nose to nose with me. The gesture was tender and intimate but tough and protective.

Finally, Mom would be happy, and he would make everything all right—right? I wanted to make him smile, to love me. He seemed to want to be our father.

But soon my mother and Bernie began fighting. They had loud, screaming arguments, pushing and hitting each other right in front of us kids. During one of them, he stormed out the door. That was when Mom told me he was still married. He had another wife, Dusty, and he had two sons, almost grown. He had another house, too, and he would leave us from time to time to go back to his wife. Finding this out was a big betrayal, but even though I was hurt and surprised at first, almost immediately I found myself thinking, *Well, of course. Things just don't work out, do they? Not in real life. Of course not. Only in stories. This is how it goes down in real life.*

After one of their whopping violent runs at each other, Bernie and Mom temporarily split up and he left the house for some time. We three kids were at home, and my mother was in her bedroom in the dark, imagining.

Tat, tat, tat, tat, tat. Short pause. Then boom, boom, boom, boom, tat. The knocks got louder, and I opened the door.

Two official-looking county sheriff's deputies stood on the porch, badges gleaming, eyes hidden behind mirrored sunglasses. "Hey, kid, go get your mother."

I went into her room and told her who was at the door.

She sat up. "Oh. Oh, um, tell them I am not here."

"Mom, I already told them you were here."

"Tell them I'm sick and they'll have to come back."

So I did. But they did not budge. I went back and told Mom to come to the door, and she made up a lie for me to tell them. She told me what to say and exactly how to say it, and I marched back to the officers with my rehearsed little statement. One policeman held up a yellow piece of paper and told me they were not leaving until we got out. By law they were not to leave the property until they had secured the house.

I could feel the heat rising to my face. Out?! What do you mean *out?* My room—all my stuff! I marched back into my mother's room.

"Get up! Mom! Get up! They are throwing us out! We have to leave! We have to get the kids and leave!"

She jumped off the bed, red hair in a knotted ball on the top of her head, and stomped to the front door, screaming. The neighborhood kids emerged to see the show. The two deputies tried to calm her down but eventually had to handcuff her. They helped me get Leenie and Lary and allowed me to grab some necessities, and then they put a special lock on the front door. Finally, they uncuffed my mother, gave her the paper, and drove off. We sat down on the curb in front of the house.

The drama over, the neighborhood kids went back into their houses. The sun beat down on the top of my head and warmed my legs as Mom went next door to call Grandpa Harry to come and get us once again.

Mom and Godfrey...The theater grew dark, and anxiety rose in the audience. Mother gripped my arm and leaned into my ear. "Maylo, you need to pay attention. This is the truth and it is coming. You need to be prepared."

Everyone else in the theater came to be scared. My mother and I came to learn.

The Exorcist, starring the teenage Linda Blair, was drawing huge crowds. It was 1973, and I was eleven years old. The movie was graphic and intense. Mom was totally into it, but I could barely watch it. One scene affected my life for many years. The young girl was possessed by a demon. She was on her bed in a white nightgown, her face green and scabby and full of evil. Dresser drawers were slamming in and out, and all of her furniture was being tossed around by some unseen force. It was terrifying, and I wanted to cover my face and my ears. I couldn't even listen.

My mother put her arm around me, moved my hands away from my face, and whispered in my ear. "You have to watch, Maylo!

How are you going to do this if you don't know? I have been telling you this for months now! It is powerful! It is not bad!"

Every night after the movie, I lay in my bed with my heart pounding and my eyes wide open. I was afraid to close them. I was waiting for it to begin. I knew what she said sounded crazy, but the thing is, she had many other people backing her up: her friends, Godfrey, even Grandma Peggy at times. I had no experience in church or any knowledge of the Bible, so her conviction was overwhelming to me. Was she right? What if it were true?

Godfrey held a strong sway over my mother. She told me that he could walk through pictures and transport himself to anywhere he wanted to be with his mind. And she believed that she could do the same. Her obsession consumed every waking (and probably sleeping) thought, infusing every word she said.

When I was ten or eleven, she took me to a meeting in Hollywood at some sort of warehouse. We entered through a side door into a room with a stage and podium at the front and many plastic chairs arranged in rows. People were setting up reel-to-reel tape recorders and settling in to hear and record their prophet.

My mother's fair skin was flushed, and she was in a high state of excitement, endlessly talking and talking and talking to me. She waved quickly to a person here and another person there, but it was obvious that this was not a social event.

Everyone quickly quieted down as a tall man with thick, black hair and tanned skin came onto the stage and up to the podium. He was extremely elegant and spoke with an aura of authority. His voice was deep and smooth and almost monotone with a beautiful accent. He reminded me of Vincent Price, an old movie star I had seen on TV in gothic scare flicks.

Godfrey's voice nearly hypnotized me, and I was overcome with a warm, thick sleep that came over me like steam. When he finished speaking, people lined up to see him and shake his hand.

Mom became quiet as we approached him. He smiled at her and she introduced me. He turned toward me, leaned down into my face, and said to Mom, "She's what I have been waiting for."

He gently put his hand on the top of my head. He kept it there as he spoke to my mother for some time, and then he looked at me again. "Good-bye, little darling," he said and smiled at me with what felt like love.

I thought Godfrey was handsome. He was obviously important—many people there that night wanted to know him better. My mother seemed to almost physically eat up his words. At the same time, I was starving for a father. It was easy, actually, to believe that maybe mother was right about Godfrey. And it was easy to pretend that maybe Godfrey loved me.

But only for a moment. I wanted to be what he was waiting for, whatever that meant, but it didn't feel safe. Not like when I was with Grandpa Harry. There was no warmth anywhere. None. Everything was secretive and chilled and hushed.

My mother spent the following days trying to teach me to conjure up visions. She tried to teach me to find the figure, the man in the dark. She mentored me in the art of what she described as "concentrating on the darkness when you close your eyes." She instructed me, "Fall deep into the darkness."

Mom explained to me the reasons we had to move so much—that we were special and people were after us. That we had a mission on this earth and a lot of people would try to stand in the way. That Godfrey was a Christ. That Godfrey brought the real truth. That she was an apostle. That she was John the Baptist. That she was also God. That she was the Great I AM. And that almost all of the apostles were present, but Godfrey was waiting for the last one, and then it could start. And that last one was me.

Huh? Yeah, it was me. She told me that I was the last Peter. She said she was proud of me and that she saw us as partners and confidantes in the great mission. She told me I would begin to have the visions, and she smiled at me just like a girlfriend might before she tells you about her first kiss. And she'd begin to laugh, but it was not her belly laugh, the one that usually cheered me when we were out of food or facing eviction from our apartment.

Her couch-bred imagining continued. When I came home from school and she had been on the couch all day, I would complain because there was nothing for me to make for dinner. She would smile smugly, as if to say, "You'll understand soon enough." And when she did speak, her words became a recurring mantra: "You don't know who you are, but I will teach you. And you will fulfill your destiny."

Bernie had gone off to be with his wife for a while. There was no other man around at the moment, unless we counted Mom's boss, who was in the habit of coming over early in the morning to have sex with her before he left for work. So it was Mom and me and the kids—and Godfrey. At least until Bernie came back, and Mom diverted her attentions to him for a while.

Bernie's Moneymaking Schemes... "There won't be any trumpets blowin', come the judgment day. On the bloody morning after, one tin soldier rides away."

It was the early 1970s. As I sprawled across my bed in a floor-length, cream, gauze hippie-style dress, my two long, skinny brown braids falling over my shoulders, I listened to the song over and over again. I had volunteered to sing it at a big school function, and the words were the perfect expression of my depression and moodiness.

Mom and Bernie seemed to draw energy from their fights, which fueled yet more fights. Their relationship was wild and out of control. Mom became more and more violent both toward him and us, while refusing to acknowledge anything good we did. If I got good grades at school, something I really tried to do, she would take credit and say she had imagined the good grades and her powers had made them come about. It was not because of anything I had done.

The kids and I had fallen into a survival routine. Every time my mother and Bernie would fight, I grabbed my brother and sister and shoved them into my bedroom and locked the door, and then together we put our hands over our ears. We heard them screaming obscenities at each other and things crashing and being thrown around, but the worst sound of all was when they stopped yelling and all we could hear was the sound of grunting and hitting and smacking.

For hope, I used music and make-believe—tools to help the kids escape. Sometimes I zipped Leenie in a dress of mine that she kept asking to wear. We turned on the little turntable in my room and whirled and twirled to "Someday My Prince Will Come." Or we turned the music up as loud as we could while playing Candy Land or Chutes and Ladders.

We had moved many times, leaving one cheap apartment for another. Bernie had multiple moneymaking schemes that always involved animals, starting with a sheep he bought when we lived in the Reseda house and continuing to raising pigeons in our second-story apartment in the Valley.

The apartment had a big sliding glass door that led to a balcony overlooking the street. In the living room Bernie stacked chicken-wire cages against the sliding doors and filled them with pigeons. The birds were filthy and would coo at ridiculous hours during the night and pooped all over the room. The filth and stench were overpowering. We got kicked out.

In the next apartment Bernie decided to raise German shepherds. Although no one in our apartment had the knowledge, patience, or inclination to train or clean up after a dog, we had many of them. They were badly disciplined and chewed up our furniture, and, again, pooped all over the apartment. We got kicked out.

I guess Bernie saw himself as an entrepreneur. He always had some scheme for the whole family that was going to save the day. Mom was always excited with each new plan. We moved into another apartment on Parker, a busy street.

My mother was working during this period, and so was Bernie. They both worked night shifts, which meant I was left with my brother and sister. I became the default recreation director. I had other neighborhood latchkey kids over, and we fooled around doing not much of anything. Sometimes boredom and lack of supervision led to arguments, and Lary got into a lot of rock fights.

To keep me occupied and out of trouble, Bernie devised a list of inane chores for me, every one of them an all-night project. "Scrub the bathroom floor with a toothbrush. Clean all the grout in the kitchen with a Q-tip."

When he got home in the middle of the night, he inspected my work. If he found so much as a speck of dirt, he pulled me out of a sound sleep. He dragged me into my mother's room, pulled my pants down, and whipped me with a thin leather belt until I had welts up and down my bottom and the back of my legs. My mother held down my arms. (Today Leenie says she could hear me crying all the way down the hall.)

My mother and Bernie had sex at all times of the day, whether the three of us were around or not. Bernie decided that we were all to become nudists. Mother walked around the house completely naked. And Bernie, who was also naked, made all of us take our clothes off while he lay on the couch with his legs spread.

As I recall, Lary and I just gave in and did what we were told, but Leenie was devastated. She was extremely shy, and it was torture for her. As Bernie yelled at her to undress, she sat on the living room floor and cried. He tried to make me take her clothes off, and I screamed back at him that I wouldn't do it. I knew I wouldn't win, though, and finally Leenie gave up. She pulled off her clothes and sat in a self-conscious ball on the carpet, crying.

Mom did nothing at all. She believed Bernie was an apostle, one of Godfrey's chosen ones, and whatever he commanded was right.

Friends and Santa Barbara...Heather was a beauty.

Her light, almost white, wavy, soft hair complimented her round sweet face, fair skin, and huge blue eyes. She was quiet and had great depth, and she was a natural actress who was in all the school plays.

She was also my best friend in junior high, and I spent as much time at her house as I could get away with. She lived in the suburbs of the San Fernando Valley in an older two-story house surrounded by huge trees that kept it cool and shady. Her bedroom sat at the top of some narrow, creaky stairs and was really more of an attic. We were sure it was haunted. She would hear noises or see shadows up there that were, it seemed to us, unexplainable, and she'd tell me about them. As girls often are, we were enthralled. I spent hours in Heather's room, listening to albums by Judy Collins, Jackson Browne, and Linda Ronstadt, whose song "Prisoner in Disguise" became my personal theme. We tried to summon the ghost of the house, wrote poetry, and talked. On the grassy quad at school, we ate lunch together, sharing herbal teas out of a thermos as we told stories to each other of fairies that lived in the grass.

My other friend, Stacy, was also pretty and blonde, with eyes like Faye Dunaway's in a heart-shaped face covered with tiny freckles. She was athletic and had a big smile and a happy disposition.

Stacy was new to our junior high school. Her mother had committed suicide, and Stacy had been adopted by a great Christian family who lived in a huge house in the hills overlooking the Valley. We became friends right away because we both had broken hearts. We were a little different from the other girls and at first were both picked on quite a bit. We talked a lot about mothers and about love and loss.

As the year progressed, Stacy began adjusting well to her new life and made more friends. I began to see less and less of her. She was healing, becoming happy. I felt a divide in our friendship.

She began attending some meetings called Young Life. She loved them and invited me to one. Because I missed my friend, I agreed to go, but I had no idea it was a Christian youth group.

Stacy's parents dropped us off at the house of the student hosting the meeting that evening, and it was swarming with kids I didn't recognize. Fun-loving, popular Stacy and her big, wide smile fit right in, while next to her I felt shrunken and clumsy. Boys were there too. We played games that seemed silly to me, and they made me feel hot and embarrassed. Other people laughed and seemed to know what they were supposed to do, but all I felt was out of place. The group seemed to be what I thought of as "the rich kids," the ones who had their own cars and lived in actual houses, not apartments.

As Stacy began to grow in Jesus Christ, our friendship dwindled. Soon she was off at great camps, making many other friends. Her Christianity was *so* not my thing! Not because I thought it was stupid or uncool or anything like that, but because I didn't understand it. I couldn't force myself to smile and have that kind of fun. I didn't know how those kids could do that. I had no clue about the source of their joy.

As I drifted from Stacy, I found a friend in a boy named Doug. Doug was short and had muscular arms, dark wavy hair, and sparkly blue eyes. He was hilarious; I laughed every time I was around him. We passed notes back and forth with drawings of stick people in them. I adored him and wrote his name all over my school books.

Doug and I made plans to get together or at least talk on the phone on a coming weekend. But when I got home from school that Friday, my mother told me to get in the car.

"We're going to Santa Barbara," she announced, naming a beautiful beach community about two hours from where we lived.

"Why?" I asked, panic setting in.

"Because Bernie bought a hamburger truck and parked it at the Santa Barbara airport. He needs you to work the front of the truck while he cooks."

I pleaded with my mother to change her mind. I was heartbroken that I wasn't going to see Doug. But there was another reason I dreaded doing things with Bernie—a reason I hadn't told anyone: Bernie had begun touching me and coming closer to me, and I didn't like being around him.

"Where are we staying?" I whimpered.

"*We* are not staying; *you* are staying. The kids and I are going back home."

"What? Why?" I was slumped in the backseat of the car by the window.

"Because there is no need for us, only you. He only needs you."

"Please, Mom, please don't make me go. Please, Mom, please, Mom, please."

Mom tuned me out and looked straight ahead as I cried in the backseat. I finally gave up. I fell silent and rested my face against the cool glass of the car window, watching the landscape change from fields bordered by eucalyptus trees to sand dunes.

We arrived at a brown, run-down, apartment-style hotel. My mother led me up a flight of stairs, knocked on the door, and quickly dropped me off.

Maybe she knew. Maybe she felt it coming. Somewhere deep inside of her, maybe there was guilt. Maybe that is why she had to leave.

I Learn to Float Away...When I walked into the apart-
ment, Bernie was in high spirits. He was happiest when he had some new venture, and this one held promise. He seemed like a child playing house or, maybe, playing restaurant. He spoke to me gently and thanked me for helping him out and asked if I had eaten. Did I want to get something?

"No," I said.

So there we were. He turned on the TV that was directly across from the bed and began to roll a joint. His cigarettes were on the table by the front door. I sat down and began to play with the pack, spinning and flicking it with my fingers, feeling uncomfortable alone with him.

"Do you want one?"

"What?"

"Do you want a cigarette?"

Hmm. I had to think about that one for a minute. A door had just been blown open—the freedom to step into a world without boundaries had just been offered to me. No kids. No Mom. He was treating me like I was an adult—like smoking was no big deal.

"Yeah," I answered casually. He shrugged his shoulders and ran his tongue along the paper of the joint, sealing it off in a tight little roll.

Well, all right then, I guess he wasn't going to stop me. I took a cigarette out and lit a no-filter Camel. I sat at the table and took one tiny hit after another, letting the nicotine flow into me, making me feel tingly and light-headed.

Bernie sat on the bed, watching TV, smoking his joint, and drinking can after can of beer.

Maybe this won't be too bad after all, I thought. Bernie seemed pretty mellow.

"So, um, what time are we going to work in the morning?" I finally asked.

"We're going to hit the lunch crowd, so we won't have to be there until about ten. I just need you to take the orders and the cash."

"OK."

"Come 'ere, Fresh. Watch some TV with me."

"Um, that's all right."

"Come 'ere." He slapped the bed where he wanted me to sit. I went over and sat uncomfortably on the edge of the bed with my feet on the floor and my back toward him.

"I'm not gonna bite you!" he laughed. "C'mon, get on the bed." He motioned for me to sit next to him, so that I could lean against the headboard and watch TV beside him.

The atmosphere of the room changed. The sound of the TV became muted in my ears, and I didn't know what to do, especially since I still felt light-headed from the cigarettes.

He put his hand on my back and rubbed it. "Maylo. I'm not gonna hurt you. Are you afraid I'm gonna *hurt* you?"

He sounded puzzled and concerned. His voice was tender, and it confused me. Bernie could be charming, but he could also seem dangerous and threatening. Was I wrong? Was I hurting his feelings? Was he a protector? A friend? Why did I still feel tense? Afraid? I couldn't answer him. I couldn't think of anything to say. He waited for me to respond but got only silence.

"I can't believe you think I would do anything to hurt you!" He sounded seriously offended. "Do whatever you want!" He leaned back against the headboard with a thud and stared at the TV.

"Um, I think I just need to take a bath. I'm gonna take a bath." My voice was small. I wanted to hide. He said nothing. I went into the small bathroom and closed the door. While the water was running, I carefully and quietly pushed in the lock button on the doorknob, hoping he wouldn't hear its small click.

The warm water rose to the very top of the tub as I climbed in. I was separated and safe in my own little room. Tension started to ease, and I sat soaking in the tub for a long time.

Then, a bang on the door. Not a knock—a bang. "Hey!"

I jumped. My heartbeat kicked into panic speed, but I sat frozen, unable to make myself stand up. He tried to turn the doorknob, and when he found I had locked it, he became enraged. "Open the door, —— it!"

He began to slam up against the door over and over with his shoulder. I cannot explain the feeling of total emptiness I had at that moment. I had no words. I stood up in the tub and grabbed a towel and listened as he slammed up against the door again and again.

There was nowhere to go. I stood in the water in the corner of the tub and let my mind float away. It was happening. It was happening for real. I knew it. I can't be here. Not mentally. Not totally. Down, down I went. Acceptance. Limp.

The door burst open, and he was across the small room and in my face before I could have a thought. He was so angry. Oh, my goodness, he was angry! Cursing at me, he grabbed me by the arms and pulled me out of the bathroom and onto the bed.

I didn't cry. I was gone. All noise was muffled, and I couldn't feel. I saw his face above me as it turned red for a moment, then he fell over beside me. Spent.

Turning on my side, I did begin to cry then, curled up into a ball. I cried and cried. I cried the tears of what felt like a hundred years. It wasn't just the rape—that violation was nothing compared to my mother's betrayal. She had dropped me off. She dropped me off. She dropped me off . . . I want my friends . . . my life . . . my sister . . . I want to be in my room . . . I want to go home. Please. Please, can I go home? My chest hurts. I hurt.

He put his hand on my shoulder. "Maylo. Don't cry." His voice was gentle. "Maylo . . ." He sighed and waited. "Maylo, I know you don't understand how much I love you. You are such a special girl. I would never hurt you."

Anyone who has ever been through something similar will understand how confusing and complicated these words were. Those who haven't may find them hard to fathom. There is no doubt in my mind even today that Bernie actually cared for me.

"I would never mean to hurt you. I wouldn't." He began to cry. I stayed on my side and he put his arm over me. I could feel him crying quietly. And I found myself comforting him.

"It's OK. It's OK," I croaked, through snotty tears.

It all gets turned around. You begin to sympathize with the perpetrator. You begin to feel sorry for him. I was a young girl who had already taken on the job of mothering her little brother and sister, and now I found myself in the role of mothering Bernie after he had violated me. For about the next five years.

Really, there was nothing left to do that evening but take the joint he offered me and get high and watch TV. The worst was over. For that night, anyway.

Borscht, Donuts, and Abuse at the Doneka-
tessen... The weekends in Santa Barbara were short-lived, but working the hot truck was the experience Bernie apparently needed to give him the confidence to open a successful deli/donut shop in the Valley.

We had moved several more times after neighbors had complained about us or landlords had evicted us. The relationship between Bernie and my mom was at once tighter than ever and more violent than ever.

When I arrived home from school one afternoon, several policemen were in the living room. My mom was at one end of the room being questioned by an officer, and Bernie was at the other. The back of his T-shirt had been shredded and his neck and back were a bloody mess. I wasn't surprised at all. We all knew that when pushed past her breaking point, Mom could be far more dangerous than any large man.

The daily dramas continued. The pot smoking and laughing and loud sex afterward were regular activities we kids could count on. Leenie became even more quiet and withdrawn. Lary, always big-hearted toward Leenie and me, became a little hyperactive and sad, and he finagled ways to spend as much time away from our apartment as he could. The three of us were doing terribly at school . . . when we went.

Bernie had become bolder and did not think twice of taking me right on my mother's own bed, sometimes in the middle of the day. Sometimes my mother was at work, but other times she was in the living room, lying for hours on the couch with her eyes closed, summoning up visions of the day the world finds out we were all apostles or imagining the chariots of gold that come down out of the clouds carrying Godfrey in them. Those rapes in her bedroom were quick and forceful. Lary and Leenie were

My dad and mom on their wedding day late in 1960

My dad and I not long after he and my mother got divorced

Me in one of those posed shots my dad and his friends were so fond of taking—I was three or four years old.

"Street Maylo," during my drug years—you can see the drug use in my face.

The three child co-stars of Irwin Allen's *Swiss Family Robinson* TV series, which aired from 1975 to 1976, until it was knocked off the air by an obscure little news magazine called *60 Minutes*

The cast of *Eight Is Enough* (1977–81), with Dick Van Patten and Betty Buckley surrounded by the five girls and three boys who made up Tom and Joan Bradford's "family"—I had a hard time believing that this family was like any real family, but many people I talked to insisted that their families were just like the Bradfords, and I guess that's why some people loved the show.

Typical "teen idol" picture—"Love and kisses, Willie Aames"

Scott Baio and I on the set of *Zapped* (1982), a comedy about a high school kid with telekinetic powers—I was on the set when Victoria went into labor, and I rushed to be with her. When Chris was born, I called to let the cast and crew know. The scene that day involved 400 extras. Through the phone's earpiece we could hear everyone cheering.

Me with Doc the chimp, who nearly bit off my kneecap on the set of *Paradise* (1982)—I ended up in a hospital having emergency surgery in southern Israel and being attended to by Israeli doctors, who just could not understand what a chimp was doing in the middle of the desert! We finally were able to make them understand that he was an "actor" on a movie set.

Singing with my band Paradise— we toured with a group of other teenage heartthrobs, such as Scott Baio, when *Eight Is Enough* was on hiatus. The show launched my singing career because the writers featured my band in the plot.

© 1989 LEE SALEM

A *Charles in Charge* cast and crew 100th episode anniversary portrait— Scott Baio is standing to my right, and Ellen Travolta, who played Charles's mother, is next to him.

A Bibleman card with a small picture of me at the time on the back.

Me with my amazing dance teacher, Pedro—dancing is what got me started, and I was determined to be the best at it.

My first job! It was a pilot called *The Home Front* (1980). The legendary Jean Simmons is on my right and Delta Burke (later of *Designing Women*) is on my left. I was eighteen.

An early job playing "Dirty Trixie," a superhero in training, on *The Kids Superpower Hour*—I guess Willie and I both can lay claim to the Superhero title!

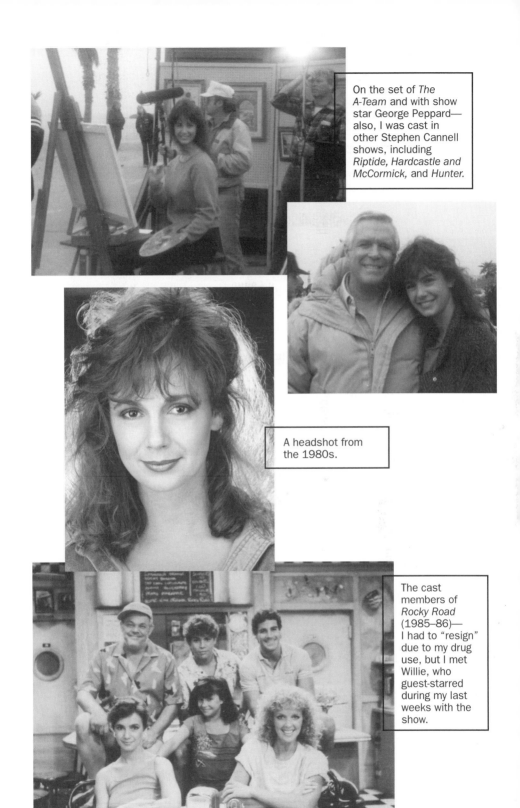

On the set of *The A-Team* and with show star George Peppard—also, I was cast in other Stephen Cannell shows, including *Riptide, Hardcastle and McCormick,* and *Hunter.*

A headshot from the 1980s.

The cast members of *Rocky Road* (1985–86)—I had to "resign" due to my drug use, but I met Willie, who guest-starred during my last weeks with the show.

Us with Willie's son Chris at the *Charles in Charge* 100th episode celebration

Chris in high school

Chris is now a bass player with the band Lola Ray.

June 1986—here we are with my beloved Grandpa Harry when Willie and I were dating. Harry was so happy that I had found a good man, and I think it shows on his face. He passed away three days after we were married. I miss him so much.

March 15, 1987

The 457-pound, record-breaking marlin that won a prize for my crew and me off the coast of Mexico—after nearly twenty-two hours of reeling him in, it turned out that he wasn't even hooked; he was tangled in the line, and that's why he fought so hard for so long. My hands had been so clenched that I couldn't straighten them out for quite a while.

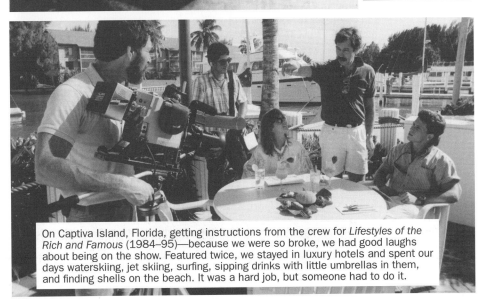

On Captiva Island, Florida, getting instructions from the crew for *Lifestyles of the Rich and Famous* (1984–95)—because we were so broke, we had good laughs about being on the show. Featured twice, we stayed in luxury hotels and spent our days waterskiing, jet skiing, surfing, sipping drinks with little umbrellas in them, and finding shells on the beach. It was a hard job, but someone had to do it.

Harleigh and I in the roles of Missy Shannon and her mother on the set of the teen video series *The Missy Files,* which Willie wrote, directed, and produced. Two films (*Changes in the Wind* and *Adventure at Sun Rock Ranch*) were released in 2003. Harleigh was twelve.

BOISSEAU FILMWORKS

Harleigh—grown and ready to leave home soon

The most recent addition to our family— Beatrice has helped us through the grief of losing Molly and Gretchen, our golden retriever and rottweiler.

directed to watch TV, so they sat without making a sound in front of the TV and stared at the screen. They did what they were told to do. We all did.

One of my mother's imaginings saw me onstage accepting an Academy Award. She was sure—she was issuing a supernatural decree through her great powers, in fact—that I would be one of the twentieth century's greatest actresses. It had to happen—it was the destiny that her imagining had arranged for me! This was one of Mom's visions that I was happy to go along with—who wouldn't want to be a great star? She enrolled me in the National Performing Arts Academy near Universal Studios, where I attended classes twice a week in the evenings.

During the days, though, she and Bernie pulled me out of public school to work in Bernie's new restaurant, the Donekatessen. It had, to say the least, an unusual menu—donuts and beet borscht, among other more typical deli items. It was in a strip mall on Coldwater Canyon Boulevard, a busy four-lane highway in the Valley. Other tenants included a Carvel Ice Cream Parlor and a Kentucky Fried Chicken, and there was a liquor store at the far end.

Every day was more or less the same. Bernie woke me up at 3:30 or 4:00 in the morning to make the day's donuts and tuna salad. We arrived so early that it was still dark outside, and I began pouring pounds and pounds of fluffy, white flour into the giant mixer. In those early-morning hours Bernie was upbeat and gregarious. While I made donut batter, he stood at a large island in the center of the kitchen, chopping tomatoes and eggs and talking cheerfully like we were great friends.

But as our food-prep chores ended, his mood would switch into high gear. He'd start breathing harder and would become impatient, demanding, and—there is no other word but this ugly one—horny. He would get angry and frustrated because I resisted his advances. Because I resisted, what would have just taken a few minutes would turn into an ordeal and the fighting would begin.

I grew absolutely determined not to be touched. He would smack my face and grab me by the upper arms and push me into a grimy bathroom in the back. After shoving me down onto the toilet seat, he would drop his pants and try to force oral sex from me by pushing on my head, and I would grit my teeth closed as hard as I could. Or he would shove me down onto the big flour bags. Or he would try to bend me over the island counter.

And he'd repeat the same words every time: "Maylo, I love you. C'mon, what is the big deal, Fresh?"

I screamed the same words every time. "I don't love you! Don't touch me, you ———! . . . Why can't you just love Mom?" I pleaded. "Why can't you just leave me alone?"

And the same answer came back every time: "This is what people do when they love each other. What is the big deal, Maylo? It takes five minutes! Five minutes! You know what you are? You are a selfish little girl! You are a selfish, selfish little girl!"

Five minutes and it would be over for me. Done. Something inside of me gave in and told my heart, "Five minutes, Maylo . . . five minutes and it is over. Just do it."

Bernie was right, I'd think. I was a selfish little girl. I was the one in the wrong. This pattern had been going on long enough now that I should know what to expect.

Many times I reminded myself how wrong what he was doing to me was. But it was such a big hassle to fight. Many times it did seem easier just to take the stupid five minutes and get it over with. And there was a weird, subtle, little-girl thing going on inside me—a strong desire to be loved that would make me want to give in to him. I did hear his words "I love you" in there, and a part of me felt selfish for fighting him. He was so frustrated with me, and if he did love me, then maybe I was pushing love away or something like that. It was a strange, confusing dynamic.

The Great Escape... At 3:30 each day I left the Donekatessen and headed home to babysit Lary and Leenie. Mom was working the night shift, keypunching, so for three or four wonderful, peaceful hours before Bernie came home, the kids and I had the apartment to ourselves. We didn't have much to eat other than what was brought home from the Donekatessen, but it didn't matter. We played our records and danced in the living room. In one apartment, we even had a small swimming pool right off of our patio, where we would swim and laugh and hang out together. I loved those kids and always had great fun being with them.

I was missing so much school that my mother began receiving delinquency notices from truant officers. So I went back to school for a while. I was so far behind that I had no idea what the teachers were talking about. My grades plummeted as low as my self-esteem.

I felt like trash, and I knew that was what I was. The only place where I got any positive feedback was at the National Academy of Performing Arts. Because of the inexhaustible supply of anger within me, my tears were always right at the surface, so I had an easy time with dramatic roles. Nobody knew that what was going on in my world was the source.

I took acting lessons there from the famous Francis Lederer, founder of the academy and an actor and teacher with a résumé as long as Santa Monica Boulevard. I also took some dance lessons there and did scene work with other teenagers who later became famous adult actors. Helen Hunt was one of the girls in my acting class, and we often did scenes or exercises together. She was beautiful, with long, straight, shiny, blond hair, and she was pleasant to me. I didn't find out until years later that at the same time she was attending the academy, she was also working with my future husband Willie Aames. Small world, isn't it?

The academy was, without my even realizing it, what I needed to help me escape for a few hours. For when I wasn't there, I had to be at the Donekatessen, and I knew what awaited me there.

Finally, at fifteen years of age, I decided I was not going to go one more day with the abuse. "Get your ——— hands off me, you ———! I am going to call the police, you piece of crap!" I screamed at him with pent-up passion and anger and power. I felt invincible. Adrenaline pumping, I bolted for the door.

My neck suddenly snapped backward, and I was stopped dead in my tracks as Bernie yanked the back of my long, brown hair in his hands. He held my head so far back that I had to lean backward onto his chest. Holding a butcher knife up to my exposed neck, he warned, "If you ever go to the cops about me, I will kill you." His tone was matter-of-fact. "I will not go back to jail!"

That time he did not even pretend to be gentle with me. He did not tell me he loved me. He did not say it would take only five minutes. He did not cry afterward.

From that day, there was no more "happy talk" as Bernie and I did food prep. He always acted angry at me. And suspicious. And threatened. And paranoid.

He watched me everywhere I went. He followed me to my acting class, driving slowly around the street over and over again. He made me give him my underwear if I had been out with friends. He took out his anger on my mother too—the pattern of their mutual abuse got scarier and bloodier.

In a rage, Bernie went after my mother with an iron one evening. I shoved Lary and Leenie into my bedroom and then tried to pull him off her.

I was yelling, "Stop it!" and grabbing at the back of his shirt when our front door burst open. Every one of us froze in our tracks. Standing in the doorway of the apartment was my Grandpa Harry with a rifle under his arm.

Harry pointed his rifle at Bernie. I don't know if Mom had called him or how he knew we were in trouble, but there he was. I will never forget it. I wanted to cheer. The scene played out like it was in a movie.

Calmly, Grandpa Harry said, "Sharon, get the kids."

She stood still. Bernie was standing between her and her father, and she could not move.

"Now!" my grandpa barked. Grandpa took two steps closer to Bernie, who simply stood there with his mouth open. "If you make one move, I will blow your head off without even thinking about it!"

Mother was frozen. Bernie was frozen. Grandpa seemed frozen. He finally spoke gently to me. "Maylo, get your brother and sister and some clothes. Pack up just what you need. Hurry up."

I jumped past Bernie and ran into the bedroom, my hands shaking. It was only a few seconds before I had the kids and a couple of pillowcases full of stuff. We ran out the front door and to the curb and climbed into Grandpa's car. I was buckling up Lary and Leenie, who were asking me a million questions, when my mom ran down the sidewalk and into the car. With his rifle under his arm, Grandpa got into the driver's seat and we left. I was giddy.

Pancakes and a Vega... Early in the morning, I woke up on the floor. My head was comfortable on a squishy, white pillow, and I was nestled inside a down sleeping bag. My brother and sister were lying beside me, and I could hear them breathing in their deep sleep.

I slowly focused on my surroundings: a brown wooden desk chair on wheels sat at a large, old desk; framed photographs of mountains, woods, and icy blue waters taken from many cruises and travels; plaques and awards; and the methodical ticking of a small clock that sat on the desk. Grandpa's wife, Nikki, was an amateur photographer, so her pictures hung everywhere. The room was creamy-colored and calm, and it smelled safe—like leather and money.

I also smelled something more. Sweet and familiar. Salty. I got up and cracked open the door. I could hear my grandpa singing. We had spent the night in Grandpa Harry's condo in Culver City, located on an upper floor of a high-rise building. I padded down the hallway and looked around the corner into the kitchen.

Grandpa was at the stove, and Nikki was setting the table. She was beautiful and calm, and she smiled at me, though I did see the concern in her eyes. "Well, hello there."

Grandpa turned and saw me. "Hiya, kiddo! Go get your brother and sister for breakfast." His eyes twinkled and he smiled.

Oh my gosh. Pancakes! And bacon! Butter and syrup and salty, crispy bacon! I trotted down the hall and found my brother and sister already sitting up and sniffing, eyes wide open.

No need to waste time talking! We were at the table in less than a minute to have our fill of Grandpa's cooking. He was an excellent cook, and he made dinner every night we were there—his special tuna casserole and his homemade rolls still make my stomach growl. While we ate, Grandpa and Nikki would tell us about the many places they had been on their travels.

During those days, I spent as much time around my grandfather as I could. When he was busy with paperwork, I worked with him at his desk. Lary and Leenie colored and played board games. The atmosphere was quiet and settled, and the three of us relaxed.

I don't remember what my mother did, or where she was, for that matter. She was in and out.

But I do remember Bernie. He showed up once or twice on the street below us and called out, "Sharon? Sharon!" He kept shouting for her until Grandpa yelled off of the balcony that he was going to call the police.

In the meantime, Grandpa was trying to find a new place for us to live so that my mother could get a new start with no Bernie. He enrolled us in the nearby school and came home one day with a brown Vega station wagon. He just gave the keys to my mother. "It's yours, Sharon."

Mom became antsy and edgy. She would sit and twirl her hair around her fingers and chew the inside of her mouth. She began to talk about the things that we had left behind—clothes, pictures, and things that she kept insisting we couldn't replace. Finally, on a day we knew Bernie was at work at the deli, Grandpa took my mother and me back to the apartment.

When we opened the door, we found all of our belongings destroyed. The TV set was bashed in, and furniture was smashed. There was acid thrown over almost everything else, so that nearly everything we had owned was burned, broken, and ruined. I grabbed what I could, just a few pictures, some poetry, some albums, and toys for the kids, and we left.

When we got in the car, we all felt awful. Mom was silent the entire drive back to the condo. Grandpa just kept repeating, "It's OK. It's only stuff, Sharon. We'll start over. Don't worry."

That sounded good to me. Even though we didn't have a home of our own, I was more than happy to sleep on the floor at Grandpa and Nikki's condo for as long as we could.

"Maylo." It was late at night a couple of days later. I had just nodded off in the sleeping bag, and her whisper woke me up just a little. She was about an inch away from my face. I could smell her bad breath. "Maylo."

I opened my eyes. The bedroom was pitch dark. "Get up. Get up." She began rousing the kids.

Lary, groggy from sleep, spoke out loud. "What? Why?"

"Shhh! Be quiet!" Mom whispered. She was moving us up and out as fast as she could. "Get your clothes. Move!"

"But . . ."

"Go! Do as I say!" She hustled us out the front door and down the elevator to the lot where she had parked the brown Vega in front of the elevator doors.

"Get in." She wasn't whispering now. She opened the doors of the car.

Lary and Leenie started to cry. "Why can't we stay?" they wailed.

By now she was angry—scary angry. We knew better than to do anything other than to obey and be quiet. She threw our things, all she had been able to carry, into the car as fast as she could.

Mom had just climbed into the driver's side when the elevator opened and my grandfather came running out in his red plaid robe.

"Sharon! Sharon, please! Don't take the kids! Leave the kids, Sharon!"

Mom acted as if she hadn't heard Grandpa Harry. She slammed the door and backed up as fast as she could, leaving skid marks on the slick poured concrete. She was cursing as she tried to throw the car into gear.

Her face was ugly with anger. Grandpa ran after us as I watched through the backseat window. He ran, crying, "The kids! The kids!"

It is still painful even to write this down. I had never hated my mother as much as I did that day. She took everything her father, our grandfather, had given her and ran off. Leaving him slumped and sobbing on the cold cement of the parking structure at four in the morning. It would be years before I would see him again.

A Tree in the Woods... My mother did get the new start she was looking for—a new start with Bernie. A new apartment. A new phone number—unlisted so Grandpa Harry couldn't find us. I couldn't come up with a way to contact him without my mother finding out. Anytime in the past when I had tried to call him or my Aunt Judy, I had had to face Mom's wrath, something no one wanted to deal with, and I also somehow felt like I was betraying her.

Bernie and my mother were honeymooning again, as they always did after fighting or breaking up. Mom was high on independence from her "controlling, backstabbing father," and Bernie shamelessly smoked pot in the living room right in front of Lary and Leenie. Marijuana was on the coffee table all the time, right next to the Tarot cards and the cigarettes.

Bernie continued to climb on me but at least had the "decency" to leave marijuana in the bathroom so I could get high and calm down afterward. It helped.

My brother and sister were growing up. I felt like they needed me less. They both had friends from school they spent a lot of time with, and they got out of the house as much as possible. I went back to the academy off and on. Mostly off.

I tried to run away. We lived across the street from a school playground that was surrounded by a chain-link fence. I'm not sure what I was thinking I was going to do once I got over that fence—hide, maybe—but it represented a way out. As I was try-ing to climb the fence, Bernie came running out of the apartment and caught me. He latched his arms around my waist as I gripped the chain links as hard as I could until my fingers turned white with strain. As he pulled, I squirmed and tried to kick at him. He dragged me across the street and I tried to grab hold of car bumpers—anything—to keep from going back into that apartment, because I knew he was going to beat the tar out of me if he got me back there. It was a pretty pathetic and doomed attempt on my part, and all my predictions came to pass. That failure did make me realize that if I was going to run away, I would have to do it smarter than that. I would have to do it right under his nose. It would take time to plan.

I began making a small effort to get back into school, where I came into contact with my old friend Stacy. She was even prettier than before, maybe because she was so happy and healthy. She invited me to a retreat.

No surprise—I was not allowed to go with her. She did something I'll always remember with love: she got so angry with Bernie and my mother that she walked home with me one day and went up to our apartment. Standing in the front doorway, she told Mom and Bernie that I had no childhood, and if they didn't let me go, her parents would become involved. Her threat played on Bernie's paranoia, and he let me go.

We rode in a school bus for a long time until we rolled up to a large cabin surrounded by several smaller cabins in a clearing in some woods. Grabbing our sleeping bags and personals, we then formed groups. We were assigned cabins and bunks, and once we got settled, we reported to the big cabin for dinner.

The weekend was packed with activities and water games, but I didn't participate in them. I was so taken by the surroundings that I longed just to stay quiet and be alone.

I don't remember much of what was said, but there was one night that stands as the single defining time in that weekend. There was a meeting after dinner in a separate building. While we all sat on the floor, a young man stood in front of us and talked. He was funny and passionate, and he made sense. He was clean—in fact, all these kids were clean—and happy. He talked about God. He talked about sin. He talked about forgiveness and love.

Stacy sat next to me on the floor. I was beginning . . . just a little . . . to understand. She had it. She had what this guy was talking about. And she loved me. She wanted me to find it. This realization was a new one. A different kind of softening began to happen in my heart. I felt really cared for by my friend. Her friendship was open, somehow bigger than before. I was very moved.

The youth pastor talked about Jesus Christ. Then he gave us an assignment—he wanted us all to leave the building, to go off by ourselves and find a tree to sit under or another quiet spot where we could focus and really meditate on God. He wanted us to call out to God and ask him to forgive us of our sins.

No one said a word, but all of us quietly got up and spread out. Stacy left my side. I wandered outside to a heavily wooded place—more of a hiding place, really—behind a fir tree. I wasn't sure how to do it. I saw the shadows of other campers here and there, praying, sitting, rocking, murmuring, or writing. They all knew how to do it. I felt awkward, totally exposed, and at the same time, expectant.

I sat down and leaned against a tree. At first I just looked around. The air was crisp, clear, and cold. But so beautiful. I was just still. I waited. And I finally said, "God?"

The name did not feel right on my tongue. Um. What now? "God?" Silence.

I could not hear any of the other kids.

"God?" And something in the core, the very middle of me, spilled out. Like someone had cracked an egg inside my chest and let it pour out, thick and full of aching.

"God? God. God. God. God." I said his name over and over, and I cried and cried. I let it go. Dropped my head, my chin on my chest, and let it come all the way out. With no audible words I cried, "My God, why? Why? Why? It's so bad, it's so awful, it's so unfair, it hurts, God. . . . God . . . I'm sorry I don't know who you are. I'm sorry. I'm sorry for everything. . . . I don't know who you are. . . . I don't know if you're real. . . . It's so . . . bad."

By the time I was cried out, calmed down, and out of clumsy words, I was alone in the woods. Everyone else had finished long ago and had gone off to their cabins—a fact I figured out after I went back to the meeting room and found it completely empty with the lights turned off.

I got mildly lost, one small cabin being identical to another, but eventually found my bunk and went to sleep, having no certainty at all if God had heard me and if we were OK with each other now. I did feel better and more relaxed. That was good enough for the moment.

Coffee, a Married Man, and Murder...The warmth
and afterglow of the retreat weekend lasted until I walked through our front door. I had felt freed up and relaxed all the way home, but as soon as I got to the apartment, I felt constricted and imprisoned again. It was just the way my life was.

I had already been smoking and doing drugs, thanks to Bernie. I had already been picked up for shoplifting—the cutest pair of shoes I had wanted *so* badly. Cursing, crying, and being angry were natural for me. So was a cutting, razor-sharp humor that bordered on mean. I could not hold God in my head. I couldn't bring him home with me.

My mother still went on and on about Godfrey. She still had visions and kept pendulums, Tarot cards, and tapes to listen to over and over. She still had her wildly big laugh, her horrible temper, and her huge sexual appetite. Bernie was still living with us, but he left now and then to be with his other family. Mom switched to keypunching on the day shift and continued her old affair with her married boss, who would use a key she had given him to come into the apartment early in the morning after Bernie had left for the Donekatessen.

Mom became obsessed with the idea of writing a screenplay about Godfrey and the prophecy, so she signed up for a script-writing class. True to form, she began having an affair with her teacher, Ken, a short, skinny man who laughed too hard and was grabby and bossy. All three men continually moved in and out of our apartment.

I was so far behind in school that getting caught up seemed hopeless. Besides, Bernie would often walk onto the school grounds and find me either to take me back to the apartment with him or inform me that he knew where I was and what I was doing. He was totally paranoid, and I could not get away from him.

About a mile or so from the school was a Winchell's Donut Shop. I started taking the public bus to school every day and then sneaking off to sit in the donut shop for hours and hours. I would buy a donut or a coffee and sit in a booth beside the giant windows that wrapped around all sides of the little store, watching the cars drive by, smoking cigarette after cigarette, and thinking about ways to hurt Bernie.

Too many times I had called the police to the apartment when Bernie and Mom were fighting, hoping they would take the three of us kids away to somewhere safe. But they always told me that my mother did not want to press charges against Bernie, so there was nothing they could do. Bernie's threats had made me so afraid that I had not told the police about the sexual abuse. Finding a way to get Bernie out of our family seemed hopeless.

I had one friend whose mother wanted to get us into a foster home, but I found out that the child welfare authorities would split us kids up. I could not let that happen. I lied to her, telling her that our situation wasn't that bad.[9]

One morning as I lit a cigarette and pulled a deep hit into my lungs, a black van rolled by the window of Winchell's. I saw the man in the driver's seat do a double take. The van came around again, more slowly this time. I was young, I was in tight jeans and a tight shirt and had long hair, and I was open to anything. Perfect. We locked eyes as he rolled by, and he smiled at me. I smiled back. Hmm. Interesting.

In a few minutes he came strolling through the door with a smirk under his sunglasses. He had long, curly hair and looked a little scruffy, a little dangerous, and like a nice way to kill some time. He sat down at my table with some coffee, introduced himself as Steve, and we talked.

He asked me if I was going to school, and I said no. He asked me if I wanted to get out of there, and I said yes. He told me I was really pretty. He asked me where I lived. He was friendly and open. We drove around for a while and listened to music, then he dropped me back off at Winchell's.

I had a friend at the academy, Stephanie, a tall, beautiful blonde from a dysfunctional show-business family. A perceptive and intuitive girl, she became suspicious of my constant "Steve this" and "Steve that" and set out to find out who he really was. I didn't know what she had uncovered about him until later—he was an ex-convict, having just been released from prison. I didn't know he was married and that his wife had waited for him while he was serving his sentence. Maybe I didn't want to know those things about him.

---

9. I didn't find out until years later that some of Mom's family members were also trying to work through the system to take Lary, Leenie, and me away from her, but they couldn't even find us much of the time.

I just knew he made me feel pretty. Every day I went to Winchell's, and Steve picked me up. He brought me some clothes that he said were leftover samples from his job as a salesman. We started having sex in the back of his van, did mushrooms, and smoked pot, and I told him all about Bernie.

He was livid and I liked that. I liked that it made him angry and that he "wanted to kill him." I felt loved, and we started to talk about running away together. The conversations fed into my fantasies of hurting Bernie. We started to talk about the things we would like to do to him. Like a joke at first, but then it got more real.

"I'd like to find that guy in an alley and cut his —— off!" Steve would say.

"I would like you to!" I would reply.

Over and over as we talked, we realized nothing was standing in our way. He told me that we could park the van across the street from the Donekatessen early in the morning. While hiding inside the van, we could use a gun with a silencer and pop Bernie while he was unlocking the deli door. After Steve had fired the shots, we could then take off and drive to Mexico.

He was serious. The more I thought about it, the more it seemed like a good idea. Bernie was garbage. I would be saving my sister from him.

The inevitable happened as we continued to scheme. One morning as I waited for Steve at Winchell's, I saw the worst thing. Bernie's car pulled up to the front of the store, and just a second later, Steve's van pulled up to the side parking lot. Steve got out and smiled at me through the window, but I knew from the expression on Bernie's face that I was busted. Bernie came through the front door and grabbed my upper arm, yelling and yanking me out of the chair.

"Where have you been? The school has been calling. You're a liar and a slut!" Red-faced, Bernie was on a roll.

Steve stood by the side window and watched as Bernie dragged me into his car. The familiar punishment came after we got into the apartment—the skinny leather belt across my bare back and legs. Many days later the welts were still there. I had no choice but to go back to school.

A few weeks later as I got off the bus, I saw Steve's van parked on the side street once again. I jumped in, happy he had found me.

"I've got it worked out, Maylo. Are you still serious about doing Bernie?"

"Absolutely!" I replied.

I left the house early the next morning. The streets were empty, and everything was still blue-gray outside. We waited across the street from the Donekatessen in the Ralph's Supermarket parking lot. Steve was resolute. Calm. Focused.

I was shaky and wanted to cry, and the only thing I could hear was my breathing. If I do this, I could go to jail forever. If I do this I will have killed someone . . . blood . . . crime . . . if I do this I will change forever . . . what is jail like . . . we'll get caught . . . my sister will cry . . . she will have no one . . . we'll get caught . . . my brother . . . we'll get caught . . . this is real . . .

"No! I can't! Stop!"

"What?!" Steve whirled around, incredulous. "What the ———, Maylo!"

"I . . . I can't do it. I can't do it. I'm sorry . . . I'm so sorry, Steve. . . . Please don't be mad. Please." I tried to grab his arm, his shirt, anything.

He was shaking his head and panting. "You can't just stop it like that, Maylo! Maylo . . . ———, you can't do that to someone! That's ——— up!"

"I know. . . . I'm sorry. Please." I was bawling.

He got out of the back of the van, and I followed. But he was different. Angry. He marched over to the driver's side, jumped into the van, and peeled out of the parking lot, flipping me off as he rode away.

That was that. I stood there in the early morning with the sky turning pale and light. Bernie pulled up across the street and opened the Donekatessen for the day.

The Interview That Changed My Life... I was sixteen years old, and I hated my life. I cried all the time. I lied to people at the academy about who I was. I hated my body. Hated it. I was consumed with jealousy of other girls, pretty girls with nice clothes and shiny hair and glossy smiles and all the attention. In the shadow of Hollywood, everyone is beautiful and thin, and the competition is fierce. I wanted to be one of the beautiful and desired. I wanted to be special. Picked out.

I wanted someone to be madly in love with me. I stopped eating anything other than lettuce and beets. I thought if I was thin enough and sexy enough, I could get someone to love me.

My mother was equally obsessed with her own looks and with my becoming a star, and her obsession magnified my hatred of myself. I wanted to believe in her visions. At least she was singled out as special in her cult. Maybe there I, too, could feel loved. According to Godfrey, I could be someone. I began to think that maybe Mom's visions were true.

And then there was my father. He really loved movie stars. If I became a star, he would be so proud of me. Then maybe I'd feel loved.

Nothing I put on made me feel appealing. Every day, I wanted to take a knife and stab at my legs over and over. Every time I put something on, I would only rip it off and throw it on the floor in a rage.

At the same time, I sizzled with hatred for Bernie. I could not stand to be in the same room with him or my mother. I could not stand our shabby apartments or the lies and the sex and the fighting. I fantasized about killing myself, convinced that if Bernie and my mother came home and found me dead, they would finally understand how much they were hurting us. I was exhausted all the time. I skipped acting classes and sat on the floor of a nearby gas-station bathroom, where I smoked cigarettes and cried.

My friend Stephanie and I talked about how I would run away. I would have to completely disappear and not tell even her where I was, not for a while. Because as soon as Bernie found out I was gone, he would threaten every one of my friends until he found me. I couldn't put any of them in danger just to keep that secret.

So our plan came down to Stephanie calling a friend who would call a friend who would hide me. That way, Stephanie would be out of the loop. I would stay at the apartment of a gal who lived far away in a part of town I had never been to before. I knew nothing about her, but she was willing to let me stay there for a time. She lived in a single-room apartment and had a pullout couch we would both sleep on.

In the meantime I had to find a legitimate excuse for leaving the house. The reason had to be casual and believable because Bernie questioned me every time I left the house.

I finally came up with an ingenious plan. I would tell Bernie that I was going to apply for a job waiting tables at a restaurant a few blocks away. I knew that would be OK because he'd want to cash in on what I earned.

I supported my story over the course of several weeks. First, I started complaining about never having any money, and then I began to float the idea of getting a job, asking Bernie, "Gosh, do you think I should?" and "What about the kids?" and on and on. He acted supportive—my asking him what he thought catered to his high opinion of himself—and said he was glad to be of help with my decision.

I finally told him there was a restaurant within a bus ride that was hiring, and the manager wanted me to interview tomorrow in the late morning. I would be gone about forty-five minutes, tops. He couldn't offer to drive me because Mom had the car. The scheme was perfect.

The morning of my "interview," I crammed pairs of underwear in my small purse. That was all I could possibly leave with. That, and a small copy of Beatrix Potter's *Mrs. Tittlemouse*, a book I had loved for many years and the only piece of my childhood worth taking.

Eight-year-old Leenie was still sleeping, beautiful and inno-cent, in her bed with floppy old stuffed animals all around her head. I stood at the door of our room, stuck. If I left, would she be Bernie's next victim? She would wake up, and I would be gone. I wouldn't be coming back. She would not have me anymore. I was torn inside. All I could see was her crying for me.

I didn't want to do it. I *had* to do it. But I was abandoning her and Lary. I couldn't do it. I started to cry. I couldn't break Leenie's heart. I loved her and Lary so, so much. But I wanted to die.

It was one of the most difficult moments of my entire life. For many years, that moment haunted me. The guilt of leaving was sometimes overwhelming, at times driving home what Bernie convinced me about myself—I was a selfish, selfish little girl.

I turned and walked to the front door. Bernie was lying on the couch. "You look nice."

"Thanks," I said.

"So, you're taking the bus? And then you're coming right back?" He looked over my purse and my clothes.

"Yeah, no biggy. I'll be coming straight home. I'm supposed to clean out the fridge before Mom gets home."

"OK, Fresh. Good luck."

Out the door I went. I walked to the bus stop as calmly as I could so as not to give myself away. All the while, my knees wobbled, and adrenaline and anxiety swelled like waves up and over my head.

I got on the bus and started sobbing. All I could think of was my sister.

WILLIE

Warning Lights and Two Women...Gentry. That's
what they call it. Sometimes known as Ferrari Red, Ticket Me Red,
Look at Me Red. There are a million names for it. But the official
name of my car's color was Gentry—Gentry Red.

It was 1982, and I was twenty-two. My Porsche 911S was
cruising at a comfortable seventy-five miles an hour as I took the
freeway off-ramp. The ramp was one of my favorites—long and
winding to a killer right curve and ending at a *T* that would lead
me to Pacific Coast Highway. I began tightening my seat belt as
the car physically sucked down on the road, increasing speed so
quickly that I was forced down into my seat, but not with a jerky,
harsh increase in speed—not this car. This acceleration was almost
imperceptible, except for the g-force that made it difficult to keep
my head from becoming a permanent feature of the headrest. The
car's engine, a 2.1 RSR racing engine, whined impressively. My
California vanity plate read "ROQ YOU."

As the smear of color that was my car blasted out of the curve,
I pressed the pedal even lower to the floorboard, keeping the car
online, its "whale tail" forcing more energy on the rear axle to
grab the road and stabilize the ride. I shifted gears as I drank a
large iced tea and expertly rolled a joint with my right hand.

The Cars' "Just What I Needed" blasted from a massive Blaupunkt stereo, and my sunroof was open completely, exposing my senses to the increasing smells of the looming harbor and the West Coast. California. My California. The greatest place on earth to grow up and live in. It was gonna be a great day.

So I told myself. Under the surface of the expensive cars, the beautiful house, the money, the fame, the constant partying, and all the cocaine I wanted, some warning lights were flashing, but I didn't, I couldn't, see them.

Three of them were women. The first two included a woman I booted out of my life and another I took into it. Later, a third one would come into my life during the making of a movie.

During what turned out to be the last season of *Eight Is Enough*, I had come off a short band tour and had some free time. Dad and Mom were in charge of Dad's annual firemen's barbecue and had asked me to help. Sure, why not? Everyone got a kick out of the "big movie star" serving everyone's food. I was cooking steaks on the grill when Mom came up.

"I have to introduce you to Victoria, Willie." She pointed out a beautiful, petite, olive-skinned brunette with a classic late '70s big hairdo. We began dating immediately, though the way my touring and taping took me in and out of her life must have been frustrating for her.

At the same time, Mom and I were trying to deal with problems in our manager/actor relationship. As my career grew more complicated, especially with the additional booking opportunities and financial issues related to my band gigs, I began to sense she was out of her league. She had been fine as a bookkeeper, and I had a business manager as well. They had kept tight rein on my income until I turned eighteen. As a manager, she also took 15 percent of my gross, and those earnings began to multiply for her.

But we both knew she needed help with managing my music career, so she tracked down a professional music manager. I'm going to call him Lyle. He came with consummate credentials, having worked with Three Dog Night, Steely Dan, Steppenwolf, and other top bands.

He stepped in and immediately began to take over, and Mom just as quickly made no secret of her belief that her authority over me was being undermined. And yet she got along well with Lyle—too well, it began to seem to me.

A nagging worry arose in my mind: Lyle crisscrossed the country with me as the band played on the Hollywood Teen tour and at other venues. Picking up girls was easy for me while on the road, and I often took advantage of the easy access to a night with a cute, adoring teenage girl. Problem was, so did Lyle, and he was married with two children. I had seen him in action and did not trust him with my mother.

The mistrust was mutual. Before I graduated to cocaine, Mom began to accuse me of doing that drug. Then she began to accuse me of hiring hookers. She began calling me to check on where I was and what I was doing. The calls picked up until she was calling me every twenty minutes.

Someone obviously had to give, and it seemed then that the worst thing a parent could do was smother a guy who already felt over-disciplined and -controlled. I fired my mom.

"Mom, this is getting ugly. I don't need you as a manager. I want my mother back," I told her, but she took my words as a personal insult and dismissal.

"I will ruin you!" she screamed at me.

Then Dad called: "Lemme hear it from your own ——— mouth!" he shouted.

I'm afraid I took the bait. "There is no way you will bully me ever again!" I slammed the receiver down.

Thus began the nasty business of a family feud, powered by a lawsuit that Dad and Mom threatened to bring against me—though, to be fair, they never did. Dad was enraged and threatened me with bodily harm if I ever came around their house. I didn't even think of going over there to try to patch things up. My brothers, sister, and extended family sided with my parents over Willie and his "massive, overblown ego." The estrangement would last seven years.

In the meantime, Willie Aames continued living the high life. Was I still looking for love? Did I still want to matter to someone? I wasn't going to find validation from my family. Mom had never praised me for any of the roles or gigs that she watched me perform. I had thousands of adoring fans, though, and they'd fill the emptiness. And whatever gaps remained in my self-esteem, well, a few grams of powder filled up the cracks just fine for the time being.

Perhaps not surprisingly, though Mom had introduced us, my parents thought of Vicki as a gold digger and were against our developing relationship. Perhaps their negativity only fueled my engagement to her, at the age of nineteen, two months after my blowup with Mom.

I had just returned from a brief band tour. I called Vicki and was brought up short when she said, "Let's get this over with, Willie. Let's just break up."

Whoa. A challenge, and Willie never backs down from a challenge. I opened my mouth to respond and almost immediately regretted it. "No, let's get married, Vicki. Will you marry me?"

Thinking about Willie at nineteen, I see now that I was dying to get married because it would show my family that I had the chops to do it. I also see that marrying Vicki was clearly an attempt to replace my lost family while showing them I didn't need them. I'd make my own family! I am sorry to say this now, because it will be hurtful to Vicki, but I didn't love her as a man should love a woman he plans to spend the rest of his life with.

We began dating in October 1979 and got married December 7, 1979. I wasn't even twenty years old. The day before we got married, I went to the set, swilling my old buddy Jack straight from the bottle. We had a magazine photo shoot that day, and I was so hammered, I had to be propped up between two of the other cast members.

"Whoa, Willie! Hold on there! We'll get through this, OK?" The photographer tried to encourage me to stay lucid long enough to finish the shoot.

By the time we married, I wasn't speaking to any of my family. Our wedding was a bit strange by the usual standards, but then, I wasn't exactly the boy next door anymore. Four hundred people attended, but the only relative who was even allowed to enter the door was Jimmy, bless him, my cousin and buddy. We posted bodyguards everywhere and had to hide in limos to get away from the media. We went directly to a band rehearsal and then on to what should have been a romantic, twelve-day honeymoon in Hawaii.

It wasn't. It rained the entire time. Had we been truly in love, I wonder if rain would have stopped our joy in each other. It did, though. Maybe it was an omen of what was to come.

The Third Woman...Vicki and I returned to California and settled into what should have been the rosy life of newlyweds. She soon joined me in using blow regularly. Let me explain, if I can, what cocaine did for me: it was both a euphoric upper and an anesthetic to the ache that was at the center of our marriage. As long as we were using, I could pretend that our marriage was legitimate, telling myself that Vicki was

content to let our maid keep the house while she shopped with my credit cards.

Eight Is Enough was winding down, though I didn't know it yet. On June 25, 1980, Vicki gave birth to our son, Christopher. We were both twenty years old. I was shooting the movie *Zapped* with Scott Baio and left the set to be with her while she was in labor. When I called the set to tell everyone we had a son, the entire cast and four hundred extras erupted into cheers.

Vicki had a very difficult time. The experience of childbirth was scary, as was the reality of the responsibility now on her. It became another reason (I'm embarrassed to say) to party harder in celebration. That day I looked deeply into Victoria's eyes and saw more pain than I had ever seen. I had more respect for her that day than at any other time during our marriage.

What a beautiful boy Chris was! I promised myself that I would be a different father from my dad and have a different family life. I would make sure my son knew I was proud of him and that I would always be there for him. I hope I have lived up to that promise. Twenty-seven years later, Chris and I still talk nearly every day. He is a talented musician and a killer bass player, and I love to encourage him in his music and see him perform when I can.

Meanwhile, I didn't talk to any of the Uptons, but I told myself everything was fine. Blow was still easy to buy and didn't seem to dent my bank account. Money was not a problem—not yet. Before long, that third woman would enter my life, and the warning lights would begin to flash.

Phoebe Cates was my co-star while shooting the film *Paradise*, the film in which Doc the chimp had attacked me. The setting was exotic, the girl was beautiful, and there had been no one nearby to remind me that I was being unfaithful to my pregnant wife. When I fell for Phoebe, I fell hard.

Lyle flew out to see me in Israel, but the visit was not unusual. We went to dinner in Jerusalem, and as we talked, I noted that he seemed tense.

"What's the problem, man?" I asked.

"I've got bad news, Willie."

"What—did the show get canceled?"

Talk about preempting an announcement. He just sat and looked at me, nodding his head. "Next!" I said immediately.

What bravado! I had no idea that Dick Van Patten had found out about the show's cancellation by reading it in the paper. The studio execs didn't have the courtesy to tell him, the main star, and of course none of the rest of us knew about it either.

When I went home on a short break, I arranged for a rendezvous with Phoebe in France. Vicki knew something was going on, but what could she do about it? Phoebe and I continued our romance at the Cannes Film Festival when we were together to do advance publicity for *Paradise*.

Paradise turned out to be a major disappointment financially and personally. As Phoebe and I screened the film prior to its release, we both sat speechless, not believing what we were seeing. We had shot some scenes nude but had been told there would be merely a fifteen-second montage, more a suggestion than actual graphic content, of us making love. And there we were, watching ourselves in color in a film that seemed like soft-core porn. We got up and walked out.

The studio, AVCO, pitted us against each other as we argued very publicly about our roles in the film. Our romance took the hit. Phoebe was the first true love of my life, and it took me years to completely overcome the loss of her. We never said good-bye to each other and have not spoken since.

When I arrived home at the end of filming, I drove my car to the studio gate, planning to go to my *Eight Is Enough* dressing room and grab all my personal stuff—posters, signed scripts (I was still collecting them), and other things of value only to me. The security guard wouldn't even let me go through the gate. He said he'd have to call to get approval first.

"What? Man, you know me! Come on! I've been coming through this gate for the past four years!"

"Sorry. Can't do it."

That response just underscored what I already suspected—the truth of what the business was really all about. I was nothing now that I wasn't a moneymaker for ABC. We were all commodities— nothing more than living, breathing props. It was all about the dollar. Was there any bitterness in these observations? Nah!

Eight Is Enough thus ended without ceremony. Suddenly I was unemployed with a wife and a baby to feed and a firmly entrenched habit to support. The warning lights were flashing, and I was beginning to see them.

From Celebrity to Sobriety in a Few Not-so-easy Lessons... "Well, do you want the part or not? It would be great for your career. It would be a good transitional role for you."

My agent tried to talk me into the part of Joel Goodson in the movie. I refused to do it. It required some nude scenes, and I had been burned. I wasn't going to let that happen again. A young actor named Tom Cruise got the part instead. The film was *Risky Business*, and the nude scenes were cut out of the theater version. So much for that moral stand.

I was still in love with Phoebe, but due to AVCO's meddling, we couldn't even be in the same press together. Still, I could not get her out of my mind. I'd find ways to get myself to New York, where she lived, on the off chance that I'd run into her.

I was miserable, with much of the misery of my own making. Obviously, with my thoughts and emotions tied up in someone else, Vicki's and my marriage was doomed. And the cocaine use had become a physical addiction and an emotional and financial drain.

The worst part was that I was nearly broke. Lyle had hooked me up with his own accountant, who had recommended that I buy into some coal mine futures as a tax shelter. That tax shelter became a rock I wished I could hide under, as the IRS turned that rock over and began an investigation of the whole deal.

I was still doing some films, which kept me away from my disintegrating marriage. I dated the beautiful Spanish star Ana Obregón while on the set of *La máquina de matar* (English title *The Killing Machine*), shot in Spain. I was still using coke and drinking heavily, and one evening Lee Van Cleef, one of Hollywood's great all-time movie villains, who was also in the film, and I went to dinner and got drunk on beer and cognac. We stumbled and sang all the way back to the hotel, lighting fires in public mailboxes as we walked by them. When I think of the trouble we could have had with the police . . . let's just say that God must have been watching over me, though I didn't know it yet.

Margeaux Hemingway was also in the film, and we did some coke together as we talked about her grandfather Ernest. She was sad and fragile and reminded me of Lani O'Grady, who was in the cast of *Eight Is Enough*. Of course, I couldn't predict that Margeaux would later kill herself with an overdose of sedatives in 1996—the fifth member of her family to commit suicide. Lani also died of a drug overdose in 2001, though it was never determined whether the overdose was intentional or accidental.

One darkly amusing anecdote comes to mind about Jose Antonio de la Loma, director of *The Killing Machine*. I came down with a virus during the filming and had to be admitted to the local hospital for a couple of days. When I reported back to the set, I sat down in my chair to watch the crew blowing up a car. Señor de la Loma walked up and looked closely at my face.

"You have fever?" he asked in his thick Spanish accent.

"No, not much anymore. I feel OK."

"Good for you, sucks for me. I like to see the fever in your eyes onscreen."

When that film wrapped up, it was back to the States, but I wasn't there any longer than I had to be. I needed to escape both my life and myself, though the second need was the difficult one.

It was on the set of the Italian film *Inferno in diretta* (literally "Straight to Hell," but renamed as *Amazon: A Savage Adventure* in English), deep in the jungles of Venezuela, that my cocaine use turned a corner. I contacted my connection, who sent me a couple of guys with the goods. They "wanted to hang out with an American actor," but they were really guards for secret coke production plants and would kill you just as soon as smile, if you crossed them.

They freaked me out. I had finally crossed some invisible line. I did not want to get caught with them, and the Venezuelan military police were visible everywhere, no doubt looking for guys just like the ones who came to me. I told them to leave, and, gratefully, they did. But they made me think, however much I didn't want to, about the direction my life was taking.

There I was in the jungle, doing drugs while lying to everybody about my drug use and reading *Wired*, Bob Woodward's account of John Belushi's battle with addiction and eventual overdose and death. It hit me: that would be me. I was going to die. Or I was going to end up sitting in front of a TV with a big pile of coke in front of me, asking myself why I don't have a future.

So what did I do? I went on a binge and destroyed my hotel room. I should have landed in jail but didn't. I realized that something—all things—had to change.

I turned to Lyle, not knowing who else to call. "I want help," I said.

"You need a vacation," Lyle said.

"I need help."

"Maybe you want more work."

"Lyle, I need help. And if I don't get it, everyone's fired today." Help arrived shortly after.

"I've never had anybody before who truly wanted help," Lyle admitted, but he set me up with an appointment.

The psychologist was one of Hollywood's finest—I'm sure he had had lots of experience with celebrities like me. "Can you walk into a meeting on your own?" he asked me at the end of one of our early sessions.

"Yes."

I went to the Pacific Palisades chapter of Alcoholics Anonymous. Sitting in the same gymnasium with me were celebrities such as Buzz Aldrin, Troy Donahue, Ann-Margret, Dick Van Dyke, and others—names and faces of great fame. Who would have thought?

There I met Bob Palmer, who became my sponsor. What an awesome guy! He had managed the careers of Dick Van Dyke and the incomparable Sir Anthony Hopkins and also had a personal story of addiction and recovery.

My first visit was the first step toward sobriety. I would stumble and fall. Getting sober was a roller-coaster ride of using, then not, then using, then not. It was ugly at times—starting over in front of everybody, doing well for a year, then falling, and repeating the cycle over and over.

I wasn't yet a new person and didn't have the power of the Holy Spirit to draw on. I had only my own determination and the support of my sponsor and AA members, and they would fail me, through no fault of their own, time and again. The path to sobriety wasn't a happy one, but it was necessary for my survival, and I knew it.

Yet I'd lie in bed at home and say to myself, "I can't go on. I can't do this." Vicki was still using cocaine and had no desire to quit. I knew I couldn't stay with her and be tempted. A year or so would pass before I decided do something about that realization.

The Mayor of the Playboy Mansion... "The meeting is with Paul Newman. Yeah, Paul Newman. He's looking for someone to play his son. Go get it, Willie."

The movie was to be called *Harry and Son,* and the role was that of Howie, the son of Newman's character, an inarticulate blue-collar worker. The audition came along just as I was trying to hang onto my sobriety. I wasn't 100 percent successful, but I was trying.

The audition itself was nothing unusual, but the detail that jumps out at me when I remember that day was Paul Newman's icy stare. He never took his legendary blue eyes off me, but I doubt he was mesmerized by my acting. He was mesmerized by something much different and heartbreaking.

Newman had a son, Scott, who had died of a drug overdose in 1978. I think Newman recognized the signs of drug abuse in me, even though I was trying to kick it and he didn't want to be near it. He gave the part to a young actor named Robby Benson, who did a terrific job with the role.

I didn't get that role, but another part came my way in 1983. I auditioned for the role of Buddy Lembeck, comic sidekick to Scott Baio for a new series called *Charles in Charge.* I was determined to get the part if I had to do backflips on a balance beam, and I practically did. At first I couldn't even get an audition. The casting director looked on both the East and West coasts for Buddy and couldn't find someone they liked, so I was given one shot. I read, met with the network, and got the job all in one afternoon.

My instincts told me that the opportunity was real. And my instincts were right. I signed for a year's worth of episodes, which aired in 1984. The first year led to four more as a syndicated series from 1986 to 1990.

The role of Buddy was perfect for me. When I stop to think that Buddy often seemed to have not a brain in his head, I also remember what I drew from to play him. The truth? Puppies! I based the character on puppies. They are comical and loyal, they don't care who or what you are, and they will always be your friend—just what Buddy was supposed to be.

I was happy to play second fiddle to Scott. The cast was congenial, and Scott and I genuinely enjoyed each other's company and played off each other for comic effect. The drug-free atmosphere on the set made the season both a pleasure and a reinforcement to my determination to stay sober.

We aired on Wednesday nights against two one-hour shows, *The Fall Guy*, starring Lee Majors, and *Highway to Heaven*, starring Michael Landon (the stories of what a gentleman he was are absolutely true). We were beating *The Fall Guy*, but the second half hour after us was a washout for CBS. The show lasted through the 1984 season. Gene Jankowski, then president of CBS, had the show yanked because CBS didn't have another half-hour show to fill the hour.

The show's ending after that first year gave me the time to focus on my impending breakup with Vicki. I moved out. Talk about a lifestyle change! When I left my house, I couldn't afford much. Vicki was just sure I was hiding money, but I wasn't. The people managing my money had bled me dry with bad investments, four-hundred-dollar lunches on my tab, and dubious tax write-offs that were turning out to be bogus.

But I was hanging in there with my sobriety, thanks to AA. I was amazed and humbled each week to meet some of the new attendees, some of whom were on Hollywood's A-list. There was complete honesty in the meetings. "Shut up and listen. Are you willing to do what it takes to get sober?" I already knew I needed to answer yes, and I did, every day, one day at a time.

I needed a place to live, and renting an apartment with another person in recovery seemed like a safe and wise thing to do. I met Juan at the meetings, and we decided to share an apartment. He'd pay me his half of the rent, and I'd pay the management company. Juan was friendly and carried some emotional baggage like I did, though I didn't know until later that his wife had obtained a restraining order against him.

The apartment wasn't the Ritz, but I had a separate bedroom and some privacy—or so I thought. After I moved in, Juan became more and more proprietary toward me. I began to resent his continual demands to know whom I was with and where I was.

One day I walked into the apartment to find Juan going through my personal belongings. "Hey, you creep, get out of my stuff! Who gave you the permission to just barge in here and start helping yourself? You're sick, you know that? You're a freak! I'm outta here!"

I tried to leave, and he tried to bar my way. He then threw himself down the stairs, screaming that I was beating him up. I grabbed what I could and ran down the steps to my car.

A couple of days later, I waited until I knew he was at work and went to the manager's office. I got out my checkbook to show her that I had been paying the rent, so she let me into the apartment.

I had no choice but to check through Juan's things for my valuables. Hidden in his dresser, mingling with his own pictures, odds and ends, records, and other personal items, were things that were very personal to me—pictures of me with people on the set, used scripts, even pictures of me with Chris.

Not knowing where else to go, I retreated to the house I had left. So there I was with Victoria and Chris, but it was obvious from the first day that our reconciliation was not going to work. Emotionally I had shut her off. I started hanging out with Scott Baio and other new pals from my recent TV series.

I had known Scott for years, with our acquaintance going back to the days of the Hollywood Teen tours and his popular role as Chachi on *Happy Days* and *Joanie Loves Chachi* in 1982.

We had several dating adventures, including taking our dates to Norman Bates' house on Universal's back lot. (Want to get a girl close to you? Try that one.)

Scott had never done drugs. I knew that for sure, and he knew of my struggle with sobriety. He was a good, sober companion for me—except for the pesky fact that I was married and he wasn't. Everyone knew I was still technically married, but a marriage certificate didn't keep me from having fun. Oh, no. Shooting a weekly series on CBS had put us in proximity to some beautiful women, and we took full advantage of the opportunities that were literally falling at our feet.

We got in the habit of showing up together at Hugh Hefner's famous home, the Playboy Mansion. Scott gave me a nickname that stuck, "Mayor of the Playboy Mansion," and it became my moniker around the beautiful women who congregated there.

The Playboy Mansion is its own not-so-little world. It has twenty-two rooms as well as a wine cellar, private zoo, aviary, pet cemetery, tennis courts, waterfall, and large swimming pool area with a grotto, sauna, and bathhouse. Hefner even got a permit for fireworks displays.

The mansion was a lot of things, but one thing it was not: a place to use drugs or to get drunk. Hugh Hefner would come downstairs briefly every evening and make the rounds as a polite, accommodating, quintessential host. Every guest knew that neither drunkenness nor drug use of any kind would be tolerated, no exceptions. All guests were also expected to behave discreetly and respectfully. A cadre of seven-foot-tall bodyguards loomed everywhere to show the door quite physically to anyone who didn't take that rule seriously. Once banned from the Playboy Mansion, always banned, end of story. Let's just say that the attractions there were too plentiful and beautiful to be sacrificed for bad behavior.

I was still in the partying mode; I just wasn't drinking and doing cocaine while I partied. Again, the desire to be accepted played its typical role in my high-profile craziness. But AA helped me stay clean most of the time.

Something bothered me, though, about AA's definition of God, and now I can explain it. I couldn't get a grasp on what kind of God I should pray to. The mantra was that we should pray to God as we understood him. I'd ask my fellow addicts, "What is God?"

"Think about whatever your idea of God is, and you can pray to that," suggested one.

"Yeah, man, take a look at this Garfield mug in my hand. For today, Garfield's my God. I can pray to that," another one told me without any sense of irony, producing a ceramic cup with the bleary-eyed cat's face on it.

What? To me the logic behind this attitude was stupid. On the one hand I would hear, "You are an addict and an alcoholic. Your best thinking got you to where you're at, so shut up and listen."

I could deal with that kind of in-your-face honesty. But if my best thinking had gotten me to this point, why on earth would I want to pray to a God of my own creation? I was a jerk and an idiot. So if I prayed to a God of my own creation, wouldn't I be following a jerk and an idiot for a God? How could my best thinking create a God worth praying to?

The question nagged at me, but I put it on a back shelf because something bigger was pressing. It was time to make the break from Victoria once and for all. I moved out for good, leaving her and Chris to have the house I had bought when I was seventeen.

From a House and a Pool to a Bunk and the Ocean...

"TV Star Aames Parties While Ex-Wife and Son Starve." "Deadbeat Celeb Dad Abandons Wife and Child." I could just imagine the headlines. I didn't have to imagine them in some cases. They were right there in front of me in black and white.

Vicki's lawyer (whom I paid for) had frozen all our accounts. I didn't have the heart to fight with her. I let her have the house and the items of value that we shared—silver, antiques, furniture. I just didn't want to fight, but even more, I knew what the press could do with such a nasty battle. And they did pick up on the story enough that some nasty articles appeared.

I wasn't a deadbeat dad, but my money supply was about dead. I needed some way to survive. Thirty dollars a day and a bunk were the going rate for a deckhand in Santa Barbara's elite commercial dive-boat fleet.

It sounded fine to me. Being out on the water—one of my greatest loves. Feeling the sun on my face. Sleeping in a dank, cool bunk, lulled to sleep by the gentle swells. Falling deeply asleep from sheer exhaustion after doing hard physical labor from dawn to dusk. Being away from the demands of my business manager and my agent, the complaints of my ex-wife, and the hounding of the lawyers and the IRS. The dive boat was a great place to hide for a while. I didn't see anybody I knew, and nobody seemed to care if they knew me, and that was good.

In essence I built myself a new identity—I became a "boat rat." I worked on three dive boats: *The Truth*, *The Conception*, and *The Vision*. I kept our gear in good working order. I also kept track of the divers' gear and helped them suit up properly. I had been diving since I was thirteen and had my master's certification in diving, so I knew the proper way to get under the tank and lift it up. Some of the divers, who were usually engineers, lawyers, doctors, and other people—mostly men with "real" jobs during the week—thought they knew all about diving, but if they had been left to their own knowledge, they could have done some real injury to themselves (and sometimes they did—we had to put divers in a basket three times to be hauled away by a Coast Guard rescue chopper). Most of the time I just kept my mouth shut and did my job.

I cleaned the boat's toilet, the head. I didn't mind it, but the wannabe divers sure had fun watching me. "Look at the big movie star, cleaning up our ———!" they'd taunt me. They obviously took great pleasure in witnessing what they thought was my humiliation.

They didn't know, though, what my new life was really like. I liked it. On the boats I met Christine, a stocky, outdoorsy Swiss-French girl from Geneva, Switzerland. She also worked the dive boats as a cook, what we called a galley girl. She was tanned, muscular, and beautiful in a European way. I called her Sturdy and joked that she was more man than I was. She was aggressive, and she was tough. I loved her un-Hollywoodish appeal.

Christine and I got into the habit of heading into town periodically, doing our laundry together and grabbing a cup of hot espresso. It was not a bad existence at all, however it may have looked to an outside observer. Early in the morning on the boat, we'd pour ourselves a cup of coffee and smoke a leisurely cigarette—that was one habit I hadn't yet given up—as we leaned over the rail, breathing in the wet smell of the seaweed and the odor of the diesel. I can still smell and taste those mornings today.

After years of experience diving, I was a sort of dive snob. In my free time I'd suit up and fall in whenever I could, looking for lobster or spearfishing. To this day the damp, old-socks smell of a wetsuit evokes memories of those days and the bragging rights for diving stories. They're fun in the telling now, but I wasn't laughing very hard when I got bumped by a great white shark while I was lobster diving.

I'd seen plenty of blue sharks and seven-gill sharks, and those I didn't worry about too much. But that time, I was in seventy feet of water, searching an area full of underwater sand ledges that looked like shelves. Between the ledges were large patches of bare sand, and over them were clouds of brine shrimp that were so thick I could not see my hand.

Wham! The impact was so hard that even in water, with such heavy drag, it spun me over three times. I cleared my mask just in time to see its huge gray-blue tail thrash the water and stir up the brine shrimp. I remember thinking that I was just part of the food chain. Then it swam away. I saw it from behind as it turned, no longer interested, thank God. It wasn't a big one. I think it had just sensed something moving in the sand that it didn't recognize and came over to check it out.

One diving duty made every deckhand nervous, and I hated it. We'd set anchors at night, but sometimes we'd have to reset because of shifting currents or tides. Occasionally the anchor got stuck in the sea bottom.

At 3:00 a.m., the captain would wake me. "Get your suit on. You've gotta go down and free anchor."

We were anchored near what we called "the shark park" on the north end of San Miguel Island where there is a rookery loaded with baby sea lions. Yum.

I'd suit up and drop into water so cold that I could see the waves of body heat floating off my body. The anchor chain would start at maybe fifty or sixty feet and then fall off the edge of the reef into blackness, down a hundred feet or more. There is almost nothing so black as water that deep in the middle of the night.

I'd make my way down the anchor line, find the snag, unhook it, and pile the chain up. It was impossible to pull it free without my dive light flashing all over the place and stirring up all kinds of reef debris, forming a virtual beacon for a cruising predator. I might as well have painted "Free Dinner" on my wetsuit. Eventually, I'd come to the surface, treading water nervously, forced to wait until the anchor was completely aboard and the OK was given. Finally I'd be up and in.

In spite of that duty, being on the sea was a welcome break from the past years. Weeks passed and then months passed. Hollywood was a memory. Then I got a call to be guest star on a 1985 series called *Rocky Road*, a call that would lead to a huge turn in my life.

MAYLO

From Shelley's Place to Sean and the Boulevard...I opened my eyes and the room came into focus. So did the pain in the middle of my back. The metal support bar in the pullout couch had mocked my attempts to get any rest all night long.

The apartment was small, really more of a bedroom with a tiny galley kitchen. The walls were brick with no windows. The girl, Shelley, was bright and cheery with thick, wavy, brassy hair and a great raspy voice. She said she had so much to show me, so much to talk about. She seemed excited to have a new friend.

I didn't feel bright or excited at all. I felt like I was on some kind of strange sleepover. I also felt like I had cut my line to the mother ship and was floating in empty space with no direction or homing device and no way to undo what I had done. Maybe I should have thought this out more clearly. I had a tenth-grade education, no clothes, no money, no work, no plan. Only freedom. Or was it bondage? I couldn't tell yet.

That first day I didn't bother getting out of bed. Shelley left for the day, and I lay there in the room. I wondered how Bernie was reacting—if he had already tried to contact friends of mine, and if he had hurt Leenie and Lary in his anger. In my imagination

171

I heard my sister's cries. I wondered if my mother herself had cried when she found I was gone. Did she?

I fell back asleep. All day. I didn't care about the metal support bar anymore. I seemed to be pushed down into the bed. I couldn't keep my eyes open.

The sleep of depression is a different kind of sleep. It captures you. It wins. I was pushed into the mattress, held down by heaviness from my toes to my head. It was bigger than I was. It grabbed my will and hid it away from me. My intentions floated aimlessly inside of me like tiny pieces of ash in a cave. My spirit felt small inside of me, like a dot in the middle of this big, black shell called Maylo, or like the tiny Whos on the dandelion fluff that only Horton the elephant hears when they cry, "We are here . . . we are here . . . we are here!"

I had to keep moving. There were people along the way who would give me a bed for the night or find a ride for me the next day. I had no money, but if I could get over the hill and down to Hollywood Boulevard, I could make a way for myself. There were places to crash in Hollywood, and I knew that many young runaways were able to hide in and around the streets until they turned eighteen. I could be anonymous there, and I knew there would be protection and resources to draw on there.

My dad lived in Hollywood off Santa Monica Boulevard, so I knew the area well. Thinking of him reminded me of the magical evenings I had spent in gay bars around town as a small child with Daddy Bill. He would lift me onto the stage, and I would sing with him. But once I made it over the hill into Hollywood, I could not contact him. He was more often than not out of the country with Lana Turner, and the few times that I had tried to convey to him how awful it was at home, I had been taken back anyway. It was not that he was coldhearted; it was that he couldn't see. Or didn't want to see—I will never know for sure.

What I did know was that Mom and Bernie would track Dad down, and I had no doubt that I would be found if I stayed with him. He was not strong enough to stand up to Bernie, nor did he have the energy to deal with my mother.

As grateful as I was for Shelley's willingness to have me stay with her, I also figured out pretty quickly that I couldn't stay there long. I was cramping her style, keeping her from entertaining her various boyfriends.

So I asked Shelley to take me into Hollywood. Once there, I would hook up with an actor I had met at the academy, an older man named Sean. Sean was the son of a sheriff and had grown up in the Deep South. He was huge—more than six feet tall with muscles everywhere and long blond hair. We were attracted to each other, and I knew he would protect me.

I also knew that if Bernie found out about Sean, he wouldn't dare try to confront him. Sean was not the kind of guy to pick a fight with. His height, muscles, and even attitude communicated, "Hey, come on. I can take you and I have nothing to lose." Not that Bernie had much to lose, either, except his life—except his life.

The Boulevard Is Not a Theme Park...The Valley's
tidy homes, apartment complexes, glossy shopping centers, trendy boutiques, small strip malls, and smog that lay atop the landscape like a dirty wig disappeared behind us as Shelley pushed her gas pedal to the floor to get her small car up the hill.

The winding, two-lane road of Laurel Canyon Boulevard hinted at hippie houses and Hollywood producer hideaways, and the secluded homes sneaked peeks at me from within the canyon's slopes. They whispered secrets to me of a different kind of life, and the canyon made promises to me with the long, gentle fingers of pot smoke and money.

Laurel Canyon was one of the main arteries that led to Hollywood Boulevard. And Hollywood Boulevard was the center of a world neither my mother nor Bernie knew anything about. The Boulevard was at once a tourist attraction and a dead end. The smooth, granite slabs of the world's most famous sidewalk, the Hollywood Walk of Fame, carried hordes of people from all over the world, who clicked snapshots and consulted maps to the stars' homes. Their feet carried them as if on a moving sidewalk, passing Grauman's Chinese Theatre (with the hands and feet of movie stars captured in cement), the Pantages Theatre (former host to the Academy Awards), the Hollywood Wax Museum (where you can stand next to "Marilyn Monroe" or "John Lennon" and get your picture taken), and all of the memorabilia stores and cheesy tourist traps along the way.

For visitors, the Boulevard was like a theme park or a circus. For residents, the sidewalks carried them like an escalator down to the bottom of their dreams, where they willingly lay down and gave up hope. They made their beds in the doorways and sat mute on the street corners as if they were resting from their lives . . . from eating and bathing . . . from dreaming. They openly urinated on the side streets.

Some of them went mad. Some were dangerous. Some were not. All of the street people knew one another. Most had stories to tell. Some of them helped one another. Some were victimized by violent beatings in the middle of the night. Some disappeared, only to be replaced by a new face with the same dead and dusty eyes. The Boulevard was its own society with its own rules.

I spent most of my time in front of the Chinese Theatre. The area was well lit and felt safe. Occasionally there was an impersonator or street performer out front, entertaining the crowds, sort of like Mickey Mouse did at Disneyland. To me it seemed like the happiest place, maybe not on earth but at least on the Boulevard.

Sean was there too. Sometimes we were together; sometimes we were not. I just stood around, doing not much of anything. Sean did odd jobs for cash, disappearing then showing up with food he'd bought. He had no one there. His family was back in the Carolinas.

Sean became my provider and protector. He gave me drugs and taught me how and where to find thrown-out pizza from old boxes behind restaurants. He brought me cabbage and clothes he found in old apartment buildings. And he found places for us to sleep in empty apartments or small guest quarters of places he was painting. Of course, we were sleeping with each other. We wandered the Boulevard together, and I fell deeply in love with him.

As bad as it all sounds, I remember those times as colorful and wild and fun. But I was young and stupid and loaded. When I try to remember specifics, there are whole blocks of time in which I can remember only a white line of cocaine or the gummy, brown bowl of a bong.[10]

There was a woman named Dorothy who showed up every night in front of Grauman's. She was in her fifties with black, shiny hair and beautiful skin. She wore wild blue eye shadow and red, red lips that made her look like an extra from *The Wizard of Oz.* She called Sean "Flash"—she thought he was Flash Gordon.

Dorothy had walked away from her family in search of fame but had never been discovered as an actress. Plucky and determined, she had decided that she would become famous as an attraction instead. She pinned every kind of button, bauble, pot, pan, ribbon, spoon, paper, bell, and anything else she could find all over her clothes. She was loaded down with things that jangled when she moved and wore so many layers that it was impossible to tell how tiny she was underneath them.

---

10. Pot-smoking pipe.

Dorothy would dance and smile at the tourists up and down the Boulevard. She would allow her picture to be taken for loose change, and over time she did become famous.

She also became crazy. But she was sweet and she was brave. She still believed in "Old Hollywood." She believed that the glamorous movie stars from the black-and-white films were still alive and that they knew of her.

Dorothy never stopped smiling. If she liked you, she would pull something off her coat and give it to you. I had several buttons from her, as well as some advice that she had given me—to brush my teeth while singing "Twinkle, Twinkle, Little Star" over every single tooth, so that my teeth would become "pearly white and never sad."

And Dorothy's teeth were never sad. Not even when we found her with a black eye and a bruised face, crumpled in a doorway off of the Boulevard, where she had been left to die overnight after being beaten and robbed. All of her precious buttons had been ripped off of her coat, and her pots had been taken.

Sean became enraged. "Dorothy! Who did this to you!"

"Oh, Flash. You are my . . . my Flash. My buttons are gone. I have nothing to give you." She smiled at me and touched my arms with both of her hands as if she were my mother, and I wondered if she had ever had a daughter of her own.

She would not let us help her. She wouldn't even let us stand her up. She simply told us she would be OK. She just needed to rest, and she lay back down in the doorway.

In that moment I became sober. My high faded prematurely and I saw a reality. The Boulevard was not a theme park. I was a girl on the streets. This was my real world.

But just as quickly as I saw, I forgot. Once I walked away from Dorothy, I put that horrible feeling in a pit deep within my soul. I stopped it. I locked it up with the rest of my feelings, my little truths.

What happened to Dorothy was her own fault. She was stupid. She is not my problem. I wonder if Sean has any money for another dime bag?[11]

A New Belief—Sort of—and a New Jar of Pot...

Sean found a place for the two of us to live for a while. He was hired by someone who owned a house off Laurel Canyon Drive to watch over the property in exchange for very cheap rent.

We lived in a tiny, one-room guesthouse that sat right off Laurel Canyon Drive. It was at the top of a steep and wooded driveway, sitting like a garden shed off to the right—a small box without a formal front door, just a steep, cement staircase that led up to a patio sliding door on a cement landing. The landing was surrounded by bright fuchsia bougainvillea bushes and was pretty private.

If you kept walking up the driveway, you ended up at the main house, a wide ranch house built with a lot of poured cement made to look like stucco, a typical 1970s California style. It had no decorative touches to give it personality—no shutters or garden or front entry other than a door. The entry was hidden behind overgrown bushes, and the whole structure blended right in with the hillside. The roof was low, flat, and sprinkled with white rocks, a popular roof choice in those days, and the fence that surrounded the backyard was a plain, cement privacy fence. The house always looked empty and in need of airing out.

This was the rented home of Chuck Negron, a famous singer/ writer for the legendary band Three Dog Night—their songs "Joy to the World" and "Just an Old-Fashioned Love Song" had already

---

11. Measurement of marijuana put into a plastic sandwich bag.

become rock-and-roll classics. He and his wife lived in that house with two very small sons.

Both Chuck and his wife were heroin addicts. I rarely saw them, but we often saw their sons. The boys were often sitting outside even in the dark, just killing time, probably because their parents were passed out after using. They were darling little boys who looked like they needed good baths, and they often came up and sat on our porch with their small, brown dog.

A lot of times I was uncomfortable with them there because I had my own drug agenda and didn't need two small boys looking into my place. On the other hand, I felt like I wanted to scoop them both up and take care of them. They made me feel guilty for not doing anything about their situation. One evening I just couldn't take their sitting and watching us, so I walked them back up to the main house and knocked on the door. No answer. The smaller boy, about three or four, took my hand and opened the front door.

I picked my way through the trash scattered all over the floors. It was eerie and still, and I got the feeling I was going to turn the corner and find a dead body. Instead, I found several syringes and used needles on the bedroom side tables.

I took the boys back up to the guesthouse, and we sat on the porch together, not talking. When Sean came home, we barbecued some chicken and fed the boys. Later he took them back up to the house. I did not ask any questions. I didn't want to feel responsible for what I knew.

Sean had a violent streak, but he was a brilliant writer, poet, and a good actor. I had seen how talented he was at the National Academy, where we first met. He was also a fascinating storyteller. He had spent a few years on shrimp boats off the coast of Jamaica. Modern-day pirates would often overwhelm the boats to steal the shrimp, and Sean told me he could never go back there because he had killed a man on the beach during one of those episodes. I have no idea if he was telling the truth, but I believed him then. I did not doubt one thing he said because his stories were consistent with his personality and interests.

For instance, Sean had a thing for weapons. He made them in his spare time. He would break off the blades of kitchen knives and insert them in one end of a broomstick and then wrap the contraption round and round with duct tape until it was a heavy ball with a knife sticking out of it. On the other end of the broom handle, he would wrap more duct tape round and round, and into that heavy ball, he would hammer nails that stuck out far enough to gouge someone if they came too close.

Sean also shot at creatures on the property. He had various handguns and gave a gun to me, a small black derringer just big enough to fit in my pocket.

He shot at canyon coyotes, rats, and birds. Once he called me out to the driveway. On the hill was a mangy coyote in a standoff with Sean. Coyotes in the canyon were common, and they were bold and unafraid of people. This one was hunched down and still, looking directly at Sean, and Sean was looking directly at it. He whispered, "Get your gun. Get your gun." I did just that and came back out, where they both stood like statues locked on one another.

Sean commanded, "Shoot it."

"Uh, here? Right now? In the head? In the body?"

"Shoot it!"

I lifted up my stocky little weapon and pointed it right at the coyote. He looked right at me. I pulled the trigger and the coyote fell over. Sean skinned it that afternoon. I will never forget the animal's bloated belly as Sean pulled the fur off, nor will I forget the wasps that circled all around him as he finished the job.

Sean also loved the ocean and snorkeled with a speargun, bringing back fish and shells. All of these treasures he skinned and laid out to dry on the cement of our patio. After each jaw, bone, or head would dry out and bleach stiff, he would nail it to the wall. Our stucco wall became a testimony of all that Sean had conquered.

Sean caught spiders and lizards and gave them new homes in dry aquariums on the porch. The Negron boys loved to come over and see the shells and bones nailed to the wall and the critters sunning themselves in their new, glass-enclosed habitats.

All of these trophies, both the dead and the living, defined Sean. They were creations—his own little works of art. For me, they were expressions of my anger. I loved the dead things. I also loved the fact that there was a live black widow in a small glass box beside the front door. And snakes. To me, their presence was like a fist in the air or a middle finger to anyone who came around to tell me life was good. It made me laugh when people said something about the critters or didn't want to come over because they were intimidating. Whatever. Stay away then. I don't care.

Sean painted houses and I cleaned them. We worked hard for very little money, always cash, and continued to live off of cabbage and marijuana. We had dreams though.

Sean's was to be a screenwriter. He once climbed the fence at Charlton Heston's home but was chased away, with Heston yelling, "Get off my property! I am calling the police!" Sean tried to tell him he had a script for him, and Mr. Heston responded sarcastically, "Are you out of your mind? Get out of here now!"

I went about finding my dreams in a more conventional way. I learned of a scholarship program for underprivileged teens at a reputable dance school in the Valley. On the day of auditions I filled out my form and was given a paper number to put on my chest. People were packed in the school's hallways, all waiting for a shot at the coveted program. We were called into the studio in large groups and were shown a routine. After we did the routine, we were slowly singled out one by one to smaller groups.

I almost fell over when I found myself standing with a little contract in my hands, signifying that I had made it. I began to spend six to seven hours a day there, dancing and working in the upstairs office. How did I keep up the pace? I bought over-the-counter diet pills from the drugstore and swallowed them two at a time to keep my energy up and my weight down. They worked, though they fueled my growing obsession with being the best, and I was very hard on myself. If someone had come looking for me, they could often have found me amped out on diet pills in the upstairs bathroom and kicking the walls because of my frustration with what I could not do as a dancer.

At seventeen, I was approached by a man at the school. He said he was an agent and wanted to set an appointment at his office in Beverly Hills. I told him that I didn't have a car, so I couldn't make it to his office. But I said it only because I didn't believe he really was an agent. He came back around a second time and spoke with me in the hallway of the dance studio.

"I don't have head shots! I don't have a car! I can't go on interviews or go anywhere other than here!" I was convinced he was a sleaze, and that like every other man, he had only one thing on his mind. I was not that talented, so what else could he possibly want from me?

Little did I know how much this man would impact my life. His name was Don Gerler, and he came around a third time. Only this time he had a car, a used Volkswagen bug in mint condition. The car belonged to another agent in his office, who was selling it for $2,500.

Don held the keys in his hand and said, "Maylo, I really believe in you. I *know* that you will be able to pay me back for this car by your eighteenth birthday. I'll even bet you that you pay me back after your first or second interview."

I'm not sure why, but I felt that his intentions were true. There was just something in his smile. I took the keys to the car and did what he told me to do. I had the head shots taken and then met him at his office and listened to what he had to say.

Now I had something that could *possibly* happen, something that would make me special. If I could be an actress . . . people would like me. I wouldn't ever have to worry about money. I would be desired. What if I could really become a great actress? What if that happened to me?

Maybe that was why all that bad stuff had happened to me growing up. Maybe there was a plan. Yeah. A plan. That must be it. I wondered if my mother somehow had been able to see this coming. Had she really had visions of this? That must be it. Somehow, the next part of my life would make up for the previous part.

So there it started. A gimpy belief system was put into place— a limited and crippled one but a belief in something, nevertheless. Let's put it this way—a hint of hope was provided.

Sean was supportive, but he did not believe in "reasons" or "plans." He told me over and over again that when you die, you get eaten by worms. That's it. End of story. You die just as you have lived, with fear and rage, and then you're gone. Eaten.

Hmm. Hard to face. Hard to imagine. I didn't know what to think. My thoughts were confused, so I focused on interviewing, cleaning houses, and getting high. Besides, I had just found a quart canning jar filled with rich, sticky marijuana behind a tile in our little kitchen, left behind by the man who lived there before us. Thank you, previous tenant! I love Laurel Canyon!

Pick Up Your Foot, Maylo!...I loved the sense of danger and drama that revolved around Sean; it fed my anger. But one evening, his anger got out of control.

Because of Sean's long hair and good looks, he was often taunted by street people. One night as we walked back to Sean's car, which was parked on a side street off the Boulevard, a skinny black guy stepped out from the alley and started making kissing noises.

"Hey, pretty boy," he said.

We both turned around. Both Sean and the other guy said something threatening, but Sean seemed relaxed to me, with his hands down at his sides. I think he assumed the little confrontation was over.

In a snap Sean was on the ground. He had been sucker-punched hard in the face, and the blow threw him backward. He slid into the street on his back. I stood there in shock.

I started yelling at the guy and just couldn't stop. And the more I yelled, the more this guy wanted to hit me.

Sean got up, and it seemed the confrontation was over. Sean put one hand out like he was going to shake the guy's hand. He smiled, said something peaceable, and took one quick step toward his attacker. The guy went down, and it got quiet. It happened so fast I couldn't even tell what was really going on.

Sean and I looked at each other. The man was holding his stomach and staring at Sean like he was surprised. Sean turned to me and commanded, "Run!"

There was blood all over the guy's hands, and he wasn't getting back up. I turned around and took off. I was disoriented and kept trying to find the car, and when I finally did, my lungs were burning and my legs were shaking. Sean was right behind me.

We hid in the guesthouse in the dark for three days with our hearts pounding as rumors of a dead body circulated the streets.

As I lay there waiting, I began to imagine what would happen to me if the police found us.

I thought of myself pleading in a courtroom. I felt the helplessness of hearing "guilty" and not being able to reverse the verdict. The panic sat in my chest as though the verdict were inevitable. For the first time since I had been with Sean, I felt a little separated from him. We were very, very quiet with each other, each of us lost in our own thoughts.

A few days passed, and my panicked feeling started to dissipate. Sean ventured out on the streets, where he found that the state of alert and excitement had passed. He bought a couple of steaks from Ralph's Market, and we tried to forget about the recent events as we smoked a joint and drank a giant White Russian. *No problems at all*, I told myself.

Don Gerler called with my first interview, a pilot called *The Home Front* for one of the major networks. It starred Delta Burke, later of *Designing Women*, and Jean Simmons, a beautiful actress who had played Ophelia to Lawrence Olivier's Hamlet. I was to read for the part of Ms. Simmons' daughter. I was terrified. Jean Simmons was like theater royalty to me.

I picked up the sides (a small portion of the script) a few days early and worked diligently on them. I drove myself to the studio and walked into an office on a studio lot that was filled with every beautiful young ingenue in town. When I opened the door, all eyes looked up from their scripts and gave me that familiar once-over—the she's-no-competition survey—and then went back to their scripts.

I wanted to throw up. I was overwhelmed with how plain I was. How ugly and fat. Fat, fat, fat, fat. I had no cute clothes. Look at all these girls. They are gorgeous! They are shiny. They have super-nice clothes. Their bodies are amazing. There must be sixty of these girls in this room alone! Don't bolt, Maylo.

What would you say to Don? Don't do it. Sit. Sit. OK. Sign in. Then sit.

Every few moments a beautiful girl would come out of a room down the hall with a big smile on her face, carrying her sides. "'Bye," she would say gaily to the producers we couldn't see behind the door. "It was nice to meet you. Thank you!" Quick turn, big white smile, long tanned thin legs, long blond hair thrown back over her shoulders. She'd confidently breeze out of the office, leaving the rest of us dying inside. I am sure we all felt the same way. "I'll never measure up. How can I compete with that? I need to lose some weight. I wonder if she was any good?" Time and again, girl after girl. And more arriving all the while.

Finally, my name was called. Down the hall I went, into a room with one chair facing a table of five people looking at me.

"So . . . Maylo, is it? What have you done?'

"Um, I'm sorry?"

"Maylo, what have you been working on lately?"

What answer were they looking for? Rolling a joint without making it too wet? Drying out a fish head on the patio? I muttered, "Um, this is my first interview."

"Oh. All right. Do you have any questions?"

Yeah, do you hate the way I look? Can you tell I am stupid just by looking at me?

"Um, no, I'm fine."

"All right, then, why don't we go ahead and get started. Shelby will be reading with you."

All the way home, I cried. I felt like I had made a fool of myself. I couldn't stop thinking about how fat I looked. I felt like a big, fat, ugly, stupid girl. My self-image, my face, my hair—everything about me was repulsive. When I got back home, I opened a bottle of whatever alcohol we had on hand and had a pity party until I passed out, stone-cold drunk.

Two days later Don called.

"Are you kidding me? I got the job?!"

I could tell by the tone of Don's voice that he was smiling. "I told you, Maylo."

I paid Don back right away. And yes, it was in 1979, right before my eighteenth birthday.

The pilot never made it to a series, but it got me my SAG (Screen Actors Guild) card, and carrying that card was enough of a boost to keep me believing I had a future. And I did—things started happening after that. For the next few years I went on interview after interview, and many of them resulted in a callback or a job. I joined a well-known theater group and worked hard to get on stage every chance I could.

Pretty soon, people were talking to me like I knew what I was doing. I was becoming someone.

Of course, I was always dieting and using. You had to diet in Hollywood. It was the 1980s and everyone was bone-thin. Almost everyone was also doing cocaine then. That was how I lived. I worked and then spent my money on drugs. I ate a little bit of rice, a lot of salad. And I dreamed of possibilities, but then I would spiral down into depression and self-hatred.

I eventually got a job on a popular soap opera called *Santa Barbara*. During 1984 and 1985 I played Sally Taylor, the best friend of Kelly Capwell, a character who was played by Robin Wright. The days were very long, but the experience was great as far as training goes. Of course, Robin was gorgeous and I felt like . . . well, I've made it pretty clear. I'll just leave it at that.

A makeup man on the set and I became good friends. He was great fun, with a dry sense of humor like mine, and we did a few drugs together. One particular night after work I went home with him, and we simply partied until early in the morning. We were not romantically involved at all; that night we just "used" together.

I had quite a bit of cocaine in my system. My nose began running continuously, so he gave me some prescription he had. I thought it was an antihistamine.

Soon after I took it, I was over the top—so hyped up that I started drinking to come down before heading back to the guest-house. Finally, in the wee hours of the morning, I managed to make it into my car. It was a short drive to Laurel Canyon. By the time I got to the front door, I was seeing stars. My knees were buckling underneath me as I pounded on the door. Sean opened it, took one look at me, and simply said, "———."

He dragged me into the bathroom and tried to get me to throw up but failed. My memory of exactly what happened is foggy, but I'm sure he was thinking he was going to try to get me to "walk it off." All that I can vaguely remember is him holding me up by my armpits underneath a concrete freeway overpass, yelling at me, "Pick up your right foot!"

I could hear him, but I could not make my body do it. I could hear my own breathing, which sounded loud to me as Sean yelled again, "Pick up your foot, Maylo!" I knew I had to concentrate. I tried to focus, and I picked up my right foot, which was shaking uncontrollably. Moving it seemed excruciatingly slow.

"Pick up your left foot! Pick it up, Maylo!" Sean continued to yell at me, forcing me to walk. I kept drooling and spitting and wanting to pass out, and he just kept making me walk. He kept at it until I was walking on my own, and the morning's early traffic was beginning to pick up.

That was my first overdose. If it weren't for Sean, I am convinced I would have died. He was in tears by the time we made it back to the house. He held me most of the day and begged me never to do that again. Ever.

Within a week he brought home some very good blow.

The Dark Day of the Dog... While the former Hollywood child star and teen idol who would eventually become my husband was swabbing toilets on a dive boat, I began what turned into a good run as a working actress. From my early twenties, I worked pretty steadily for thirteen years, landing guest spots on *Hardcastle & McCormick, Riptide, The A-Team,* and others—many of them directed or produced by Stephen Cannell.

As I became more confident, I also grew to love the business of television. I loved being on the sets and working with creative people; I just loved the whole family feeling of being on a show.

The interview process always gave me an attack of nerves, though, and I was always dieting, never eating properly. I started the day with lots of coffee and maybe a spoonful of rice from a box of leftovers in the fridge or a bite of meat from the night before, but really never more than a bite or two, just to keep the edge off my burning stomach. Lunch would be nothing at all, and dinner might be lettuce with blue-cheese dressing or cabbage washed down by alcohol of some type. My drug habits also continued to evolve, as drug habits do when they go unchallenged.

Between acting jobs I waitressed in various restaurants around Hollywood. I had two life skills—acting and asking, "Would you like fries with that?" One more: I made a mean White Russian.

My relationship with Sean was in and out. As I became more stable in my work, I began to worry about Sean "going off" on somebody. I contemplated leaving him many times, but it was a difficult break to make. I didn't believe I really wanted to do it. Besides, every time I got sick or did too much blow, Sean would be there—all soft and tender and scared—and the love he showed me just made me melt. I loved being loved. That was it, really. I loved having someone love me. I loved him because he loved me.

One day I was driving down Laurel Canyon in my little gold VW bug, dressed in a tiny purple halter dress and wearing purple high-heeled slingbacks, on my way to a nearby French restaurant for a job interview. My foot slipped off the gas pedal as the heel of my sandal buckled over to the side. The shoe completely slipped off my foot. There was not much traffic, and I was so familiar with all the bends and curves of Laurel Canyon Highway that I had a pretty good speed going. I tried to keep my eyes on the road as I reached down to get my shoe off the floorboard and out of the way.

The next thing I knew, I was upside down. The car had gone up the side of a hill and had started to roll back down onto the street when it was halted by a tree. The driver's side window was on the floor below me, and the passenger window was facing the sky. The roof of my small car had been smashed all the way in, and the car was totaled. The only thing that saved my life was what caused the accident in the first place: I was bending down.

A woman was screaming. "Are you OK in there? Hello?" Trapped inside, I could hear people trying to get around the car to find me. Every time I moved, the car would rock and threaten to roll the rest of the way down the highway. I waited forever for a tow truck and the fire department and was finally removed from the vehicle.

Sean had already heard about the accident because a friend of ours had been driving down the Canyon and had seen the car hanging in the tree. The friend had called him: "Dude, I think Maylo has been in an accident. Her car is gold, right?"

So Sean was there with me almost immediately. Once again. Holding me, with his giant blue eyes filled with tears. "You could've been killed!"

The days settled into the familiar pattern. I continued to work and get high. Sean seemed to get into one bloody fight after another. Although his episodes were starting to bother me, I stayed with him. He had been the first true love in my life, and we had a history together.

The more I tried to ignore the fighting, the harder I became. The more I did drugs, the more selfish I became. Most of the tender parts of my heart were shut off. My attitude became "whatever . . . that's their problem." Anytime Sean hurt someone, it was the other person's fault as far as I was concerned.

But there was one day that I could not ignore—one act of violence that replayed over and over in my head for many years. It's one of those things I wish I could go back and erase.

The youngest Negron boy had a small dachshund. Sean hated it. The dog got into our trash cans and stood in the center of the driveway, barking at whoever tried to drive onto the property. The driveway was on a hill, and Sean's car was a stick shift, so it was an ordeal to stop the car, set the brake, get out of the car, and move the dog.

I was in our little guesthouse when Sean climbed up the stairs, carrying the dog. I opened the sliding glass door to see him kneeling on the patio floor, holding the little dog down.

"Sean, what are you doing?"

"Nobody is home up there. They all went out."

"So?"

"So, I am going to take care of this ——— dog!"

"What do you mean, Sean? What are you going to do? You can't do anything to the dog, Sean; that little boy will be devastated!"

"I'm just gonna tell them it was hit by a car. It runs out in the street all the time anyway."

"You can't do that, Sean!"

"Watch me. Come here and hold him down." Sean had a giant framing hammer in his hand and was holding the dog by the back of the neck with the other.

Revulsion and fear made me feel physically ill. "Please, Sean, please." I begged him not to do it, and he told me to get out of his way.

I ran into the house, slammed the sliding door, and closed the drapes. And then I stood in disbelief in the middle of the room as I heard three hollow sounds—thunk, thunk, thunk.

Oh my gosh. He didn't just do that. He couldn't have just done that. I feel sick.

The slider opened and Sean came in. "OK. I'm gonna go and get rid of it. If they come here looking for it, tell them it got hit by a car and I took it. I'll be right back."

He was so matter-of-fact. He left and I just kept imagining that little boy's face. My head was full of an image of Sean hammering the dog's head that would not go away. I stumbled into the bathroom and threw up until there was nothing left.

Afterward everything happened just as Sean had predicted. The Negrons came home, and Sean told them that the dog had been hit by a car and that he had disposed of it so the boys would not have to see it. He was the hero. The Negrons thanked him. The child was heartbroken.

I cringed when Sean touched me from that moment on. Our relationship was over. There was no way I could stay in that house.

I could not look at him anymore. He tried to believe I just needed space. I had always been with him, and he tried to wait for me to get over it. We got back together temporarily a couple of times, but it was no use. Something died in me the dark day of the dog.

That's What Friends Are For... "OK, Sean, I'll see you

soon." I got out of the guesthouse without acting as if leaving was any big deal. But I knew it was.

I had found an apartment back in the Valley in a huge, cement complex that sat right off the freeway. It was a single room with red carpet, a small kitchenette and bathroom, and a bed that also served as a couch. It was tacky, but the rent was cheap and it was my own. I also got a dwarf hamster and a kitty. Life was good. I was going on interviews, doing occasional shows, and had enough money put away to be comfortable for a little while.

Then I met Tim. He lived on the third floor of the same complex with his girlfriend, Teri—a beautiful, sweet, gentle blonde. Tim had played keyboard for years with a famous, quirky musician who had a sort of cult following. It took me no time to realize that Tim was dealing cocaine.

We became fast friends. We did blow for days at a time, playing backgammon and drinking vodka and grapefruit juice to take the edge off. I was managing to make it to interviews, but many times I was not on my game at all because I was so buzzy. Job opportunities started to dwindle, and my savings was also disappearing because I was buying from Tim almost on a daily basis.

When I got low on cash, Tim was understanding—no surprise there—and came up with little jobs for me to do to earn my next gram of blow. I soon was weighing out the cocaine in his back room and putting it into little baggies. Always jumpy and excitable, he seemed even more nervous when people came to buy. When there was a knock at the door, he hid in the living room while Teri or I would check the person out to make sure everything was cool.

Sometimes Teri did the exchange. When there was a problem with someone, Tim told Teri what to say and instructed her not to let anyone in. When I think of him today, I realize what a coward he was. He had his own little world set up in that apartment, where he ruled with cocaine, using the people who would come and hang around, trying to earn some or get some for free if Tim felt generous.

I was one of them. We would get loaded and sit around and talk about God. Or we would talk about other people. Tim would talk about music and art, and I would talk about acting and dancing. It was absolute crap. It was self-serving and pathetic and classic denial, but we all thought we were somehow so deep and creative.

Things finally got to the point that I didn't care about art or really anything deep at all. I needed the drug. I *needed* it. If I didn't get it, my nerves would be shot and I would go into horrible depressions and isolate myself. I couldn't go on interviews because my face looked so bad from not eating and from crying all the time. At five-foot-seven, I weighed only 110 pounds.

I was doing more and more for Tim. I had convinced myself that he really cared about me as a friend and that I really cared about him. Once I agreed to drive Tim to his contact in the city to do a pickup. I waited in the car while he left and got a big package. I was so wired, I wasn't thinking straight—I had been awake and high for three days. He returned with a giant block of cocaine covered with a towel—enough to put me in jail for a very, very long time if we had been pulled over—and put it in my trunk. And all I could think of was how much Tim was going to give me.

One evening while at Tim's, there was a bold knock at the door. Tim jumped up and went to hide in his bedroom because the knock sounded purposeful—like the cops might be on the other side. I opened the door and recognized a man who had come to the apartment several times to buy drugs.

"Tim can't come to the door right now," I informed him. The man merely pushed me out of the way. He was in a rage. He dragged Tim out of the bedroom, yelling at him about money and threatening to kill him.

Tim started talking as fast as he could, but the man just yelled, "I'm not going to listen to this. No excuses!"

Tim begged the man to give him more time, but the man was about to clobber him. Tim seemed so pathetic that I felt sorry for him and tried to get between them.

"Please, leave him alone!"

The angry man shouted, "Stay out of it, Maylo!" He pushed Tim against the hallway wall. Tim tried to run out the front door, but the man grabbed him by the neck and bent him over the metal railing of the outside walkway.

"Help me!" Tim yelled as the man choked him. We were three stories up, and there was nothing but concrete beneath us.

I screamed, "No! Stop it! Please! Please!" But my cries were wasted. I finally stepped backward and watched from a few feet away, waiting to see Tim's body go over the rail.

But the man relented. He gave Tim three more days, telling him that if he didn't come through, he would have no trouble killing him. He called Tim some names then took off, leaving Tim bent over his knees, trying to get air back into his lungs.

I wasn't shaky. I did not have any reaction at all—just a "business as usual" feeling. Whatever. I was interested only in whether Tim would remember he had promised to get me high. I wondered if I would get extra for sticking up for him.

Thai Food and Spain... "Maylo? You got the job!" Don

was on the phone, but it took me a few minutes to rouse myself from my nap to understand what he was telling me.

Really? I didn't remember going on an interview. I sat up as things came into focus. Wow. A job. That was great.

It was the leading role in a new series by the Arthur Company to air on TBN, Ted Turner's new television station. Cable TV was a totally new thing, and a lot of serious actors didn't hold it in high regard. But I was thrilled; a steady gig was not an easy thing to come by.

The name of the 1984 show was *Rocky Road*, and it aired for two seasons. It was a silly little three-camera situation comedy, and I was to play Jessica, a character fashioned after Mary Tyler Moore, who had come home from college to raise her younger brother and sister and run the family ice cream store after the tragic death of their parents. It was very fluffy and not all that good, but it was a lot of fun.

Part of the fun was a friendship I made with a co-star who was ready to go just as fast and hard as I was when it came to using. We worked all week in rehearsals and taped in front of a live audience on Fridays. By Friday night wrap-up, we were at the ATM machine, pulling out our drug money for the weekend.

Some guys on the crew introduced me to a whole new pleasure: freebasing. When you freebase, you smoke crack (rock cocaine) and hold big hits in your lungs as long as you can until you feel your entire body flush with the drug. We just went deeper and deeper and partied harder and harder. Once I did it, there was no turning back.

But the consequences could be very dangerous. One time after a three-day binge, I was in my friend's bedroom. She laid out more lines of blow, and I just kept on until my heart was racing and pounding out of my chest. It felt like it was going to explode. My legs got shaky, and I felt like I couldn't control my eyeballs. I could hardly speak. When I did manage a few words, my friend just answered, "Oh, sweetie, you are just coming down. You need another line."

No. I didn't. I knew exactly what I needed, and it wasn't more drugs. I had been there before. I told her to watch me in case I stopped breathing, and we stayed up and waited for my body to calm down. It took all night.

I would clean up my act for a day or two or go see Sean, where I'd smoke some pot and hang out with him to get away from the temptation of going to Tim's apartment for more cocaine. I couldn't seem to get completely away from Sean, but he did not know the extent of my addictions. He did not know that I was driving deep into the Valley to some hole-in-the-wall house to buy crack whenever I could. He didn't know that I was not above getting on my hands and knees and picking up any little white thing, any little speck, off my rug and putting it in a pipe and smoking it with the hopes that it was some little piece of "rock" I had dropped.

I couldn't hold it together anymore. One of the show's producers confronted me, demanding to know whether I was using drugs. Of course, I lied. I decided to leave the show, though it really was a "mutual decision" because I was unable to keep my energy up on camera anymore and had lost my drive for anything other than drugs. I didn't care about the show. We would make the announcement at the table reading the next week.

In the meantime, during my last weeks of the 1985 tapings, there was a buzz going around the set about some famous guy who was going to guest-star the next week. It was a guy I was supposed to know about. Some guy from a show called *Eight Is Enough*.

"Never heard of it." I hadn't. After all, watching TV had not been the entertainment of choice when I was on the streets.

Some guy named Willie Aames. "You know, Willie Aames. Tommy Bradford. Willie Aames."

"Never heard of him." I hadn't. And I was way too tired to care. While everyone else was all aflutter, I stayed off by myself. Whatever. My motto.

The first day of the next week, we all met—cast and writers and producers and our extra special guest star, Willie Aames—for the table reading.

Willie was sitting a couple of people down from me. He was introduced and I looked at him briefly and he looked at me. Whatever.

Then the announcement was made that I would be leaving *Rocky Road*. The kids in the cast, who inexplicably (to me) had bonded with me, burst into tears, and a whole big deal was made over it. Whatever. Let's get to work.

Over the next week, my co-star spent time with Willie. He was nice enough, she told me. She thought he was really nice, actually. And she *really* thought he was a lot nicer than Sean.

"Maylo," she said, "you should go out with him. He's nice."

"No."

"You should go to lunch with him, Maylo. He is six months sober. He is doing the AA thing, but other than that, he is really nice and funny."

"Sober? Yeah, right! That's gonna happen! No way!"

"Why not?"

"He is short, not my type; I don't care if he's funny. He is *sober*. He is a geek! What could we possibly do together? Talk?!"

After a few days she came back. "Maylo, I know you would like him. You need to go to lunch with him!"

I finally said, "OK, OK. He can take us *all* to lunch. The entire cast and crew. Somewhere nice! But only if it is everyone!"

Fifteen to twenty people were involved with the show, by the way. I figured Willie would think I was out of line and would drop it. Uh-uh. Willie apparently took my answer as a challenge.

Before I could come up with anything clever to say, I found myself sitting in his black Jeep with the top down and the stereo blasting the Dream Academy's "Life in a Northern Town": "A Salvation Army band played / And the children drank lemonade / And the morning lasted all day."

We drove through Hollywood to take everyone to lunch at a very nice Thai restaurant he had already reserved. He sat across the table from me and smiled as he ate.

Arrrggg. He is cocky. I do like Thai food, though. His teeth are big. He looks like he is challenging me or something. Like he is going to say, "Your move."

Did he say that? Did he just say, "OK. Your move"? What a cocky little jerk. Hmm.

What is he saying? He is talking about Spain—about the food in Spain and the sun, about the siestas and the pavilions and the people. And now I am listening, because he is taking me to Spain with his memories. And his eyes are . . . what color are they? Gray? Green! And he won't stop looking at me!

And everyone ate. They ate and ate, whatever they wanted. And after a while, they all thanked him and we got back into our vehicles. And as he drove me back to the studio, I remember thinking, *Hmm. Willie Aames. He is pretty generous.*

Roots...I don't know what finally broke me down. Maybe his tenacity. He was so annoying! But something inside me cracked open the tiniest little bit when I realized that he actually liked me. I became curious. I thought, *If I look at him sitting down and forget how short he is, he's kinda cute!*

That week we found time to sit on the couch right on the stage and talk and talk. For the first time in years I wasn't thinking, *I gotta get outta here.* There I sat in black, fishnet stockings with long, red fingernails and lots of black eyeliner, talking to someone without thinking about when I would be able to get high again.

When you meet someone like Willie Aames, you expect him to be all about showbiz, but he wasn't. He was into, of all things, islands and fishing and diving and the beauty that was in all of those different places. He seemed desperately tired. He had been broken—I didn't yet know why—and he was so different from anyone I had ever met. He wasn't about doing drugs or about the tiresome questions everyone in Hollywood asks upon first meeting you: "What have you been doing? What are you working on right now?" There was something homey about Willie—in a way, he reminded me of the feeling I had had years ago at Grandma McCaslin's house.

As the week wound down, he kept saying he had something he wanted to ask me. But we were working, and when we did get together to talk, he would just smile and say, "Nah. I'll ask you later."

I was becoming impatient and irritated. "What? Ask me already!"

"Nah, forget about it. Maybe later."

The last day he walked me out to my car. We stood in the parking lot and talked for a short while, and he said, "You know, I've wanted to ask you a question. I've wanted to ask you if I could maybe kiss you."

OK. That was really sweet. That was really tender. "Um, yeah. All right. I guess so." I probably didn't sound too enthusiastic.

He pushed me against the car and planted a big, giant, time-stopping, Italian-movie-style kiss on me. Then he turned away and left me standing there with my stomach flipping over as he jumped into his Jeep, put his aviator sunglasses on, and looked back at me like, "There ya go, baby!" So cocky. And ornery. And . . . fun.

He came crashing into my life. Our first date was to a concert where we met some of his old band members. Sadly, I had no respect for the fact that he was sober. I did some lines beforehand and even brought along a girlfriend. I ordered one drink after another, and he eyed me but never said a word of criticism.

After the concert he drove me out to Orange County, where he lived. It was a long drive from Los Angeles, and we talked the whole way. I spilled out everything about my life. Willie just drove and listened. He didn't talk about himself at all. He was focused and intent on what I was saying. His face was soft and thoughtful in the dark, and as he drove, he reached over and held my hand. A great, deep friendship was born that night on the road between Los Angeles and Orange County—an invisible commitment already growing roots underneath the surface . . . roots that would be tried, tested, and proven over the next twenty years.

You're Cute, but Not That Cute...Most of the time
I was with Willie, I didn't give drugs a second thought. But that didn't stop my habit, not at first. I had two sets of friends—my using friends and the sober friends who revolved around Willie. I stepped in and out of both lifestyles. I didn't have a regular gig anymore and was running out of money, so cocaine was no longer an option—crystal meth was cheaper.

No one, including Willie, knew the state to which I had sunk. I found myself in the worst parts of the Valley, trying to make small talk with the two "coke hos" who lived with my dealer, a huge black guy with dreadlocks. When I did drugs, I did them alone. And I was beginning to become ashamed. Ashamed of where I was going to get them. Ashamed of my lies, my double life. Ashamed of dangling Sean out there, in and out of my life.

Willie and I were seeing each other more and more. He was honestly making a go of sobriety. He was stubborn about it and picking up the pieces of his life. He was in the process of cleaning up his messes, and I started to want that. I wanted to walk that road with him and get my life on track. So finally, in a move long overdue, I completely broke off my relationship with Sean. We had been through this so many times before that it was hard for him to take it seriously, but I told him there was someone else. Someone I really loved.

Sean didn't take the news well. "He can't love you! He is an *actor!* Is he skinny? Is he soft?! Who is he?"

"Sean! Leave it! He isn't any of those things! I am really, really sorry."

Maybe I should have been scared instead. Sean began stalking us. One night Willie understood just what he had gotten himself into with me. He was talking with me in my apartment when someone suddenly started pounding on my front door. There was no question that it was Sean, and there was no doubt that he was angry.

"I know you're in there! Open the door, Maylo!"

When I looked through the peephole and saw him, I became flushed and scared. I turned back around to Willie, but Willie was . . . gone! As Sean kept pounding on my door, trying to open it, I crept through my condo, looking for Willie. I lived three floors up, and there were bars on all my windows, so I knew he still had to be there somewhere.

"Psst. Psst. Willie? Willie?!"

I turned down the hall and opened the door to my roommate's closet. OK. This was one of the first things I loved about Willie: first I saw his feet, and when I pushed the clothes aside, he said with a totally straight face, "You're cute. But you're not *that* cute!"

Well. I was not used to someone walking away from a fight, and that comment, in the middle of such a tense situation, cracked me up. It was so funny. *He* was so funny. We both just laughed. When all was quiet, I stuck my head out my front door and looked down the hall. No one.

"I think he's gone, but let me just look from the balcony at the parking lot to be sure before you leave," I told Willie.

Sure enough, there was Sean's old car parked right where I would be sure to see it.

I received many scary phone calls over the next three days. Willie was stuck in the condo with me the entire time, threatened with death if he left the building. It was very romantic. It's ironic to think that Sean's threatening both of us just drew us closer.

WILLIE

The Rocky Road to Love... Here's my version of the day we first met: she was tall, brunette, slender, and cute but in a different kind of way from the supermodels who congregated at the Playboy Mansion. The last thing I wanted at the time was to meet someone. No more women, not for a long while.

She seemed not to care whether people liked her. She stood by herself with leg warmers on her long legs, doing deep bends and stretches, picking her leg up in a pose almost like that of a horse prancing. She seemed aloof.

Just being professionally friendly, I asked, "You into horses?"

She looked at me like I was the worst pervert she had ever met. "Whoa," I backtracked, "I didn't mean it like that. You just did this little thing with your leg and it reminded me of . . ."

"I'm a jazz dancer," she said. Her answer was more an attack than a response.

She talked to her co-star, who seemed to be a good friend of hers, but otherwise she looked like she was lost in her thoughts.

Maybe her detachment had to do with what happened the first day of my guest appearance on an episode of *Rocky Road*. As we sat around the table, reading through the script, the director, Patricia Palmer, announced that Maylo was leaving the show. One of the children in the cast had started crying, and everyone else had bummed. Gee, what a swell time to join the happy family.

Although she didn't talk to me, her co-star was friendly. When I asked about her, she said that Maylo's boyfriend was a jerk. "Ask her out, Willie. Go ahead. She's trying to break up with him."

Red flag. I didn't want to meet anybody, especially someone with baggage. Still, there was something about her that intrigued me. On the second day of taping, after we wrapped up, I tried to talk with her again. Slowly she began to talk a little. We were still onstage, the show's "living room" behind us, and we both ended up sitting on the couch, just talking about stuff. Our conversation rabbit-trailed for a couple of hours. The same thing happened the next day, but each of us began to share more personal things about ourselves.

Maylo's co-star began a campaign to get me to take Maylo out. "Not if she has a boyfriend," I answered. She was cute, true, but I'd had my share. Finally I gave in.

I decided to take the risk. "Would you like to have lunch?"

Lukewarm to freezing. "Yeah, sure. As long as you take the whole cast and crew with us."

Little Miss Jazz Dancer must think pretty highly of herself, I thought. What she probably hadn't figured out was that that kind of challenge only pushed me further. The scary part was that I was broke. I had no way of knowing how I was going to pay for all of those people to have lunch. But the gauntlet had been thrown down, and I wasn't in the mood to be bested.

I called my favorite Thai restaurant and arranged for a private dining area for everyone, all twenty-plus of them. The same day we all went. The staff had set up the tables with their best white linens and dinnerware, and the buffet and drinks were plentiful.

I sat across from her. I could tell she was trying not to look at me. When she did, I simply smiled and said, "Your move." Her face was hard to read, but I think she smiled a little. She seemed intent on what I was talking about and asked me questions about some of the places I'd been. I found myself talking about surfing, scuba diving, fishing, and islands. I worried that I might be boring her, but I hated the typical Hollywood kiss-kiss conversation: "So, Willie, what are you working on right now?"

There was something about Maylo that I couldn't put a name to. I could tell there was a huge amount of unconventional personality behind those deep-brown eyes. When she smiled, her teeth were perfect and beautiful. But those eyes . . . there was a lot to learn about her behind them. And even though she tried to put me off, there was an honesty in her that intrigued me. She wanted absolutely nothing from me. And, oh yeah, she had a great rear end.

Back at the boat, I told Christine about Maylo.

"What kind of girl can pull you away from me?" She asked in her French accent and rolled her eyes, as if expecting the obvious answer to be "No one, Christine. No one is as good as you."

But I didn't say it. I couldn't. Christine had already damaged our relationship beyond repair. She had recently had an abortion without even telling me she had been pregnant. What her reasoning had been was beyond me. Did she think I wouldn't have cared about the baby? Who could figure out what she was thinking? Things were over between us—that demonstration of distrust told us both a lot about our dead relationship. I have to say that I often wonder who that little person would have been. It tears at me and is a source of melancholy. I know that one day when I get to heaven, there will be this beautiful little curly-haired child who will come running up to me, squealing, "Daddy! Daddy!" And with one huge hug, I will lift him or her and we'll laugh together. Finally I'll know that little person who already knows about me.

Rocky Road wrapped up the episode, and I asked Maylo the question I'd been wanting to ask all week. She looked at me a little strangely but gave her permission. When the kiss was over, Maylo was staring straight at me. She didn't speak. The rest of the cast had seen everything, and they stood clapping and cheering and laughing at us standing there in the parking lot. I quickly asked Maylo if she'd go to a concert with me.

Her repeated cocktail of choice that night at the concert was a Greyhound, which I bought for her. "You go ahead and have as many as you want," I told her, "but I won't be having one."

That's it. That's how it all began. I was trying to hang onto my sobriety, while Maylo had a possible drinking problem. It didn't take me long to figure out that drugs were a big part of life for Maylo too.

Almost from my first conversation with Maylo, I found myself wanting to know more about her. Underneath the "whatever, who cares" attitude was a gem that just needed polishing, and then, wow. The longer I was around her, the more interested I was. But from the beginning I decided that Maylo was Maylo, and I was not going to try to change anything about her. Whatever she was, she was, and if I was going to spend time with her, I wanted it to be truly unconditional. No hiding things between us. No relationship games—I had learned to hate them. *If that's what you want,* I thought, *I can tell you right now, it's over. If you want to be honest, there's hope.*

And there was something about her that satisfied my need to matter. Early on, I remember thinking that she needed a knight in shining armor, whether she knew it or not. I wanted to be that knight in shining armor. It was an honorable goal— just not one I could achieve. It would take me a while to figure that out.

Out of the Closet...OK, so I saw myself as a modern
Sir Galahad come to rescue the fair damsel. Maylo's old boyfriend,
Sean, didn't exactly want me to be a knight of any kind. Intimida-
tion. Threats. I knew he'd kill me.

"No one else is going to put up with your crap!" Maylo told
me he'd yelled at her when he found out she was seeing someone.
"No one! You're not going to find anybody else!"

Sean appeared outside Maylo's door one afternoon when I
was visiting and began pounding on the door, demanding her
to open it. "I know you've got someone in there, Maylo! Now
open up!"

Still, our relationship was evolving from friendship to affec-
tion to love. So something had to change in my living arrange-
ments.

"Hey, Willie, you can rent part of our apartment. You can pay
us $150 a month." One of my fellow AA members offered to share
space in an apartment he shared with another member. It was in
what was the Costa Mesa barrio, not three streets from the tiny
home I was born in. Supreme irony—I had sworn over the years
that I would never go back to that neighborhood, and yet there
I was.

Well, the "space" they let me share was the floor of a closet.
I built a few small shelves in it, set what belongings I had left
on them, and laid out a sleeping bag. On weekends, I picked up
Chris, and the two of us slept in that cramped space together. I did
my best to make it special because he was with me. But I had never
felt so low. *This isn't how I am supposed to end up*, I thought.

I didn't have many options. I was out of money. Maylo was on
her way to being broke too when I met her. We recognize today
that our similar positions were part of God's plan, but we didn't
know it then.

I have to back up a little to describe what happened during those days. My partying had paid off in spades. I had continued being persona non grata to my mom and dad, but some alarming symptoms had made me realize I needed to see a doctor, so I made an appointment with our family's longtime physician. The VD test came back positive, so he started the treatment immediately—two shots of penicillin, one in each cheek. Youch.

What neither of us knew was that I had developed a life-threatening allergy to penicillin. As I was sat in the waiting room after the shots, I went into anaphylactic shock. Next thing I remember, the doctor and a couple of nurses were standing over me—one holding an oxygen mask over my nose and mouth and the others yelling, "Breathe, Willie! Breathe!"

They lost my pulse once but injected me with epinephrine and soon had me stabilized. After a night in the hospital, I realized how close I had come to dying. I began to think of Mom and Dad and the seven wasted years. It was so stupid. I found a pay phone and called the house.

Resuming the ties with my family was not easy. There was no rosy, return-of-the-prodigal-son-fatted-calf reconciliation. Mom accepted my apologies, but Dad was a tough nut to crack. And in true Dad fashion, he set up some caveats for reestablishing our relationship. But I was just tired. Tired of the grudge match. We began a hesitant little walk toward each other. They had no idea of what my real living conditions were (or they might have offered to let me stay with them), but I wasn't going to tell them.

As the relationship between Maylo and me deepened, we moved into a small apartment together in Huntington Beach. I did have enough residual income coming in from time to time that, with her waiting tables, we had barely enough to afford rent, but it didn't matter. We were definitely poor. After several months we were so broke, we were counting pennies. We'd roll them in aluminum foil and take them to the local market.

But we were also happy. I'd spend nearly every afternoon on *Screw It*, a little skiff I had bought when I'd had money to spend. (The boat's name was a Willie-esque play on words, but it also had a straightforward meaning because *screw* is a sailor's word for the propeller.) I'd come home with fresh fish, and we'd cook it up with fragrant jasmine rice that Maylo would buy in quantity at a local oriental market. There's nothing like the delicate taste of bass when it's fresh.

Now you know my side of the beginning of our relationship. Before long I'd be offered the role of Buddy Lembeck again for a syndicated version of *Charles in Charge*.

MAYLO

Blast from the Past... "Maylo, if we're going to get serious with each other, you're going to have to deal with your problem."

The time came for me to make a choice. Willie confronted me about my drinking and using, and I agreed to go with him to his AA meetings in Pacific Palisades near the beach.

Willie's sponsor was an older man whom I just loved. He had a face like a weeping willow and a solid spirit that wouldn't take any grief from anyone. He had been around a long time and had helped many famous people get sober, so he wasn't impressed with stardom. The friends at his table were a virtual "who's who" of Hollywood—we even called it "the night of a thousand stars."

Of course, at first I was awed by the fact that I was actually hanging out with these people, but that initial feeling quickly gave way to what was really going on. People were being honest. People were talking about their struggles, their failures, their victories. A lot of talk seemed to be about "making amends, cleaning up your mess." The tone was direct, and I had to admit it was the right thing to do. I couldn't deny it. I had to do it. It definitely was time to quit.

You would think that putting drugs down would have been difficult. You hear all of these stories about withdrawal, but I can honestly say that I don't remember having any of that. Though I wasn't a believer yet, it surely was God's grace because I simply quit. I never went back.

What *did* happen soon afterward was unexpected. Willie had signed to a syndicated version of *Charles in Charge*, so finances were looking better than they had been. I was newly sober and was honeymooning with my sobriety. I was getting my act together, and it seemed fitting that I should also take care of something I was long overdue for—my first gynecological appointment. Since I had health insurance through the Screen Actors Guild, I called a random doctor out of the organization's providers booklet.

Willie went with me. I didn't think much at all about the appointment. I assumed I would go in, get checked up, and leave. I did the deal, stirrups and all, and when the exam was over, the doctor said, "OK, Maylo. You can get dressed now. Then would you please come to my office? The nurse will show you where it is."

"Sure," I said uncertainly.

His nurse tapped on his door and led me in. As I sat in a small chair in front of his cherry-wood desk, he leaned forward and handed me a business card—for a counselor.

"How many years were you sexually abused?" he asked me.

Before speaking, my mind began racing. *I don't know . . . I, um, I can't think. I can't . . . think . . .*

"Um, a lot. Why?"

"Maylo, your cervix is badly damaged, and we need to do a biopsy right away." He took out a pencil and paper and drew a picture of a cervix and a birth canal and told me about a procedure called a conization. I heard only about every other word until he asked, "Do you have any children?"

"No. No children."

Then he told me that he was not sure I would ever be able to carry a child full term because he would have to remove so much of the cervix, but he would do the best he could.

The biopsy proved what he already knew. I had cervical cancer. An operation was scheduled immediately.

I was livid. Enraged. I had thought I had run away from that. I had thought it was over. I got flush after flush of red-hot anger. Bernie, whom I hadn't even thought of in years, was here . . . in my body . . . taking, violating, robbing me all over again.

And even worse than that was the utter hatred I had for my mother. No kids! The doctor said I might not be able to have kids! You took it all, Mom! You never protected me! You never once protected any of us kids! You let him in! I didn't matter! You gave him my future!

I wanted to kill someone! So I took out my rage that afternoon on Willie, who had not known what was coming. "Leave me! Leave me alone! Don't you dare stick around and use my operation to make your fans feel sorry for you! 'Your girlfriend has cancer. Oh, poor Willie.' Don't you dare do that! I will do this by myself! Leave! Leave right now! Go on!"

I dared him. I pushed him away. There was no one else around to punish but him. And he took it. He didn't push back. He put his arms around me and didn't say much of anything. He let me cry.

And I could not stop crying. While I had been using drugs, I had learned to hold everything back for so many years. I had self-medicated. When I finally got sober, I cried years and years worth of tears. I woke up crying in the morning. I cried in the middle of the day. And I had night terrors for more than three years. I saw Bernie's face over me and body parts and violent scenes with the bodies of strangers. I never fully slept. I was constantly afraid. I had no bravado left. I was a train wreck. Much more than any man would want to take on.

And both before and after the surgery, Willie simply held me. He woke up every single night without fail and wrapped both arms around me and held me tight enough to stop my shaking.

WILLIE

Stick Around, There's More to Come... Leave
Maylo or stay with her? Bail out or hang in there? To be honest,
Maylo didn't know what I was thinking about when we found out
about the cancer.

I hadn't really committed myself to a relationship that centered around the *L* word, and the memory of Phoebe held me
back a little, even though I had begun to recognize that what I was
most in love with was the romance of our time together.

Then there was the weight of IRS payments, penalties, and
attorneys' fees that never failed to crash through the rosy memories. Lawsuits flew around me like a swarm of wasps. Finances
were always a problem, and Vicki continually demanded that
I send more money for her and Chris. Did I need yet another person with needs that were far from what I could fix?

There was also the part of me that wanted to enjoy my freedom and the women who were making themselves very available.
Maylo was beautiful, sure, and I had a steadily growing recognition
that she was somehow unique and solid. But I didn't know if I was
capable of giving what Maylo needed. I didn't know if I wanted
such a heavy responsibility when my divorce wasn't even final.

Once again I did the manly thing—I broke up with Maylo. What a jerk. There was Maylo facing surgery, and she just packed up some clothes and left to stay with her manager.

As she walked out, my head began to buzz, and I couldn't think straight. I thought, *Willie, you have never had someone in your life who is so loyal, so ready to be your closest friend—someone who honestly wants nothing for her own gain. She only wants to encourage you and to love and be loved.*

I picked up the phone and called my sponsor. "Bob? What have I done? I've just broken up with the love of my life."

"Willie, you gotta quit screwing around someday. She deserves better than this. Grow up." Let's just say that Bob's sympathy was a little lacking. And he confirmed what I knew in my heart.

I made a conscious decision to let go of my sophomoric memories of Phoebe. I called Maylo and after several attempts that were flatly rejected by her manager, I got through to her and asked her to come back. The ordeal lasted less than eighteen hours, but it felt like a lifetime.

When I think about it now, I realize that staying with Maylo when she needed me was perhaps the second adult thing I had ever done, after facing my addiction. I had always wanted to matter to someone and now I could, but it would be for the right reasons.

After Maylo recuperated, life continued in a pleasant routine. I had been offered a second extended run with *Charles in Charge* as a syndicated series, one hundred episodes—four years of steady work. As an actor, I was always wondering where the next gig would come from, so knowing that for four years I was guaranteed to work offered freedom and security. During this second run, Scott and I could take risks and make mistakes, trying dialogue or stunts that might bomb or might work, all without worrying that the show would be canceled.

Maylo calls those days magical. She got to experience the

atmosphere on the set firsthand as a guest star for one episode. I had decided to invest myself emotionally in the show and became friends with everyone. I set a personal goal each week of making my old friend Scott laugh.

I've already described how different sets have different atmospheres. On *Charles in Charge*, you knew the minute you walked onto the set that the show was a comedy. You might see the stage manager keeping track of the rehearsals while playing with his yo-yo, or you might see Scott and me heaving rotten fruit at the stage ceiling to see if it would splatter or stick. Really, the entire set came to work just to play and to joke around.[12] Everyone, from makeup artists to the stars, treated one another like family.

At first Scott and I hung out together in off hours, jet skiing and generally just having fun being seen as we dared each other to do silly things. We got to where we could learn all sixty pages of lines in one day and end up with extra time. We'd get lines that weren't all that funny and figure out what was funny about them. We'd insert jokes into the script that came from our escapades off the set. Each episode was filmed before a live audience, and the audience picked up on our obvious attempts to make each other laugh. When this happens in a sitcom, it makes the audience more receptive. They feel like they're a part of the show and laugh even more enthusiastically.

Memories from those days, especially from the first years, are some of my fondest. We had a standing date to play three-hole golf on a course near the studio with Tony Danza, who was in the middle of *Who's the Boss?* Scott and I finished our taping so early that we would have already played a round by the time Tony even showed up. It used to drive him nuts. He couldn't figure out how we finished so fast.

---

12. It wasn't until later in the show that the risqué nature of some of the jokes began to bother me, but I'll explain that change of heart as my account continues.

Besides the wonderful Ellen Travolta, who had a recurring role throughout the series, we had young actors on the show from time to time who were on the brink of stardom. Meg Ryan was on in the early days of the show. The beautiful Nicole Eggert, who would go on to star in *Baywatch*, played the part of Jamie Powell for three years. There were always guests on the set: Christina Applegate (*Married with Children*), the dryly funny Jerry Van Dyke (*Coach*), Sally Struthers (*All in the Family*), Charles Nelson Riley—a comic stage actor whom I also appeared with on the game show *Hollywood Squares*—and even, in a nod to a sitcom classic, the iconic Tony Dow (*Leave It to Beaver*).

Maylo reminds me that some of the events during those days could have caused me some problems if I had been unattached still. I received bouquets of roses regularly from women who would insert a card in them with their phone numbers. And on one memorable occasion, I was standing offstage in the dark when someone tapped me on the shoulder. When I turned around, a girl grabbed me and planted a huge kiss on me.

"I always wanted to meet you. I just love your show," said the breathy voice. It was Lisa Bonet, who was in *A Different World* at the time. Whew!

Tom Hanks, always congenial and pleasant, rode around the lot on his bicycle. "And there's Willie Aames!" he'd call, waving. "And there's Scott Baio!"

Another person passed by the set every day as well, and she was as unfriendly as Tom was friendly. Every day I said, "Hello," and every time she gave me a look of sheer disgust. She was involved in shooting *Dick Tracy* with her then-beau Warren Beatty. So I had to make a game of it just to tick her off. I kept saying, "Hey, you're Madonna, aren't you? I'm Willie Aames." She just made that face and kept going. Not once did she greet a lowly TV actor like me.

One day in the first year of filming, I went to work on the set but was barred from the stage. Soon I wasn't the only one standing behind the locked door. The rumor was that a commercial featuring pyrotechnics was being filmed. It was so top secret that we didn't know until much later that it was the famous Pepsi commercial featuring Michael Jackson, set to the tune of his song "Billie Jean."

During the mid '80s, Robin Leach, host of the show *Lifestyles of the Rich and Famous,* booked Maylo and me on an episode shot in New Zealand. Being on the show was hilariously ironic, since my obligations to the IRS and alimony payments put me on the other side of the block from rich. But we had a wonderful time hang gliding, yachting, and sunning ourselves. We certainly got the celebrity treatment, but one event was especially memorable.

We were invited to a formal dinner with the prime minister, and toasts were offered. A dignified, decorated general in full regalia stood up and made a speech that went something like this: "I know it's not popular right now to be too friendly with Americans. But I remember a time in the not-so-distant past, during World War II, when America was the only country standing between us and Japan. Japan was intent on conquering us. Thanks to the Yanks, we meet here as free citizens of New Zealand. And I demand a response!"

And everyone shouted, "Hear, hear!"

I looked at Robin Leach, who started laughing and said, "Don't look at me! I'm English! You get to represent the United States to the prime minister and the admiral!" I stood up and responded to those kind words in the most gracious way I knew how.

It's been rare for me to be at a loss for something to say. But on one memorable occasion, I ran into the great, the only Tom Petty— one of my all-time musical heroes. I was tongue-tied. Word got around that he and Bob Dylan were going to rehearse on the lot. I happened to be in the right place at the right time. Petty was driving around, looking for the stage he needed to find, and stopped to ask me for directions.

I was such a big fan that I couldn't talk. I finally was able to give him directions. As he drove off, I said, "You're really cool, dude!" I must have sounded like a complete doofus. He just looked at me as if to say, "What a loser!" At least that's what I felt like, but who cared? I had met Tom Petty!

Before I knew it, most of the shows had been filmed. During the last two years, the atmosphere on the show changed, and with it my joy in what I was doing. Scott began saying more and more frequently, "I don't want to do *Charles in Charge* anymore." He seemed suspicious of me, telling other cast members and guests that I was trying to steal the show from him, so I confronted him. "Look, Scott, I'll be your co-star for as long as you want to go. We're good together."

I have to give him credit; he was honest. He just insisted, "But I need to show people that I can do a show without you." He'd heard that I had received a raise, so he threatened to walk off the set if it went through. That cost me one hundred grand.

I don't know why he began feeling the way he did, but his comments and attitude put everyone on edge. The joy of working together was slowly sucked out of the atmosphere.

Things deteriorated to the point that I wasn't allowed to talk to the crew and they weren't allowed to talk to me—Scott's orders. I felt forced into getting ready to move on, but it was time to go. Some life-altering events in Maylo's and my off-screen lives during the past couple of years of the show had changed my attitude about many aspects of Hollywood. And bigger changes were on the way.

In the next chapter Maylo backs up a little in our chronology to catch up the sequence of our two stories, which, by the time *Charles in Charge* ended in 1990, had become forever intertwined.

MAYLO

A Small Gift with Huge Significance... The hallway was wide and gray that day in 1985. Gray walls, gray floors, large, shiny gray tiles with little specks of blue and black—impeccably clean.

My feet were cold. My hair was tucked inside of a cheap shower cap with gathered elastic that pulled the tiny hairs on the back of my neck. The gurney I was on had a stiff, thin mattress that crinkled when I moved. I had been wheeled into the hallway and pushed against the wall to wait. The hall was totally empty. I lay on my back and stared up at the ceiling tiles. Willie could not be in this place with me. I did not know Jesus Christ. I had no God. I couldn't find a nurse to get me another blanket. I was still. Hollow. Alone.

I realize now that the operating room's double doors were a sort of starting gate for me. Only I did not yet know there was a race to be run, and I could not see the track.

It was in this clean, gray hallway that I felt my soul, the essence of what made me Maylo, somehow detach itself from my body and look at what lay on that gurney. The eyes of my heart saw a thin young woman . . . but it was just my body, my flesh. I am not my body, I realized. My body was at the mercy of the surgeon. He

221

would cut and work on my body, but my heart, my mind, all of my emotions, were not his to deal with. They were wadded into a ball, separate from my body, and they did not belong to anyone or anything.

When I was wheeled into that room at the end of the hall, if anything went wrong, I belonged . . . where? What would happen to me if I died? Would I rest? Would I cease to exist? My heart, my thoughts. What would happen to them?

I had no distractions in those moments. I had no children to think of. No future. I thought of Bernie. I thought of my mother and her so-called spirituality. I thought of how many times Bernie had been on top of me. I thought of how it didn't matter. Whatever. It is just flesh—flesh and bones. I thought of surgery and the conization. Of my cervix. Just tissue. It doesn't matter. It is already gone, anyway. I was submitting my body to the surgery, dehumanizing it. But in my mind I kept hearing a small voice. "Whom do you belong to, Maylo?" It wouldn't go away. "Whom do you belong to? Who is Maylo? Maylo without the body?"

This is taking forever. Where is everybody? I thought surgery was at 9:00 a.m. It must be at least 11:30 by now. My feet are freezing.

Again. "Who loves you?"

I don't know. Willie. Willie loves me. I think. Willie *says* he loves me. Does he love me? Does he really know me? I don't know.

"Who loves you, Maylo? Whom do you belong to? Where would you go? Who are you? Who loves you? Whom do you belong to? Who are you? Who loves you?"

Geez! I don't know. Let's just hurry up. Do they even know I'm still here in the hallway? I am cold and uncomfortable and haven't eaten and . . .

"OK. Maylo, they are ready for you. Let's go, hon."

I was wheeled down the hall and through the double doors. This room had life in it. There were people working and the sounds of tools being prepared—sounds like silverware being put back in a drawer.

I was underneath a huge, round light. It was much warmer. Right away a man came to stand over me. He explained that he was my anesthesiologist and that he would be giving me an IV. He would then put a mask over my face, and I would begin counting backward from ten.

"Yes. Yes. OK. I understand."

Then my doctor came in. He leaned in close to me and spoke quietly. "Maylo, you are going to go to sleep, and while you are sleeping, I am going to do more than a conization, OK? I am going to go inside and cut out every part of you that was used and violated. I will go everywhere that man was, and I will take out all that he touched. When you wake up, there will be no part of you that belongs to him. There won't be anywhere inside of you left that he has touched, OK?"

I nodded. The impact of what he said settled on me. The last thought I had as the mask was being put over my face was of a clean body. A clean, pure body. The past would be cut out and thrown in the trash.

I did not know Jesus Christ. I had no God, but I woke up feeling clean, and I knew something very special had happened. Some sort of healing had taken place, healing that began with words that were spoken to me. A promise was given to me by a doctor: I would be clean and new.

When I came to, Willie was standing in the recovery room beside me. I felt clean and I felt new. Simply that. And introspective.

I listened a little more closely to the speakers at AA, feeling myself opening up to possibilities I had never considered before.

Hmm, maybe I needed to consider some answers for those questions that would not leave me alone in the hospital hallway.

Willie and I were not only falling in love; we were becoming best friends. We were building a life together in our small apartment in Huntington Beach. One day as I was driving home and listening to the radio, just flipping from station to station, I caught a talk show. This guy was good—really, really good. Willie would love this guy.

I did not know what station I had found; it was just one of those quirky things that I stumbled upon. The man was funny. He talked about life honestly and touched on the "higher power" theory that had been preoccupying me lately.

When I saw Willie that evening, I kept repeating, "This guy was like the best AA speaker we have ever heard, Willie. I was totally cracking up, but what he was saying was so true. It was like he hit the nail on the head. You would love him. I wish you had been there."

"Well, who was he?"

"I don't know. I just caught the last twenty minutes or so. I have no idea." Willie shrugged, and we both forgot about what I had heard.

As we drove in the car together another evening, I was flipping through the radio stations and heard his voice once again.

"Willie! This is that guy! That guy I was telling you about! You have to hear this!"

Willie pulled the car into our parking lot, and we sat in the car. We listened, we laughed, and we were moved.

At the end of the segment, an announcer's warm voice said, "Thank you, listeners. That was Pastor Jim of Southside Church. For more information call . . ."

A pastor? Are you kidding me? I had no idea. I really didn't! Southside Church? That's only about three miles from where we live! What a coincidence!

"Hey, Willie, we should go." We were still sitting in the car.

"To church? Right. What, are we going to become Christians now? Give me a break!"

I knew he was right. Every Christian I had ever known I had made fun of, except my old friend Stacy. When I was still in school, a super-cute boy "got saved," and us girls practically wept because we felt it was such a waste. Oh no! A Christian? How sad!

Yeah, Willie was right. I wasn't going to become a Christian. That was stupid. Ridiculous. Funny, actually. Willie and Maylo as Christians. Ha, ha.

We had to admit, though, the man we heard was a good speaker. He was funny. Hmm. Maybe we should go.

Hope Is More than a Pretty Word...This was a bad idea. I had never seen more nylons and barrettes in one place in my life. It was Sunday morning, and Willie and I were standing around with a group of other people waiting for the church to open. It was warm out, and we were in a cement courtyard. I was smoking a cigarette. And fidgeting. Even in our "Sunday best," we looked different from these people. My pants were too tight; my shirt was too tight. My makeup was suddenly too heavy. My nails were too long and too red.

Nobody seemed to notice or care about what we wore. They actually all looked like very nice people. Good people. Like Bettys and Janes, Jims and Bobs. People you can rely on.

The big double doors finally opened, and people started moving into what appeared to be a lobby. I was still holding my lit cigarette when we approached the door, and I was stopped by a greeter.

"I am sorry; you will need to put out your cigarette. There is no smoking in the sanctuary."

My face flushed. I stepped out of the line. To be honest, I was ashamed. I was ashamed of my smoking, ashamed I was so stupid as to try to bring a lit cigarette into a church. But my shame only lasted a full second before it turned into anger.

"I knew it! I knew I wasn't good enough for those people!" I went with Willie to the side of the building to finish my smoke.

"I have *tried* to quit smoking. I have! They think they are so much better than me. You know, I came here because I am a mess and can't fix myself. If I have to clean up my act just to get inside the building, I will never make it! I may as well give up right now!" I had a good rant going by the time I stepped out my cigarette.

Willie and I stood by the side of the building, trying to decide whether we should leave. We were angry and jaded and not very open. Finally, one of us said, "Let's just go in. We are already here." And so we did. The service had already started.

We found two seats together just as someone stood up at the podium and announced that the pastor would not be speaking today. I snorted. That was who we came to see! And he wasn't even speaking today? What a waste of time. I rolled my eyes and crossed my arms.

Instead of a sermon, several testimonies were going to be given by several different people. Huh? What the heck does that mean? I looked at Willie. He was looking at the stage and thinking.

Several people sat down in chairs on the platform. One by one each got up and spoke. They told powerful, real stories about their lives. About what was happening to them. Their struggles. Several had been through horrible divorces that devastated their lives and their children's lives. These people were sharing their weaknesses—sort of like AA, with one difference: Jesus Christ.

AA is awesome; don't get me wrong. It was part of what led me to God. But these people pointed to Jesus Christ alone. And they weren't all on the other side of their troubles with a lollipop and a banner with "God Loves Me" printed on it. They were in the middle of their storms. They were clinging, and they weren't bitter. They weren't angry. Their humor was not jaded or mean.

Somehow, they were getting through it all with Jesus Christ. Without giving up. They had hope for their future. Hope. Hope. Willie said it best: "I didn't even realize I needed hope until someone presented it to me!"

That was it. I needed hope. Hope beyond Willie. Willie can't be everything. He isn't the answer. How do you get hope? Why is Jesus the hope for these people? Was Jesus really real? More than a picture in Grandma McCaslin's bedroom? How could she have sung those songs about him and believed in him? How does a person believe? How do you get to be like these people? I don't know about the Bible, but it seems stupid to believe in someone who is just a historical figure. I believe that George Washington lived, but I know for sure he isn't going to do anything at all about my current situation, whatever that may be. What is all this?

When we got into the car after the service, Willie said, "That was really good."

Yeah. It was. We were quiet on the drive home. I remember feeling lifted inside for the rest of the evening. Another gift. An almost imperceptible change was beginning.

We went back to church week after week, and each week I came home feeling soft. I felt like I wanted to be nicer to people. Corny? Yes. But it was true. That was a small part of our hope. There was hope that I could become a better person. Now, all of this was fine, but I was still waking up every night with night terrors and still would hardly eat anything. Willie was threatening to call the Minirth Meier Clinic and have me put into rehab for an eating disorder. He finally came to me at the end of his rope.

"Maylo, when I first met you, I wanted to be your knight in shining armor so badly. I wanted to just scoop you up and love you until you were well. And, Maylo, I am loving you as much as I can, and you are not getting any better at all. As a matter of fact, you are getting worse. You gotta do something, honey. I am not big enough to fix you; you need something bigger than me."

What?! What does that mean? Are you breaking up with me? If you love me and that is not enough, what am I supposed to do? I can't wake up crying every night for the rest of my life. Why? Why can't you wait?

It never occurred to me that I was exhausting him. It never occurred to me how much of his patience was being tested and how much sleep he was losing.

"Maylo, you need help. Like, you need to see a counselor or something."

I promised him I would ask the associate pastor at the church if he knew where I could go, as long as Willie promised he wouldn't leave.

"I am not going anywhere," he said and took my hand.

Hope.

Decisions... Joe Hemphill, an assistant pastor at the church, was tall. He had a face like Grandpa McCaslin's and a slight twang that suggested he was a transplant in California. His broad shoulders and height made him seem like a tree trunk—big, solid, and permanent—that had been rooted in the ground forever. I met with him, and he referred me to a young counselor.

She and I met twice a week. We did a little of the "pretend your mother is in this chair and tell her how you feel" therapy. That just did not work for me. I wasn't having any major breakthroughs talking to the chair. But I did have several conversations with Pastor Hemphill during the same time. I had questions about Jesus Christ.

Mostly, I needed to talk. I needed to tell someone other than

Willie how much I hurt. How much I hated myself and all that had happened to me. Because Pastor Hemphill would not meet with me alone, Willie had to go with me.

Willie had his own questions and frustrations, so Pastor Hemphill's counseling us together worked out well. Over the next few weeks as we continued to go to church, I was aware of an opening slowly developing inside me—a willingness. Things that once were hard to believe began to make sense to us. Sort of.

This was a completely different world, but it looked and felt safe. Here I could be just Maylo. I didn't have to work so hard to be hip. I didn't have to compete with anything. I didn't have to work the "I'm fine, I'm tough, whatever" posture.

It was great to let go and let some softness come in, but there was the other Maylo, Street Maylo, who was so afraid of losing her coolness if she became a Christian. I was afraid that I would lose my edge, and all of the musicians and übercool people we hung around with would write us off as one of those "born again" nutcases. Then Willie and I would have nowhere to go on Friday nights.

I wanted to be a secret Christian—a double agent, working both worlds. But Pastor Hemphill did not mince words. Nor did he let me linger in my own hurt and self-pity. He offered a solution. He pointed to Jesus Christ, crucified in my place, risen and alive now in those who call him Lord. I heard the words, but I did not know how to let go of my doubt and receive the love of Christ. I couldn't get my arms around what the love of Christ was.

I kept stumbling over my childhood. Where was Christ then? How can a God who loves me allow those things to happen? How is claiming him going to make me heal from all of that? Pastor Hemphill didn't even have to think about it. His answers came swiftly and without wavering.

"Christ was with you every step of the way. He did not forsake you. He loves you so much, Maylo. He was there. When you were hurt, he was hurt. He wept for that little girl . . . and he wept *with* her. He has saved every tear that has fallen from your cheek in a bottle, and each one is precious to him. That is the truth. And he wants to take all of those hurts and throw them in the deepest sea, as far as the East is from the West, and then he wants you to learn how not to go fishing."

I got it. When he said that Christ wept for me as a child—that he saw all of it and wasn't distant and aloof but heartbroken over the magnitude of what was going on, heartbroken over the sin— I understood because I was heartbroken too. I needed to hear that Jesus Christ related. He had compassion and empathy.

Pastor Hemphill led both Willie and me to Christ that day. It was very simple and very mysterious. We bowed our heads together, and after we were finished with the sinner's prayer, he said, "My dear, you are a virgin in the sight of the Lord." And I felt like one. I can't explain it, but it was extremely personal and it was very real. Purity was restored in my heart. I was new and clean both inside and out, and my childhood was my childhood, not my future. I was unstuck. I could move forward now.

Willie and I both wanted to do everything the right way. We didn't want to ruin what was going on, so even though we were living together, he moved into a separate bedroom. *Very* shortly after our "separation," he asked me to marry him.

We were baptized and married on the same day in March 1987. My whole family was there. I found my mother in the same apartment she lived in when I ran away from home—now married to her scriptwriting teacher. She came to the wedding, as did my brother, my sister, Aunt Judy, Grandma Peggy and Bud, Grandpa Harry and Nikki, and my father. That was one side of the church; the other side was filled with actors and comedians and Uptons.

It was a truly fun day. After the wedding, Willie's dad and my Grandpa Harry greeted each other like long-lost friends, as Willie and I watched in surprise. Turns out that they had known each other when serving with their local fire department. Grandpa Harry was very ill in the final stages of cancer, but he made it. He came into the bride's room while I was getting ready and buried his head on my shoulder and just cried and cried. I know that he was so happy to see me marry a good man. He passed away three days after my wedding. The last dance he had was with me on my wedding day. I cherish that memory. I still miss him so much and think about him. I love him and always will.

Did this story have a happy ending? Not exactly, but it had a happy beginning. I still had all of the same struggles. I struggled with food, I struggled with depression, and I still had occasional nightmares. But I was plugged into a good women's Bible study and was growing and learning how to walk through those things. I was learning to rely on God's Word and promises.

Our relationship was being built brick by brick, with God proving himself to me over and over again with peace and fellowship. There were times in my morning devotions when all I could do was slide out of my chair to my knees and cry. At other times I would just thank him over and over again. He gives me overwhelming joy to be alive. To just live.

I was beginning to see through such different eyes.

The To-do List... Willie and I both brought so much baggage to our marriage. While I was praying about and working on my issues, Willie was piecing together his own life. His ex-wife hated him. We had his darling four-year-old son, Christopher, with us on weekends, but saying good-bye each Sunday afternoon was difficult for both father and son.

Willie was also still in the IRS torture chamber, locked in a lawsuit with no end in sight. He went to the IRS on his own. "I don't want any part of this lawsuit. I don't want to be lumped in with all those people. I want to settle right now and pay you. Please." But the IRS said he could not do that. We simply had to wait.

On top of that, his ex-manager was suing him for more than a million dollars. We got served with the papers on Christmas morning. We lived in a tiny apartment near the beach, and I was the one who answered the door. So many people scampering for what was left of Willie's money, while we struggled just to make ends meet, even though Willie was in the middle of good years with *Charles in Charge*.

In spite of the financial difficulties, we were happy. There was a big roadblock in my way, though: I could not get away from the *F* word. It was there every time I went to Bible study. It convicted me and I knew I had to confront it, but I didn't want to. I didn't know who I would become once I had dealt with it.

Forgiveness. I have received such forgiveness. I am washed over and over with forgiveness. My Father in heaven understands my humanity. He knows the motive behind every single offense of mine. And he has forgiven me. And he calls me to forgive as I have been forgiven. That means that I cannot hold on to my anger toward Bernie. I cannot aim my poisoned arrows at my mother anymore. My spirit cannot march around being mad— mad at them, mad at God, mad at myself . . . mad at everyone. God knows that this anger will kill me. It will kill off everything soft inside of me. So he says, "Forgive them. Give it to me. Let me be their judge. You are a child. A child of mine, not a judge. I am a just and righteous God. Give it to me."

Turning my anger over to God was monumental. I had hung on to what happened to me with such a tight grip that I didn't know how to be without it. Maybe that is why people grow bitter. They take all that has happened to them and drape it over them- selves like a thick cape, wrapped up in feeling sorry for themselves.

They make others feel badly for them and eventually believe that their past is who they are. It defines them.

It certainly defined me. I was a rape victim, a runaway. I was the kid who grew up with a psychotic mother. If I were to forgive all of that—forgive the rapes, forgive my mother—who would I be then? Who would I be without all of that to hold in my fist and show to everyone? A scary thought. How do you even begin to tackle that?

I think I'll stay here for now, I'd protest to myself. *I can forgive later when I am older and know more of God's Word and stuff. I'll forgive over time. Yeah. Time heals all wounds, right? This is the Maylo that I am right now. I don't want to let go of her. I am comfortable with her.*

So that is the decision I made: to "get around to" forgiving when I was good and ready. My prayers remained shallow and safe, and my relationship with Jesus remained safe and easy. I was still learning to read my Bible. I was still grateful and full of worship, but I only wanted to learn more about him, not undo myself wholly before him. I didn't want to see what he saw in me that broke his heart. I still could not come close to understanding how much he loved me and how much he wanted me to be healthy.

But that was going to change. All of the forgiving I was going to put off or let happen "in its own time" was about to become first on a new to-do list. A list that suddenly appeared with the utterance of three life-changing words.

"Willie, I'm pregnant."

Welcome, Harleigh Jean... I was tired of being angry. I wanted to nurture my baby and build a home with Willie. I knew that forgiveness was the only way to move past all of the memories and hurts. I just didn't know how to begin.

I knew that in my own strength, I could not forgive Bernie or my mother. I mean, how in the world do you start something like that? What was I supposed to do? Just say, "I forgive you," over and over until I convinced myself that I had done it? And then I can get up and walk away all better and tidy and released? Wouldn't that be nice?

Nope. That's not how it works. I simply could not muster up the mercy in my heart. There was only one way I could even begin the process, and that was to pray for them—consistently.

God's Word tells me over and over to forgive. It is a running theme. In Mark 11:25 Jesus says, "And whenever you stand praying, if you have anything against anyone, forgive him, so that your Father in heaven will also forgive you your wrongdoing." *Whenever* I stand praying. Anything, against anyone. And in Luke 6:27–28 Jesus says, "Love your enemies, do good to those who hate you, bless those who curse you, pray for those who mistreat you."

Pray for Bernie, pray for my mother. My insides boiled when I sat before God to pray for them. At first I couldn't think of one thing to say, mostly because I didn't want to be doing it at all. "Lord, I pray for . . . Bernie (ugh). Lord, I pray for my mother."

That was all I could do. And I only did that out of obedience to God's Word and because I was in love with the One who forgave me. I wasn't motivated out of love for Bernie or my mother at all. The motive was immature, but it was enough. God doesn't get angry just because we are immature. When I become a mature Christian, he isn't going to love me any more than he does right now. I was simply willing to do it.

Every day I prayed the same thing. And I always asked God to forgive me for having such a hard time forgiving them. And eventually, I began to soften. I began to feel something for them both when I said, "Lord, I pray for them." My grip loosened. It was no longer about what they did to me. It wasn't between me and them—it became something intimate between me and God.

Eventually I was able to ask God to show me Bernie and my mother as he sees them, so I would see them through his eyes. I kept asking for that and for wisdom and mercy and discernment regarding *any* enemies I had. When that happened, I found myself weeping for them.

My heart and my spirit belonged to God—no longer to the past—and I could see them as the terribly broken people they were and are. And I knew that I had moved on and that they were still sick. They needed the one true God so badly. Today when I pray for them, the motive of my heart is decent and real. I hope God is merciful with them and that they can find him and be set free.

I did not lose my identity when I forgave. Not at all. There was a Maylo that was much truer underneath all that stuff. I was released from the bondage of attaching myself to what had happened to me and was free to discover who God created me to be. I was learning that the closer I got to Jesus, the closer I got to myself. When people say, "I have to find myself," I think, *You can't find yourself without Jesus.*

I was learning this. I was a very happy girl. My innocence was being restored little by little.

My husband was also healing. He was broke financially, but we were having a good life. He often took week-long fishing trips and would come home with a couple hundred pounds of tuna that we would put in our freezer. With a twenty-pound bag of jasmine rice from the nearby Asian market, we were set for fresh, fragrant dinners that cost us almost nothing.

Willie had made amends with his family, and he took a fishing trip with his father for more than a week. Willie's mother and I enjoyed each other's company very much, but I woke up feeling bad the day the men were expected to return. I began to cramp and started to run a fever. As Willie and his father walked through the door that Sunday afternoon, I tried to meet him, holding a little pacifier in my hands that I wanted to show him, but I didn't make it to the door. I was having a miscarriage. Willie's parents called their physician, and we met her at her office. Willie waited in the lobby. That was the first time that I can remember seeing my husband cry.

The miscarriage was pretty tough. Afterward I wondered if my body would be able to carry a baby to term because of the conization surgery. I thought about Bernie and my mother, and I was angry. But it wasn't that raging, burning, awful anger that consumed me before. It was sort of calm; it didn't toss me around. I was angry, but I could take it right to God. I could get on my face and just give it to him.

"Lord, I belong to you. My children belong to you. My future belongs to you, and I totally and completely trust you. Lord, it hurts. I wanted that baby. I pray that your will would be done in my life, Lord. Help me, Jesus. I love you so much."

Of course, there were times when I would just get on my knees and cry. He was there for all of it. His presence would quiet me. And then peace would come. No words. Just peace.

Life began to return to normal, and just a few weeks later we found out I was pregnant again. Or maybe I should say simply I was pregnant because the doctor told me he suspected that this pregnancy was, in fact, part of the original pregnancy. That's right—the baby to come was probably a twin of the baby who had miscarried. Is God amazing or what?

This time my OB/GYN had me lie down and rest for the third term of my pregnancy. I gained sixty pounds and felt like a human water balloon. I was bored to tears from lack of activity yet totally excited at the same time, watching *Oprah* every day and living on cold strawberries.

It was mah-vel-ous! It was July in California and hotter than I could bear. I got myself a kiddie pool, filled it with water, and took my big belly and ridiculous hat and lay down in the tiny pool in the backyard. That was where I stayed most of the time until the day of our daughter's birth, July 21, 1990.

It was a difficult birth. Harleigh Jean Upton, whom Willie today calls our miracle baby, got stuck in the birth canal, and, of course, the epidural numbed only one side of me. I was told afterward that another pregnancy would be problematic, which at the time was fine. I was grateful to have one child, considering all that my body had been through, and besides, I needed to experience passing a Mack truck through my body only once in my life, thank you very much.

We Can't Stay Here...So why did I suffer from postpartum depression? I don't know. But the baby blues were awful.

While I was doing my best to cope, the IRS notified us that the lawsuit had finally come to an end. The firm lost, and all of the clients were stuck holding the bill. The lawsuit took almost seven years, and the penalty fees were made retroactive, turning an original $32,000 bill into hundreds of thousands of dollars.

At the same time, *Charles in Charge* was wrapping up its last few episodes. Every month that went by without a payment to the IRS increased the penalty, which grew and grew no matter what we did. Making the huge monthly payment was nearly impossible, and the payment never seemed to put a dent in the principal. Child-support payments, alimony, attorneys, agents, and, of course, income taxes meant that there wasn't much left.

Willie was trying to think of what we were going to do. What would come after *Charles in Charge* went down? He began to feel a burden and talked to me about it.

"Maylo, we can't stay here."

"What? What are you saying?"

"We aren't going to make it here in California. We will stumble as Christians, and we won't be able to make it financially."

I understood, and he was right. It was too hard in Hollywood for us to really grow in the Lord. For years we had established ourselves as totally different people than we were now, and our old contacts didn't get it. They thought the whole God thing was a phase or something. It was too tempting to go back to our old ways. Even with a passion for Christ, the old friends and the good times we had together at the bars sometimes just sounded easier.

But where would we go? We didn't have family anywhere but in California. We didn't have jobs anywhere. We had only acting. We had only auditions and waiting tables and construction.

We decided to rent a motor home and go looking. We tooled through Idaho, Utah, and Washington. Harleigh screamed the whole way, and we came home with no real plan, but having seen the difference in the cost of living, we were more open to a life somewhere outside of California.

Then Willie got a phone call from a friend who owned a bait and fuel dock in the harbor. His father holds one of the world's richest marlin fishing tournaments in Mexico every year. Would Willie consider filming it and making it a show they could possibly air on ESPN? They would not be able to pay us—we had to laugh at that—but Willie could fish the tournament with the other anglers and maybe receive some sort of back-end payment.

Willie was more than happy to take the job. He has always loved Mexico and had fished for marlin all over the world but hadn't caught one. Willie's marlin story is his to tell, and he will,[13]

---

13. Willie's story of the marlin tournament is in the transcript of our conversation in the last section of this book.

but here is what he told me after he stumbled home: "God and I had a twenty-one-and-a-half-hour talk the whole time I was pulling on that fish, Maylo."

Yep. The fish story is one of those that, in retrospect, really show the hand of God in our lives. We both were in prayer for guidance as to what to do. Willie, being a strong man who had spent much of his life on the ocean, needed his own personal experience with God that would just knock him out. Willie needed for God to show him, without a doubt, that he was there. Real. The fish was it. God was huge. He was mighty. He was real, and he was getting ready to pack us up and move us to a whole new place. A Kansas City producer who saw the tournament on TV offered Willie a job working on a weekly fishing show.

Leeks and Onions... That fish is how the Lord got us to the Midwest. We boarded a plane thinking, *No more slavery! Yea! New Promised Land of milk and honey!* We were relieved to kiss the financial burden of living in Southern California good-bye. The cost of living in the Midwest was so much lower.

It was exciting to start over. We had no way of knowing that the job Willie took in Kansas would not exist within seven months, leaving us in a strange city with no job and hardly any contacts— like the children of Israel in Numbers 11:5 who cried out for leeks and onions. At least in L.A. we knew people. At least we had this . . . at least we had that—the negative thoughts went on and on. We were like the Israelites in more ways than one.

All we had in Kansas were our little Calvary Chapel church and our home Bible studies. And a ton of fear and stress. And a beautiful, curly-haired, happy girl who knew that bunnies ran wild everywhere, snow came down silently while Mommy baked, and *Sesame Street* was there for her every day. God had put us right where he needed us to be: at a loss. Dumbfounded. With nowhere to turn.

There in Kansas, over the next several years, was where my faith was hammered out. There on the prairie is where God kept his promises, one after another in real, tangible ways.

He taught me to cling to him by removing all other stable footing. Sometimes the only thing that didn't seem to be spinning out of control was the floor, and I spent many, many hours with my face on it, praying, leaving wads of wet, mangled tissue behind me from room to room. God's Word became my only hope and my peace.

Still, learning to trust was *hard*. I wasn't getting out of bed every morning and cozying up with coffee and a blanket to have a sweet time with Jesus then acting gracious and peaceable afterward. Of course, some days were like that, and those days were the reward—the hope. A lot of the days in the beginning were too honest to be cozy. They were convicting. They burned because I had to face what was in my heart. God's beautiful Word revealed everything about me. And I could see it for what it was, for what I am in the flesh, without him.

But I never felt that he was ashamed of me. His Word told me over and over, everywhere, that he loves me, that I am the apple of his eye, his beloved who is more costly than the finest gold. And the more I stayed in his Word, the more *consistent* I was in my devotions, the more God's Word began to define my reality.

The forgiveness—all that work I had to do—had to keep going. The walk was just beginning. God's reality, which is the only true reality, was growing deep roots. I came before him so many times, asking for forgiveness for my selfishness, my gluttony, my laziness, my doubt.

And even with all that, his Word tells me in Isaiah 61:3 that he will give me a crown of beauty instead of ashes. I give him my ashes; he gives me beauty. And for me to have ashes, something had to burn up. Fire is devastating and hot and feared. No one willingly walks into a fire.

That being said, let's talk about Bibleman. I know you want to. You are curious or angry at Willie. Or you feel confused, right?

Bibleman came to us unexpectedly. All that I can say is this: When you throw open your arms and cry out to God with all your heart, "I am yours, Lord! Do whatever you want to with me. Slay me. Humble me. Use me. Only love me in it. That is all that I need," be prepared to go the distance with no safety net. You will have no choice.

Why would God use Willie in this way? We do not know. We are so flawed. And Willie never would have thought that he would ever minister to anyone. When we got the phone call to consider doing Bibleman, Willie said no. But the phone kept ringing. They would not give up. One producer even said, "Willie, you need to face it and get on board. It has already been decided—you are Bibleman."

Willie's stock answer for everything is "I will pray about it for three days." That's what he did. And soon he was hopping up and down in a dressing room, trying to get blue spandex over his hips. A cape, a mask, groovy boots, and, most likely, no pride left—there he stood. Ta da! Ex-teen idol, Christian superhero extraordinaire. "Hi, kids." (Cheesy smile.) "I'm Bibleman."

We had no idea what we'd gotten into. We did not speak Christianese. Willie was never the tucked-in, clean-cut example of what a Christian man looks like . . . whatever that is. He was a regular broken man with pride and issues and a willingness to do whatever it took to get the message of Jesus Christ to kids.

A lot of things happened during those ten long years while at home I was raising our daughter almost as a single parent. I could feel opposition to what we were doing—spiritual warfare—and even objections from some within the church who felt that Willie's place was at home leading his family, not out on the road. The thing is, no one can speak for another man. No one was with Willie when he prayed about yet another year on the road. No one but our family was in the living room when it was discussed, and no one on the outside could make those decisions for us. It all was between Willie and the Lord. And I was always asked about it. If I had ever said, "I need you to be home," the touring would have been over. After God, his family is the most important thing in the world to my husband, and I never once felt anything less from Willie.

Jesus Christ stepped in for my husband while he was on the road. I felt his presence in my loneliness many times. (You never notice how much church is centered on family activities until you are alone.)

Harleigh and I went through so much together. Once we even got hit by a small tornado that tossed our six-foot privacy fence around the neighborhood like toothpicks and ripped off pieces of our roof. We were in the basement underneath a mattress with two dogs and two cats and water pouring down the walls, but the solid presence of the Holy Spirit surrounded the small space with stillness and peace.

I understand being lonesome at night after the kids are in bed. I spent years praying, "Lord, be my husband. I need to feel you . . . to be kept company. I need for you to be here with me when Willie cannot."

And I learned that my prayer is one that should never be neglected—even when a husband *is* home all the time. I learned that Willie is my best friend, my partner, and my companion, but that Jesus Christ is truly my husband. He is perfect in every way and trustworthy.

Men make mistakes. Women make mistakes. We make decisions for the wrong reasons. We try not to, but we struggle with our pride, our lusts, our weaknesses. We are works in progress. If someone is in the public eye, that person's mistakes are there for everyone to see. In our case, they are rerun on national TV over and over.

We can feel the judgment of others.[14] It is humiliating, harsh, and hurtful. And it is not wasted on Harleigh, who is now a teenager. All I can do is allow my husband, my daughter, my neighbors, myself, and the congregation to be human. I can't expect any of them to be God. Only God is God.

I can trust God to stay true to his Word. As much as I love my husband, he is just a man. I love him because he *tries* to do the right thing. He certainly does not hit the bull's-eye every time, and, God knows, neither do I. I have all sorts of issues: I have ridiculous fears, I cry too easily, or I am always in some sort of health crisis.[15] But we accept it all. Every single morning I walk into the bathroom and see my husband on his knees in the shower. *Every* morning.

So whatever the fear or issue, I know that I am praying about it and my husband is praying about it, and I can exhale.

We are grateful for the Bibleman experience. We thank everyone who ever bothered to show up for a live show or purchase a video. If any good came from any of it, you all know by now that it had nothing to do with us. It was God ministering to your children and to my family.

Willie finally suffered a severe back injury after so many years on the road. His knees have been operated on, and his back surgery was the final blow to his superhero body. Good-bye, Bibleman. Thanks for the memories.

---

14. We felt judgment particularly in regard to Willie's appearance on *Celebrity Fit* in 2005, which he talks about at the end of this book.
15. After years dealing with some puzzling symptoms, I was diagnosed with lupus in 2004. I explain more about my battle with lupus in the conversation at the end of this book.

WILLE

Bibleman Goes on the Road...

They were grown men—strong, travel-toughened men who were used to being away from their families for weeks and months at a time. And they were crying. Crying. And all I could do was to say, "OK. After this show, we're going to head home. After the next gig, we're turning around. We're going home, and we're taking some time off."

I called the church where we were to appear next and found out that, like many of the previous churches, the next church did not have its contracted safety constructions and other requirements in place for the show. I simply told the pastor, "Gig's canceled."

"Well, I'm just going to trust God that he'll deliver you to our church."

"No, sir. We're heading in the other direction as we speak. We're not coming. You've had eight weeks to get everything in place, and I cannot expose my guys to the safety hazards."

This was one of the lowest points in the entire Bibleman touring ministry. Grown men so let down, so disillusioned, and so exhausted emotionally and physically that they simply stared at the unprepared auditorium and wept. Let me backtrack a little.

I had become a Christian during the last days of *Charles in Charge*. Both Maylo and I accepted Christ the same day in

Joe Hemphill's office. After some months of discipleship, we were baptized together one Sunday morning, March 15, 1987, and married the same afternoon. There have been few moments as deeply emotional and as spiritually beautiful as watching the love of my life, my best friend, become my sister in Christ and then having her presented to me that evening as my new bride in Christ.

For more than two years I'd felt a deep urge to leave California. It's one of the few times I can say that I was being called by God to make a change. In fact, the urge was bordering on panic. We had to cut the ties; we had to leave if our faith was to survive. A door finally opened and led us to Kansas City, Kansas. Our new environment seemed tailored to the spiritual needs of my family.

When we arrived in Kansas City, we were exhausted and needed to heal and rest. The pastor of the small church we started attending said that as he prayed to understand why we had landed at this unlikely location, he kept hearing the word *exploited* in his prayers.

We spent nearly five years just studying the Bible and looking for direction from God as to what he wanted us to do. I paid the bills by working for an advertising firm and a cable installation company. I didn't think that I was automatically going to be a Christian celebrity. In fact, I was betting against it. I told God that I was completely his. "Lord, I want to be obedient," I prayed. "Whatever you want and wherever you want me, tell me to do it. I'll do whatever you want me to do."

Be very careful what you pray for. It wasn't long before I was confronted with becoming Bibleman, the visible personification of the Christian superhero in the video series.

To be honest, the last thing I wanted was to be in children's ministry. I don't even like kids all that much. I'm just not the type that's dying to get down and play with the little guys. I think my own kids are great, but I don't expect anyone else to. In fact, I get very uncomfortable when people show me pictures of their off-spring. Show me pictures of your dog, your goldfish, your belly-button lint collection—*anything* but your kids. What if they're not exactly pleasant to the eye? What am I supposed to say? "Gee . . . yep, that's quite a child!" I can't bring myself to lie that well. Before you start writing angry e-mails and accuse me of being a fraud, hear me out.

I was not all that thrilled about a concept I found to be cheesy at best. Give me a break. Bibleman? So what's he do? Battle Koran-man? Worse than that, as I spoke with my pastor about the role and we prayed about it, I grew fearful of the responsibility. Adults can make up their own minds, but teaching the "lambs" about God's Word is a very different story. I would become accountable to God for everything I taught or didn't teach. The Bible is very specific about the consequences for false teachers.

But the more I tried to get out of the situation, the more I couldn't escape the growing evidence that God wanted me there. And the more I thought about the possibilities, the more I realized that a touring Bibleman could be an opportunity to reach huge numbers of children and teens at a time that might mark a turning point in their lives. It was a spiritual beckoning to obedience, and I had to accept it. It was great that the Bibleman videos were out there, but if we really wanted to make a difference in children's lives, we had to be there with them. To talk to them. To look them directly in the eyes.

I don't want to leave you with the impression that I hate kids. I don't. I just wouldn't say I had a "heart" for children's ministry. And I think God wanted to take me out of my comfort zone.

I like to look at Paul's example. Paul was a Jew's Jew. He abso-lutely loved Jewish people. You would say that Paul had a "heart" for the Jewish people. But God didn't call him to the Jews. He sent him to the Gentiles. And through Paul's obedience, we have one of the greatest ministries of all time.

The Holy Spirit would give me the patience, the passion, and the vision to turn Bibleman into a productive children's touring show. At the end of those ministry years, God's blessings on our team's obedience showed itself—nearly 900,000 children had come forward to accept Christ through the Bibleman ministry.

Once I took on the challenge of touring, I began ten years of great blessing paired with great frustration. I learned about my tolerance for imperfection in myself and others, and, unfortunately, I learned some things about people who call themselves Christians.

The *Bibleman Live* show was elaborate, featuring full costumes along with jaw-dropping special effects (including the largest laser light show in the country and pyrotechnics). At the end of each show, I would take off the mask and make it clear that neither wearing the suit nor Bibleman defeating villains made me Bibleman. The only thing that made me Bibleman was my relationship with Jesus Christ. Without that, I was just a man in a suit. I asked that the kids never follow Bibleman or any man. Instead, follow Christ alone because as a man I would let them down. Jesus would never let them down. I also insisted on an invitation.

For the first four years, the company behind Bibleman sent me out on the road with a crew of three guys: Marc Wayne, who played the character Coats; Brian Lemmons, who played all of the evil villains; and Chad Plummer, a kid we found at a church in Fort Smith, Arkansas. Each of us had multiple tasks, from running lights and sound to climbing the ceiling-high pedestals and inching our way across the swaying trusses to focus the lights. One year turned into two, two into four, and four into ten, touring all over the United States. We were sometimes gone for forty-five to fifty days at a time. We rarely went home even on holidays, with the exception of Christmas.

We traveled in a twenty-four-foot box truck that we had converted into a motor home, towing a twenty-eight-foot trailer loaded with gear and equipment. Most of the bookings were in large churches, and their contract rider with us specified that they were to have "X" number of assistants, "X" feet of stage, a ramp for us to unload our heavy cases and props on, safety regulations in place for pyrotechnics, and so on.

It became almost routine to arrive at a gig and discover that not only was the church unprepared, but they were going to try to negotiate us down on our requirements—specifications that were put into place for stringent safety reasons, not for our egos.

Before arriving at each booking, one of the guys called ahead to make sure the contracted measures were in place.

"I'm calling from the Bibleman tour. We are checking to make sure that you have the twenty-four feet of space for our lighting equipment before we arrive."

"We don't have twenty-four, but we have twenty. Will that work?"

Inevitably I would have to get on the phone. "This is Willie Aames. No, we need twenty-four. We can't safely light the pyrotechnics with only twenty feet of surround space. This is a minimum requirement."

Similar discussions would ensue about how high the lights were supposed to be, if platforms were in place, and so on. More often than not, our church contacts would think these items were negotiable. We would arrive at the venue only to find that the show's equipment and safety specifications were not met. So off to Home Depot one of the crew would go, with me fronting the money for plywood, circular saws, screw guns, and other necessities. We would build the stage ourselves within a day, and the show would go on.

We charged a moderate, flat ticket price, and we did not take up an offering. The goal of *Bibleman Live* was that an entire family could enjoy a top-quality laser-light show without breaking the bank—a show with first-rate special effects that presented the gospel in such a cool way that no kid of any age, adults included, would cringe at a cheesy, churchy show.

To make a show work for different ages, the fun is in the writing. I'd write dialogue that specifically spoke to boys aged six to eleven, making them laugh. Then I'd write in some gags for Mom and Dad, catching them off guard and getting them laughing too. Perhaps the most fun was inserting some underground, hip, dry understated humor to haul in the teens.

Bibleman Live did seem to cross the age barrier. After each show a four-hour-long line of children and their parents would form—each person waiting to shake hands, take a picture, and be encouraged or prayed over.

We did not get behind a counter to sell T-shirts, videos, or anything else. All of the money went directly to the corporation, not to us, for the items sold. If churches wanted to sell them, fine, but we did not get involved—doing so would have compromised our message.

Unfortunately, we witnessed some unethical behavior in making money off the show at more than one church. One church stands as a disheartening example of pastoral money-mongering. It was in Florida, and the local ABC, NBC, CBS, and Fox news affiliates showed up to interview me for the evening news.

Just before I came on, the senior pastor stood up and announced, "Well, kids, it's time for us to take our offering." And the cameras rolled on. "We've got to give some money to Bibleman so that he can survive! Bibleman's just trying to make it down the road, and without your donations, Bibleman won't have gas or food. Kids, I want you to stand up."

The seats creaked as three thousand children rose from their seats with their parents. "Now, kids, scream in your parents' faces, 'Give Bibleman money!'"

Backstage, I was doing backflips. I was so angry, I was spitting rubberbands—well, almost. At my instruction, one of the guys called all the reporters backstage. "I want you all to know that in no way do I have anything at all to do with that request for money," I announced. "We have never taken money. We take a flat fee." Let's just say that we were never invited back to that church.

I had no problem with a church taking a love offering to offset its costs of putting on the event, and in fact, a majority of the churches did take one. It was no small commitment to have our show there. But claiming the money was for Bibleman was another story.

We also experienced some freak-show treatment from people who were supposed to arrange sleeping accommodations for us. One night's lodging we'd rather forget was in either Michigan or Indiana. We had been driving late into the night, and we arrived, exhausted, at 3:00 a.m. A church member took us to the hotel. As we opened the door to each room, we immediately noticed the smell of urine. But that wasn't the worst of it—there were bedbugs and fleas. We called the night auditor and had him send in someone with new sheets, but then we just fell onto the beds—we were too tired.

The next morning the senior pastor arrived. "How's everybody doing today?" he asked cheerfully.

"We're exhausted," I answered. "And I think you should know in case you bring anybody else into that hotel that it is a dive. It's filthy and disgusting. Even the cockroaches think so."

"Yeah, well, I know," he said. "I would never put my family there, but it is owned by one of the church elders, and you know church politics. "

What's the right answer for such a comment? I said, "You mean you put a guest in a dump that you wouldn't let your own family go into but then pass it off as church politics?"

And yet, my crew kept on. In spite of the negative experiences, we often met some of the dearest, most honest, most caring people I have ever had the honor to call friend, brother, or sister in Christ. For ministries that had little to give, we often waived the flat fee or gave it back to the church. Most of the people we worked with were the real deal, reflecting the love and joy of Christ in their eyes.

One was a pastor in Miami, Oklahoma. His church wasn't a big one, but that didn't matter. *People* were what mattered to him. That man's name is Carrol, and I have watched him sacrifice his own needs for the sake of someone less fortunate for years. I look up to him and only hope that after I've been a Christian as long as he has, I will have his joy and selflessness. What an example.

And then there was Sondra Sonders, the children's ministry director at a megachurch that seats eight thousand to ten thousand per service. For forty years Sondra has watched her church grow; she's lived through church splits, gossip, and heartache but has kept on. Her gifts and her wisdom I deeply admire, but even more amazing is her relationship with Jesus. Her personal walk is as evident and vibrant as any new believer's.

So many believers who have grown up in the church think that if you haven't slept with rats, shot heroin through your eyeballs, or been in prison, your testimony is nothing special. Nothing could be further from the truth. You are the encouragement that keeps the rest of us going. Your stable, caring attitude and your forgiveness are what we came looking for. I think of that day Maylo and I walked into that church. Without people like you, Sondra, and Carrol, we might not be Christians today.

The rewards of *Bibleman Live* were mostly worth the sacrifices. The ultimate rewards were the kids' responses.

We got to Oklahoma City not long after Timothy McVeigh's truck bombs blew up the Murrah Federal Building, killing 168 people. We arrived emotionally and physically used up and ready to go home. We sat down and prayed, "Lord, if this isn't your will, let us know, because we're near the end of our rope. If this is just ego and the flesh, pull the plug, tear it down. It's got to be for your glory. If it's not your will for us to continue, please give us a sign." We got up and dispersed to our assigned duties.

The show started. I walked through the middle of the set onto the front of the stage. In the very first row sat a small boy, nine years old. Someone backstage had told me his name was Ben. He was missing both his legs and had walked on his hands to see Bibleman because no one would give him a ride. As the show started, we all looked at each other and said, "OK. All right. Let's give this our best shot."

That night about 30 percent of the kids in the audience were either victims of the bomb blasts or friends or relatives of someone who was. They wanted to know why God had taken their parents, brother, sister, or friend. As usual, I stayed around after the show, signing autographs, talking, and praying. The hurt, the anger, the loneliness—God put us in that place to address those issues in the name of Jesus Christ. We knew it, and that's why we kept on.

A time in Kentucky also encouraged us. A really likable boy showed up as part of the church's work team. Something about him pulled at me, and I told him, "You're going to work with me all day, OK?" I taught him how to set up the pyrotechnics, and he hung around with us that day.

Just before the show started, he asked, "Can you come and meet my mom?"

I asked one of the guys to bring her backstage with the boy. When I met her, she was crying. "You have no idea what you've done for my boy."

"I'm just hanging around with him. He's a great kid."

She said, "I know. You don't know, do you? His sister was the first girl shot in Paducah. She was the one who said she believed in God, and the kid shot her in the head. She's been in the hospital."[16]

The mother said that she herself had that day been released from a psychiatric hospital where she had been getting counseling to cope with her terrible ordeal.

I was just being obedient. That's what it's about. Obedience. It isn't glamorous, and at times I wasn't an outstanding example of the trait. If I sat the crew down today and we reminisced, I have a feeling that they'd say, "Yeah, well, Willie was not exactly the perfect role model, truth be told."

They'd be right. The deep-seated hostility underneath my personality would surface from time to time, and I'd let fly with some choice words from my past. I'm not proud of pre-Christian Willie. I am flawed, and I know it. I am just a man. But through Christ even the toughest of old habits can be stamped out, and they will be.

We *all* worked hard, and I think it was to the glory of God. In the years we were on the road, nearly a million kids filled out cards at the end of our shows. We'd stay around for as long as it took to talk with any kid who wanted to learn more about Jesus or just share a heartache or a need with us. We knew that some of the children wanting to meet us might not be returning to a Christian home. Some would be returning to a dysfunctional family and maybe even a violent existence. We had to make it clear that it was safe to speak their needs and fears with us. And speak they did. We had many children open up and tell us things they wouldn't or couldn't tell anyone else.

In October 2002, during the last year of the Bibleman tours,

---

16. In 1997, a fourteen-year-old student at Heath High School opened fire on a large prayer group that met before school, killing three students and wounding five others.

John Muhammed and Lee Boyd Malvo were carrying out their sniper shootings in the D.C. area. It was a scary, uncertain time for children and their parents since some of the shootings occurred right outside a school.

We had a booking at a church that could seat ten thousand. Thirteen shootings had already occurred, and the suspects were still at large. I called the pastor.

"How far are you from where the sniper shootings have occurred?" I asked.

"A few miles . . . well, really, about a mile."

I said, "I don't think we're coming."

His answer surprised me: "You have a spirit of fear."

"I'll tell you what," I answered. "I don't like it. Let's keep an eye on it."

Shortly thereafter the sniper wrote a note: "Your children are next."

I called the church and said, "Sorry, but we're canceling."

"But you can't. We'll sue you."

"So you want me just to serve up four thousand or five thousand kids at a highly publicized event with dates and times printed in the newspaper—you're an idiot. Gig canceled unless the sniper is caught."

The snipers were caught the next day, and we did do the show.

But we did have to cancel personal appearances from time to time. Death threats against me were not uncommon—after all, as Bibleman, I had a high-profile Christian persona. A lot of people hated everything I stood for. But the real concern was the hordes of children who would be in the same area with me. We had no choice but to cancel at times, sometimes making our local contacts angry.

Sometimes, though not all the time, those people were the same ones who wanted to compromise our safety or expected us just to make do with the supplies they provided. That last year financial support was nonexistent.

By the time I began the last tour, many changes had taken place. All of the original team was gone. I was physically worn out, trying to keep going with a cervical disk problem that was getting worse every day. I was looking forward to being home more with my family, who had sacrificed years of birthdays and holidays with Dad for our ministry.

Unfortunately, I did not have the opportunity to decide when and how I'd make my exit as Bibleman. I didn't see what was coming until it hit me like a brick at the end of 2003.

I had notified the backing company that surgery was necessary to correct my seriously herniated disk. Within days of that notification, I was released from the company. Being let go sent me into a tailspin like I have never experienced or thought I could experience. And worse, I was disillusioned with other Christians.

But when I think of those times when we were worn out and lonely and then would spend five hours signing autographs and praying with those kids and their parents, I'm amazed that I have been blessed so much. Laughing and sharing with kids, I know it was God who made those evenings what they were.

MAYLO

Season to Season... I am sitting here now on the threshold of a new season. It is almost as if the sun has changed. The light is different, and the shadows of the past are cast behind me now, and I see the outlines of all of those people—my mother, Bernie, Sean, and all of those in between—only when I turn my head to look back. And they are only shadows. They don't look real anymore. In front of me are light and open space. Possibilities.

Harleigh is fully grown and ready to leave home soon. She has watched me bend my knees and open my hands all her life. Her expectations of this world are realistic, and her faith in God is limitless. She has seen him work. She has met my mother. She knows it is a miracle that I am who I am today. It is only because of Jesus Christ.

My mother is institutionalized now, and I have no idea where Bernie is. My father lives near us in Kansas City, and my brother and sister live in other states and have families of their own. I pray that they find freedom from their painful pasts.

Willie is off in the Yukon for weeks at a time, shooting wildlife shows for the Outdoor Network. He lives in tents and sits still in trees as bears and elk and moose and all kinds of living creatures come out of the woods around him. He misses his family, but this is Willie. This is the man I married. God meets him in the wild. Willie is the truest Willie when he is in the wild or on the ocean. Creation grounds him, not Hollywood.

During the course of writing this book, we suffered the losses of Molly, our beloved golden retriever who sat at my feet for fifteen years while I did my Bible studies and prayed, and of Gretchen, a gorgeous tenderhearted rottweiler who was the best mother I ever had.

I have canned twenty-eight quarts of tomato sauce from my garden. But now it is almost time to put the ground to sleep for the winter, to clear away what was once productive and fruitful and let it all rest and breathe and prepare for next spring. The kids have started school for the year, and the neighborhood is still. My house is quiet. Women's Bible studies are starting up at church. The familiar rhythm of the season of harvest has begun.

This book has been a work of my heart. And even with all that was said, so much more is left. So many "God moments" I would love to share. Maybe another day.

For now, I can only testify of his faithfulness. I can only encourage those of you who are lonely, broken, ugly, selfish, addicted, hopeless, immature, imprisoned, and afraid. He is real. I scoffed once too, but it is true. He heals. He forgives. He loves you. He loves you so much more than you are allowing yourself to believe. Don't be afraid to let go of your edge, your anger.

If you look my way, you will see me leaning on my Beloved. I am just like you. I wasn't sure. I didn't want to do the work. I was too lazy to be devoted. But he loved me anyway. He fed me with his words and with bittersweet experiences. He allowed me the room to doubt—room to find my own faith in the simple choice to believe him. He let me think. And when I wavered, when I wanted to fall, just to stop trying and fall backward, he showed up. Smiling. An answered prayer would land in my lap or show up in my living room, and I would feel his embrace. No falling. Only believing.

He knows where you have been—physically, privately, and emotionally. Every tear you have shed is in his hands. It was squeezed out of his heart. He felt it with you. Believe it. You are the apple of his eye, his precious child. You have a testimony. You are a trophy of his grace, and I know that he wants to give back to you what was taken. He desires to see you heal and love you and for you to know him.

There is a puppy in our house now—a small, energetic ball of fluff who thinks she is big. All things are new to her: the rain, a bug, cheese, a rotten tomato that has fallen off the vine. Every day is exciting. And she is in training, discovering what the boundaries are here. She is evidence to me of God's love. I wept and wept when Molly died, and soon after I absorbed the blow of Gretchen's death. It was so painful, but he who loves me knew my heart. He knew how to restore my joy.

"Maylo, I will give you Beatrice. She will be warm and will sleep on you and snore and bark at your cats and chew your nose and hair, and you won't be able to catch her when you want to. She will need you, Maylo, for everything. She is a baby. And it is a new time. For you, for her, for us. You do not know the plans I have for you. Enjoy Beatrice and rest in me. I am here always and forever, and your future in me is more than you could ever hope or dream because I love you."

I love you, too, Lord. Thank you.

WILLIE

Of Spandex and Hope... There are so many great memories from my time of wearing spandex for Jesus that I would need another several hundred pages to share them, plus another few hundred to write of the craziness of growing up in Hollywood. The message I continue to believe in is one of unending grace, unconditional love, and hope. So many miss the message. We have access to the one true God—the God of all that wonderful creation. It is a message of hope. If we have that hope, we can endure.

People ask me how to start a ministry like Bibleman. And I say that I don't know. Go ask God.

I never set out to be a Christian role model or a national children's pastor. And never could I have imagined the blessings that have been lavished on me by my Lord Jesus Christ. I have one last story that may illustrate more vividly what I am saying.

A couple of years ago the Make-a-Wish Foundation contacted me. They had a boy with a wish to spend a day with Bibleman, going bowling and eating pizza. I was burned out and wanted some rest before I headed back out on the road. All I could think of was me, me, and more me. But I agreed to go.

What a day we had. I arrived by limo, decked out in full cos-tume—battle weapons and all—with some genuine props and keepsakes from the Bibleman set. I picked up my new friend, a rosy-cheeked boy who wore thick glasses. We bowled a few rounds and ate pizza, daring each other to eat more than the other. His neighborhood friends and family came to his house afterward to enjoy cake made by his sweet, godly mother. His father and I exchanged fishing and hunting stories and life lessons we had learned in our walks with Christ.

As I leaned back in the limo after warm hugs and promises to pray for each other and stay in touch, I reflected on the depth and reality of what had happened that day.

Imagine that you have a terminal condition. You know your death is certain. Someone tells you that they will grant your last wish—anything you want. If you want to go somewhere, name it. If you want to meet someone famous, just tell us who.

Think about it. If I were dying, I cannot think of anyone on this planet outside of my family whom I would want to see. I can't think of anyone else or anywhere else that would qualify as my last wish. Yet that ten-year-old boy wanted to spend the day with Bibleman.

I am not suggesting he wanted to spend the day with *me*. No, not at all. He wanted to spend the day with Bibleman, the charac-ter. I believe that the power of the message brought by Jesus Christ became a foundation of hope for my friend. Bibleman became an ambassador of God's promises.[17]

At times, I loathed squeezing into that spandex. And on some days I was so tired that I would have given anything to get out of

---

17. I saw him several more times when his parents brought him to cities where we per-formed. We also talked often on the phone. Sadly, the last few phone calls were to him in his hospital bed. Several times he stopped eating and his parents would call me, and I'd call him to encourage him to eat. I still remember him daring me to race him down the hospital corridor—him in his wheelchair, me lying belly first on a skateboard to keep the race even. I'll see him again in heaven.

signing autographs for five hours. But God blessed our efforts. In spite of me, in spite of what I had a heart for, his grace and power blessed both the show and the video series.

The only thing I set out to do was be obedient. That's one thing I'm glad I did.

WILLIE AND MAYLO

A Conversation... *The following conversation took place recently at the Olathe, Kansas, home of Willie Aames and Maylo Upton when the two were interviewed by Carolyn Goss.*

CAROLYN GOSS: As you became Christians and got into the Christian life, did you meet any other Christians in the TV world?

WILLIE AAMES: There weren't any other Christians on *Charles in Charge*. When we made our commitments [to Christ], I don't remember any huge changes at first. I had been quite a partier before that. I just didn't do drugs anymore. At first I just had to look out for what I was saying. I was watching out for double-entendre stuff in the show jokes and so on.

Toward the end of the series, there was a lot of stuff I didn't want to be part of. I would say I didn't want to do a gag, and there was that whole battle between me and them and between me and myself as to what I could get away with. Our pastor was visiting me on the set, and everybody knew I went to that church. So you try to lead as much of a Christian life as you can, but it's sort of a double life.

Maylo Upton: All of a sudden you're changing. All of a sudden it's like, I can't do that anymore. So what happens is that it's really, really hard unless you quit your job because everyone knows you. So they either think, it's just a phase . . .

W. A.: They wait for you to get over it.

M. U.: Or they think you've suddenly gotten all self-righteous, so there is this tension.

C. G.: You knew you had to get out of Hollywood and that whole mentality, that whole orientation toward life. You knew *Charles in Charge* was winding down during that time, and you also had Harleigh.

M. U.: Here's the thing: Willie had made a commitment to God, and when Willie makes a commitment, he makes it full force. And we were almost ready to lose our house, and he had this feeling that if we didn't get out of California soon, we were going to spontaneously combust. We had no money and no prospects of any money. Then here comes an offer that I think was from the enemy: "Willie, I have a series for you!"

W. A.: I had two series offers after *Charles in Charge*. One was a regular role on a show called *She Wolf*, and the other was on a show called *They Came from Outer Space*. They were both by the same producer. They were guaranteed twenty-two episodes on the air. I walked in the office, and there were pentagrams everywhere.

The guy was real nice and he said, "We're offering you twenty-two on the air."

And I said, "No. I can't do it."

And they said, "You're nuts. You're turning down twenty-two episodes on the air?"

M. U.: "Because of something you believe?" And they said, "So go to church! I mean, who cares if you do this show?"

I'd get offers and I'd say, "I cannot be in bed in a teddy with this guy."

And my manager was saying, "Oh, for crying out loud." We had more and more of a burden to get out of there. We were going to get ostracized for being Jesus freaks.

W. A.: I also had another offer to do an infomercial for a set of CDs called *The History of Classic Rock.* They offered me $500,000 for three days of work. I have no problem with classic rock. I love it. But the project was sponsored by *Rolling Stone,* which at the time was promoting some sexual behavior that I couldn't go along with as a Christian. I turned down the offer and then promptly threw up (just kidding).

M. U.: And then there is this hope that hey, God, you must have some million-dollar opportunity waiting for us! Right? It was still hard times. It was all about making hard decisions for Jesus Christ. It was all about . . .

W. A.: Making the hard decisions as a Christian. It was about toughening up your walk, your resolve. It was about "let your yes be yes and your no be no." I don't know many Christians who would turn it down. They would just go ahead and do it.

M. U. [*laughing*]: But we were just so used to being broke that we were like, yeah, whatever. I was tied to the house. Harleigh was a screaming, difficult baby, and no one else would take care of her. People would not believe us when we said how difficult she was. People would say, "I understand. I had a baby who had colic."

And then they'd take care of her for an hour, and we'd come back and they'd say, "I'm so sorry!"

W. A.: Yeah, they'd say, "I don't know what to say! I've never seen or heard anything like it!" [*Laughter.*] She'd cry and cry until she had no more voice and then she'd croak. "Aagh! Aagh!"

M. U.: And then the doctor gave me this book about "active alert" babies. The deal is, the child's brain is ahead of her body. It said that when she can stand up, this should stop. Harleigh skipped crawling and just stood up one day and walked, and sure enough that was the day she stopped crying.

W. A.: That's true. She just toddled over to me, and I picked her up, and from that day, she was like a different child.

Anyway, I got an offer to write, produce, and direct a sports special for a marlin fishing tournament and also to be on camera as host. And then, the show's creators said, "We can't pay you. Do you need to be paid for it?" [*Laughter.*] "Of course not! I'll do it for free!"

I started thinking about fishing shows, and they were boring. It was scheduled to air on ESPN. At that time, anything on cable was just garbage. I decided that since I had never caught a marlin, I would enter the tournament and I would make them an on-camera bet that not only would I catch my first marlin, but I would win the tournament. And if I didn't win, I'd dress up in drag at the awards banquet. I figured people would watch to see me make a fool out of myself. There was no way I was gonna win this thing with the world's most competitive marlin fishermen. So that's the way we set it up. There were all kinds of gags wherever I was. Guys were throwing women's wigs and clothing at me. It was all in good fun.

So we entered the tournament. The first day my crew and I caught two. One was 200 pounds and the other was 330 pounds. We were in first place.

M. U.: His crew was all Mexican, very poor, living in shanties. Good men.

W. A.: The second day we got nothing. We were then completely out of the running. We had one day left in the tournament.

That morning I said to my crew, "Hey, watch this." I looked up and said, "Lord, I need a big fish. And I need it now."

About ten minutes later we got bit. The line got yanked from my hands, and I started fighting this fish. I fought it for twenty-one and a half hours and won the tournament. It dragged the boat twenty-six miles.

M. U.: There was a hurricane coming.

W. A.: Sixteen hours in, at about 2:00 a.m., I was sitting there and the radio came on. "We've got some good news and some bad news. The good news is that the tournament rules say that as long as you're fighting that fish, the tournament is not over. We have to wait for you to land that fish, so we're postponing the awards banquet. The bad news is that there are two hurricanes coming up the coast."

They sent a couple of boats to refuel us.

M. U.: The tournament was worth so much money. One of the rules is that you're not allowed to leave your rod during all that time. Willie was sitting there. If you have to go to the bathroom, you have to do it right there. People were dumping water on him. Another guy sent out a boat to videotape him to make sure there was no funny business. People were staying up all night, waiting to hear what happened. It made the front page of the sports section in the *Los Angeles Times*.

W. A.: When I finally got it, the fish wasn't hooked. He was wrapped in the line. He finally gave up from sheer tiredness—earlier at about 2:00 a.m. I saw the water light up with mahimahi—they glow. I'd see the line chasing the school of fish. I couldn't believe it. I thought, *Sixteen hours and this thing isn't even hurt! It was trying to feed!* He never jumped. We never saw him except for once. The crew said, "Oh my gosh"—or whatever the equivalent is in Spanish.

M. U.: When [Willie] finally came in, he couldn't stand up straight. He couldn't open his hands. And he said, "Maylo, I just had a twenty-one-and-a-half-hour talk with the God of all creation." God always, to this day, meets Willie in nature.

W. A.: I won $150,000. We tithed and then split it with the crew.

M. U.: They were sobbing. It helped them finish their houses. It was so glorifying to God. Willie had called upon the Lord, and everybody got provided for.

W. A.: They were believers when they came off that boat. They were jumping up and down, crying, "Thank you, Lord!"

That show was seen by a guy out here in Kansas who was doing fishing shows. He thought it was the best fishing show he had ever seen. He asked if I'd come out and be on his show. I came out and fell in love with the place. I thought that Kansas had everything you'd want. It's a great way of life. I came home and said, "Honey, we're moving to Kansas."

M. U.: And I fell apart. I thought, *Cows and freckles.* [*Laughter.*] I was a city girl. And there was that California, materialistic, beachy, money thing . . .

W. A.: We'd tell people in California that we were moving to Kansas, and they'd ask, "On purpose?" [*Laughter.*] "What's out there?" And I'd say, "Nothing. That's why we're moving there."

M. U.: They'd think, *OK, yeah, they've flipped.*

C. G.: So you moved out here to work on that show . . .

W. A.: It lasted about six months with him, and the show was canceled. We had sold our California house, cut all ties, so now I had to work, and we're in Kansas. We have no contacts out here, and my parents are saying, "I told you so. You'll never get back in."

And I'd say, "What makes you think I'd want back in?"

M. U.: We got into a little grassroots Calvary Chapel in Olathe, and it was hard-core Bible study. We learned to cling to the Lord. This is where we were formed.

W. A.: Everybody at that church was broke.

M. U.: We were like, "We go to the Church of the Hard Luck." [*Laughter.*]

W. A.: The church was so poor that the pastor could not take any pay or insurance. So he worked for the city and was our trashman. We called him our "trashtor." We'd go out and pray over the maggots.

M. U.: But that's one of the things I loved about being here. I learned to garden. I went to the library and found this whole book of journals of pioneer women, and I read of the hardships they had endured. I read of the things they had to leave behind— how they had to leave their china on the trail and so on. But in their journals, God is just all throughout. I began to think of this concept of the study of pioneering faith. And I thought, *This is our pioneering faith.*

As I gardened, God showed me and taught me so many things in the dirt about how things grow. Things about areas I wanted God to deal with in my heart. When pulling weeds, if I yanked them out too fast, they would break off at ground level, but the root would still be there. And I thought, *Wow, Lord, some of this stuff will take time for you to weed out.*

So even though we were broke, I was learning to find God in everything—in the earth, in his provision. I learned to can our own food. We became friends with the farmers in the area and would help them harvest potatoes. We'd follow behind the tractor and pick up potatoes and put them all in bags.

W. A.: We helped butcher animals. If you learn to live like they do on a family farm, you can really reduce the stress level. The house may be precarious, though they're going to have a hard time getting it away from you, but you'll have food.

M. U.: God has always provided—through the fish in the harbor and now by the land. We had Bible studies at our house twice a week. We were constantly at church, or we had fellowship in a home. If it wasn't Bible study, it was *koinonia,* [the Greek word for] New Testament-style fellowship. We would break bread together, be together.

W. A.: Five years of hard-core study. In a church that had no more than thirty people.

M. U.: And no matter what your problem was, if you went to the pastor's wife and said, "Can I counsel with you?" the first thing she would say was, "Are you in the Word?"

We were taught that the Word of God is *it.* I began a study and devotional habit every single day of meeting with the Lord, my dog across my feet. I got up before everyone else. To this day I still do that. I journal and study in the Word. There are days when I am just hanging on. All I can do is cry out to God, "Help me get through today." I learned to live every day with him. I didn't know then, but I know now that God was preparing me for Bibleman.

W. A.: There were so many days when all I could do was cover my face and I couldn't even pray. It was just, "Lord, Lord." That's all I could say. There were no words. I was so down, so out, so broke. That's what it means when it says the Holy Spirit will pray for you. You are so done, so consumed; you're without words.

M. U.: It's the worst place, but it's also the best place to be. In the middle of all this, we had no work, we were renting a house, we didn't know what we were gonna do. And I got this phone call. My Grandpa Harry had died three days after our wedding. It had been years. This was about 1992. "Maylo, Grandpa's estate is finally settled." I didn't even know there was one.

My Aunt Judy said, "There's a trust for you, and there's $27,000 in it."

There was a temptation to live off it. But I had this burning desire that it had to go down on a house. I didn't know what to do, and I had Harleigh in the backseat, and I was driving down a country road out toward Olathe. I saw this sign. I'm praying, "Lord, Lord, what do you want me to do?" The sign said, "Wooded Lots." I pulled in and I turned into a cul-de-sac, and I was facing a lot with a sign on it that said, "$27,000."

I called Willie. "You are not gonna believe where I'm sitting. I am looking at the most beautiful quarter acre in the woods." He drove out with me. We had our "trashtor" come and pray over the lot with us. And we built the dinkiest little house on it, surrounded by a picket fence. And I planted the biggest garden ever.

C. G.: Let's fast-forward a few years. You've covered the Bibleman days in the book, so let's talk about the time they ended, when you [Willie] discovered you needed surgery.

M. U.: This was a terrible time for Willie. Nobody called. I left his room for a little while and came back, and his pillow was soaked with old blood. He felt completely abandoned. He was told that he was 66 percent disabled, that he could never lift anything heavy again, and here he had no job.

And then *Celebrity Fit* called soon after his surgery. It offered enough money to live on for a year. He had gained weight in recuperation and had gone into a huge depression. He could not get out of bed. He told me he thought we would be better off if he died so we could collect the life insurance.

C. G.: Tell me more about your battle with depression.

W. A.: I had never experienced debilitating depression until the past two years, after Bibleman came to an end. Oswald Chambers is one of my heroes, and he was an extremely depressed man who believed that he had absolutely nothing to offer Christianity whatsoever and that every sermon he preached was a failure. Well, we all know now that *My Utmost for His Highest*—bits and pieces from sermons from a man who was not well known until after he died in 1921—has changed the lives of millions by just reminding them of simple little truths.

Brennan Manning has a story he often tells of an angel at a well who periodically stirs the waters so that people can come and be healed of various ailments. Everyone seems to be getting healed, and everything is fabulous, and then a doctor comes. He has suffered gravely with some ailment. He stands in line to get to the well, and the angel puts his hand up and says, "No. This is not your time to be healed." And the doctor says, "How come everyone gets this but me?" and the angel answers, "This is not your time. You need to remain broken. That's where your strength is."

M. U.: It's one of my favorite stories. My battle with depression is different from Willie's, rooted in a lifetime of mourning. I'd be fine for a while, and then this overwhelming grief would pour over me for not having had parents who seemed to care, along with debilitating low self-esteem and a feeling of loss for so much that was taken and picked away from me. Add to this the years of being alone while Willie was on the road.

Everything has slowly made me understand that there is only one source for everything I need. The church can't save me, feed me, or heal me. I had many times when I just crawled to the Lord and spent days, afternoons, hours, minutes—whatever it took in his presence, weeping.

I would not trade those times of prayer for anything on earth. If you told me, "I can give you your life back with all of the happiness and the greatest family and all that kind of stuff, but you won't have the relationship you have with Christ today," I would say no. I would go through it all over again because the relationship it drove me to when I was and am broken is so sweet. We have an amazing God who saves, restores, and builds and then helps us help other people through that. That's what the angel story is about.

C. G.: How did the experience of depression play out?

W. A.: I got to the point that I was way beyond self-hatred.

I felt sorry for anything or anybody that had to be around me because I was such a disgusting piece of worthlessness. My only thought about myself was how horrible it had to be for people I loved to be near me. Then *Celebrity Fit* came along and gave me a chance to get back in shape, which I thought might help me climb out of the depression too.

M. U.: And then comes the *Celebrity Fit* footage of him getting mad. I mean, he never cussed! And everywhere on the Internet, anti-Willie blogs. A lady wrote us: "He has tattoos!"

I wrote her back. I said, "Ma'am, we come with a testimony. We come from the streets! I'm sorry we got a tattoo!" So everywhere he turned, people are saying he just wasn't righteous enough.

C. G.: So what you've got is Christians who think you're a fraud, and you've got non-Christians . . .

W. A.: Who think I'm a fraud. You're a heretic to one and a lunatic to the other. You're a lunatic to people outside, and you're a heretic to your own.

M. U.: No grace from anyone.

C. G.: And you came down with lupus when?

M. U.: In 2004. I had been in and out of hospitals and treatments and in pain for years and years. When I was finally diagnosed, I was told it is like chasing phantoms. I was diagnosed first with Hashimoto's Thyroiditis, and all these other things were going on while Willie was gone on the road.

I had scabs all up and down my arms. I had an internal infection from my hip all the way up to my clavicle. I had to be opened up in my chest and irrigated, and the doctor said the infection looked like egg-drop soup inside my body. My thyroid died completely. I had been sick, sick, sick. So then Willie was let go, had the surgery, and the church seemed to abandon us.

W. A.: And I was in a complete depression in a dark room, unable to move. And suddenly Maylo couldn't walk.

M. U.: My bones felt like chalk to me. They felt like they were going to crumble. The doctors told me there was nothing wrong.

I was in a Bible study with a gal around this time who had MS. She said, "Maylo, get yourself a little book and take your temperature every day at the same time. Write down your symptoms every day in a log. Do it for two months. You have to be your own advocate. Do this for two months and then go to a rheumatologist." It was the best advice anyone had given me.

I did go, and he finally took the right blood tests and he said, "You have lupus." I got every book there was, and this was at the same time Willie had surgery. And people seemed to forget, we had a thirteen-year-old girl who watched her family do nothing but give in ministry and then get completely shredded. She was angry and confused about God: "Are we all just talking about being Christians?" It was my responsibility as her mother to still get up in the morning and get on my knees and have my devotions. Because I can talk, talk, talk, but unless she sees the walk and sees Jesus' work and healing through my being on my face . . .

W. A.: I watched Maylo's pain and couldn't do anything about it. I was done. Over. Totally incapacitated both physically and mentally. And I truly believed that Maylo was going to die. She was nearly comatose for two weeks.

M. U.: He lay in the guestroom for days. I would open the door and say, "Honey?" He'd turn over and say, "Don't look at me." He thought of himself as a beast. He had all of these people in the media and the press talking about how "over" he was. There were people posting notes all over the Internet like "I saw Willie Aames waiting tables, and he weighs four hundred pounds," and things like that. But what people don't realize is that we have a daughter, and she gets on the 'Net and reads these things about her daddy. We'd have to say, "Harleigh, God knows."

And then there was *Celebrity Fit*, and it was like it would never be over.

W. A.: Why was it that I was so ostracized?

M. U.: The man from *Celeb Fit* showed up, unannounced, at 7:00 a.m. after a night in which I had had a temperature of 104, and Willie was afraid he'd have to take me to the ER. And then the guy marched right into our backyard as if he owned the place. But people don't understand that. Willie said, "You are getting me so in the flesh right now" and slammed the door.

W. A.: They don't know what that phrase means. Thank God I did have a chance to redeem the way I appeared so angry. I recently did a "Where Are They Now?" show. The *Celeb Fit* people came out and interviewed me, and I was able to affirm that, yes, I still believe in Jesus Christ, and no, I'm not gay, and no, I'm not marrying Paula Abdul. [*Laughter.*] That was one of the rumors, believe it or not. It was actually kind of funny.

From this point, we're hand-to-mouth, putting together a hunting show for the Outdoor Channel. It's going well.

M. U.: I just keep telling Harleigh, "God has a plan; we have a testimony. Even if all of this is only for me to have a testimony to show to you, it's been worth it."

W. A.: At this point, it's a matter of healing. There are still good days and bad days. I think the thing we can always say is that there has always been—OK, there *is* always hope. Sometimes it's the faintest thing you can possibly see. There is also a choice. You have to choose at those moments whether or not you are going to continue to believe. It's a choice to say, "This is who God is, this is what he said, and I'm going to continue on, because he's given me enough reason to believe he is true throughout these years." These have been the hardest two years of my life. Had he not brought us through so many other circumstances, I don't know what I'd do.

M. U.: There have been times when God showed us in physical ways that he is there. Once I was going to have my car taken away, and I needed $237 to keep it. And I had been praying. I went out to the mailbox, and there was an envelope in the mailbox—no name, no stamp—and inside was $237 cash. We had no idea where it came from.

W. A.: There was a time when I had only about ten dollars left in my pocket. I got home, and all the lights were on and there was food burning on the stove. A message was there: "Willie, meet me at the hospital. Harleigh has hurt herself." She had had one of those childhood playground accidents.

We hadn't eaten all day and were at the hospital late that night. And I had cleaned out our bank account to pay the bills. I said, "Let's just go to Taco Bell."

We finally went to pay the bill, and the cashier said, "The person up ahead told me to say, 'Jesus loves you,' and he paid your bill." And I just started crying. It was God's little way of saying, "I'm here." We call that food "the spiritual burrito." The person who did that will never know how God used him or her that day.

M. U.: There have been enough times in our lives that God showed up, not with a winning lottery ticket, but he just showed up when we were down, falling underneath the cross. We couldn't carry it anymore. I think of all those times in our past, back to Joe Hemphill, to Dr. Farhat [the gynecologist who performed my conization], all the way back to that time at the camp in the woods with Stacy. All the times I almost died.

There is a real gritty hanging-on-for-dear-life in a woman's walk. There's a sifting that goes on—being submissive to God, submissive to your husband and an example for your children. And if you haven't had a mother figure, a grandmother figure, to be an example for you, you have to carve it out from women in the Bible, pioneer women through their journals, and a little bit of Martha Stewart. [*Laughter.*]

C. G.: Let me ask you this, getting back to the theme of "Without these wounds, where would your strength be?" Is there anything else you'd like to say about it?

W. A.: Ultimately, I've had this experience as a Christian, when God asks you what you're going to do. Just like when everybody fled, and Jesus asked, "Are you going to leave me, too?" And the disciples answered, "No, Lord." I've always read the passage a little differently—the disciples answer him a little sarcastically: "Yeah, right, Lord, what do you think we're going to do? We've left everything behind. We know you're God. Where are we going to go?"

You have a choice because you have human will, but in a way you don't have a choice because you know what the truth is. Ultimately, God asks us the same question every day. Are you going to flee too? For some of us it's harder, but ultimately when I've been curled up in a ball and I'm so miserable that I'd rather die, I have to ask myself what I am going to choose. Some days it's hard to get up and walk. It's difficult to get up and pray. It's hard to face another day.

But God asks us before we make that final decision to give up, "What are you going to choose to believe?" And I flash back to all the things I've been through, and I realize he's been there. To me that's Scripture. It's tough. It would be easier to curse God and die.

It would be nice to end this book and say that we're rich. But that's not the truth. And God never promised that we'd end up rich.

There are two things, ultimately, that I need. I need my God, and I need my family. The rest I can suffer through.

M. U.: For me, "Only the wounded soldier can serve" means that when I'm in the hardest place, the neediest place, the most-afraid place, I am hard and bitter and I have no peace. As a Christian, "in me is no good thing." The only way I get through the day with peace and grace and decency is through the daily renewing of my mind. If I am not wounded almost every day, how can I say to another woman that she needs to be with her Lord every day? How can I explain that to my daughter? My daughter has the faith that she has today because she has seen the wounded serve.

She's seen God show up, even if it's she and I lying in the hammock. Once a dove came and landed right on her knee and looked at her, and it was just a moment, and she said, "Thank you, God." There is a depth from being broken and being broken again and being broken again.

Now after all of this, the prayers before of "Please, God, please don't let us lose the house" or whatever, thinking we're going to be OK now, and we never are, now my prayers are, "God, just take it all. I don't care. I want only you, and I want to be around enough to tell my grandchildren about you."

W. A.: Ultimately, Christ is all you've got. I don't care who you are. Ultimately, you're going to get asked that question. You may face tragedy; you may face joy. But every single day you will face the question, What are you going to choose today? The fact is, you're going to make a choice as to where you stand each day. And every experience, good or bad, begins to bring you closer to the Lord. Through that process we find forgiveness, grace, and, most importantly, his love that will bring you into peace.

M. U.: As long as you are in pain, you understand. If that's what it takes . . . this is the love of my life—the only thing that holds it together. Like a bumper sticker that says, "Whatever, Lord."

Willie Aames'

FILMOGRAPHY

Film and TV Series: Acting Roles

Bugtime Adventures TV—Narrator

Bibleman (2004)

The Missy Files (2003) TV

"An Eight Is Enough Wedding" (1989) TV—Tommy Bradford

"Eight Is Enough: A Family Reunion" (1987) TV—Tommy Bradford

Inferno in diretta (1985)—Tommy Allo

    aka *Amazon: Savage Adventure*

    aka *Cut and Run* (USA)

    aka *Straight to Hell* (International: literal title)

Charles in Charge (1984) TV—Buddy Lembeck (1984–85, 1986–90)

Goma-2 (1984) Chema

    aka *Killing Machine*

    aka *Máquina de matar, La* (Mexico)

The Edge of Night (1983) TV—Robbie Hamlin

Dungeons & Dragons (1983) TV—Hank the Ranger (voice)

The Tom Swift and Linda Craig Mystery Hour (1983) TV—Tom Swift

Zapped! (1982)—Peyton Nichols

Paradise (1982)—David

Scavenger Hunt (1979)—Kenny Stevens

Eight Is Enough (1977–81) TV—Tommy Bradford

Family (1976–77) TV—T. J. Latimer

Rich Man, Poor Man—Book II (1976) TV—
   Young Wesley Jordache

Swiss Family Robinson (1975) TV—Fred Robinson
   aka *Island of Adventure* (UK)

We'll Get By (1975) TV—Kenny Platt

The Family Nobody Wanted (1975) TV—Donny

Benjamin Franklin (1974) TV—Benjamin Franklin (twelve years old)

Doctor Dan (1974) TV—Adam Morgan

Unwed Father (1974) TV—Gum

Pssst! Hammerman's After You! (1974) TV

Runaway on Rogue River (1974) TV

Frankenstein (1973) TV—William Frankenstein

Director

Bibleman (2004) TV

The Missy Files (2003) Video

Writer

Bibleman (2004) TV

The Missy Files (2003) Video

Himself

"Celebrity Fit Club: Where Are They Now?" (2006)

Celebrity Fit Club (2005) TV

Dickie Roberts: Former Child Star (2003)

Child Stars: Then and Now (2003) TV

"Eight Is Enough: The E! True Hollywood Story" (2000) TV

"Circus of the Stars #14" (1989) TV—Performer

"Circus of the Stars #10" (1985) TV—Performer
"Battle of the Network Stars IX" (1980) TV—ABC Team
"Battle of the Network Stars VII" (1979) TV—ABC Team

Notable TV Guest Appearances

Hollywood Squares (September 8–12, 2003)

Blacke's Magic

"The Revenge of the Esperanza" (22 January 1986)—Eric Wilson

The Love Boat

"Audition, The/The Groupies/Doc's Nephew" (6 November 1982)—Doc's nephew Danny

Little House on the Prairie

"Injun Kid" (31 January 1977)—Seth

Medical Center

"Torment" (22 September 1975)

"The Enemies" (4 March 1974)—Jeff

"The Nowhere Child" (15 December 1971)—Eric

The Waltons

"The Beguiled" (16 January 1975)—Danny

Adam-12

"Credit Risk" (17 December 1974)—Billy Ray

"Extortion" (15 September 1971)—Little Boy

Disneyland

"Runaway on the Rogue River" (1 December 1974)—Jeff Peterson

Adam's Rib

"Katey at the Bat" (12 October 1973)

Gunsmoke

"A Quiet Day in Dodge" (29 January 1973)—Andy

"P.S. Murry Christmas" (27 December 1971)—Tom

The Courtship of Eddie's Father

"Time for a Change" (23 February 1972)—Harold O'Brien

"In the Eye of the Beholder" (16 February 1972)—Harold O'Brien

"The Karate Story" (12 January 1972)—Harold O'Brien

"To Catch a Thief" (10 March 1971)—Scott

Cannon

"A Flight of Hawks" (22 February 1972)—Macklin Boy

The Odd Couple

"Win One for Felix" (3 December 1971)—Leonard

(*Primary source: imdb.com, 26 September 2006*)

Maylo McCaslin's

FILMOGRAPHY

Film and TV Series: Acting Roles and Guest Appearances

Bibleman (2004) TV—U.N.I.C.E., L.U.C.I., Gossip Queen

The Missy Files (2003) TV—Mrs. Shannon

Charles in Charge
    "Buddy Comes to Dinner" (1987)—Lauren Andrews

Rocky Road (1985) TV—Jessica Stuart

The A-Team
    "Beverly Hills Assault" (1985)—Peggy

Santa Barbara (1984–85) TV—Sally Taylor

Hardcastle and McCormick
    "It Coulda Been Worse, She Coulda Been a Welder" (1984)—guest star

Hunter
    "A Long Way from L.A." (1984)—Lainie

Blue Thunder
    "The Godchild" (1984)—Lisa Ritchie

Riptide
    "Hatchet Job" (1984)—Alison London

Nine to Five (1983)—guest star

The Powers of Matthew Star
    "Jackal" (1982)—Cindy

Superstition (1982)—Sheryl Leahy
  aka *The Witch* (USA)
Kid Superpower Hour with Shazam! (1981) TV—Dirty Trixie (voice)
The Home Front (1980) TV pilot

Herself
  "Celebrity Fit Club: Where Are They Now?" (2006)
  Celebrity Fit Club
    aka *Celebrity Fit Club 2* (USA: second season title)
    "Welcome to Fit Club" (2005)

(Primary source: <u>imdb.com</u> 26 September 2006)

7/09 6 4/08